Fishing Key West and the Lower Keys

UNIVERSITY PRESS OF FLORIDA

Florida A&M University, Tallahassee
Florida Atlantic University, Boca Raton
Florida Gulf Coast University, Ft. Myers
Florida International University, Miami
Florida State University, Tallahassee
New College of Florida, Sarasota
University of Central Florida, Orlando
University of Florida, Gainesville
University of North Florida, Jacksonville
University of South Florida, Tampa
University of West Florida, Pensacola

University Press of Florida
Gainesville
Tallahassee
Tampa
Boca Raton
Pensacola
Orlando
Miami
Jacksonville
Ft. Myers
Sarasota

Fishing Key West

and the Lower Keys

David Conway

Aerial photos and satellite images contained in this book are provided by the United States Geological Survey's National Aerial Photography Program (Project NAPP), which began in 1987 and continues to this day. More can be learned about NAPP and the USGS's other aerial and satellite photography projects and products by visiting http://edcsns17.cr.usgs.gov/photofinder. Dry Tortugas map image used with permission of Maptech, www.maptech.com. Photo of Captain Tony Tarracino courtesy of Monroe County Library, Key West.

Printed in the United States of America on acid-free paper

18 17 16 15 14 13   6 5 4 3 2

Library of Congress Cataloging-in-Publication Data
Conway, David, 1964–
Fishing Key West and the lower keys / David Conway.
p. cm.
Includes index.
ISBN 978-0-8130-3294-8 (alk. paper)
1. Saltwater fly fishing—Florida—Key West. 2. Saltwater fly fishing—Florida—Florida Keys. I. Title.
SH456.2.C67 2009
799.1609759'41—dc22   2008027421

The University Press of Florida is the scholarly publishing agency for the State University System of Florida, comprising Florida A&M University, Florida Atlantic University, Florida Gulf Coast University, Florida International University, Florida State University, New College of Florida, University of Central Florida, University of Florida, University of North Florida, University of South Florida, and University of West Florida.

University Press of Florida
15 Northwest 15th Street
Gainesville, FL 32611-2079
http://www.upf.com

Contents

Part III. Species

Part IV. Appendixes

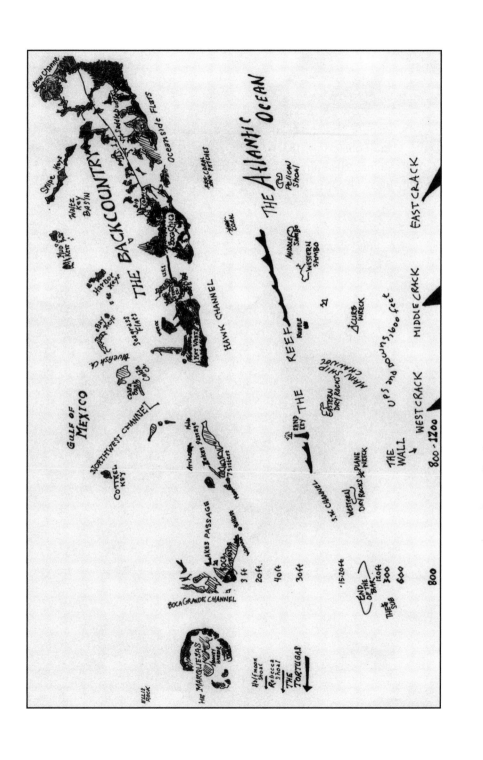

part 1

Tour of the Key West Fishery

1

Welcome to Key West

360° of Fishing, 365 Days a Year

While New York, Boston, and Chicago sit under blankets of cold, gray winter sky, you might take off from a Key West dock at 8 a.m. to look for sailfish, dolphin, and tuna, as we did aboard Capt. Richard Houde's boat, *Southbound.* First we loaded up on threadfin herring using sabiki rigs and cast nets at a channel marker in the Gulf of Mexico. Then we headed to the Atlantic. On the way, we passed light-tackle fishermen jumping tarpon in the harbor and other anglers after yellowtail working jigs and baits along the reef.

With winter temperatures topping out at about seventy-six degrees and the skies bright, we had prime conditions for bluewater fishing off Key West. Easterly winds met the east-bound current to give the seas a slight chop, with water temps in the low seventies and a distinct color line where blue water met green.

We set up to troll, not the only way to catch sailfish but a popular method to cover a lot of territory and increase your chances of running into any number of other species, including cobia, wahoo, and tuna. We motored along the color line into a strong current, running two outriggers and two flat-lines with threadfins on 3/0 hooks, 20-pound monofilament and 50-pound leaders.

Between Sea Buoy "KW" and Eyeglass Light, Captain Houde spotted a sailfish free jumping. Mate Brice—who has since graduated to run his own boat, *Double Down*—leapt from his perch on the tower ladder. He hooked another threadfin on a spinning outfit and cast. The sailfish took it and the rodeo began.

Looking northward over the harbor to the Gulf of Mexico. In Key West, you're never far from the action.

You're 150 miles out to sea and you haven't even left the docks. You're surrounded by an ocean and a gulf, the world's third-largest living reef and the Gulf Stream to the south, world-class flats to the north and west, more than 200 wrecks, and a sub-tropical town. You can fish every day of the year.

The tiny two-by-four-mile island of Key West offers anglers plenty of temptation and limitless choices. Sometimes, it's hard to know which way to turn when the Atlantic Ocean is your front yard and the Gulf of Mexico is your backyard, but it's good to know your options.

It's a six-mile ride from Key West harbor to the reef straight out of the main ship channel into the Atlantic, seven miles southwest to the Sand Key Light, which can be seen from Key West on clear days. Past the reef, depths drop to about 110 feet and rise again to about forty-five feet on the bar, which is a submerged reef. The bar starts at American Shoals and stops south of Boca Grande, where deep-water currents swirl into the Gulf and draw pelagics. Out past the bar, depths drop quickly—from 250 feet to more than 2,000 feet in about six miles.

Any time of year at the reef, anglers anchor up over bottom structure, day or night, to catch yellowtail, mutton and mangrove snapper, and groupers. A day of yellowtail snapper fishing is a classic Keys trip and a good starter for anglers unfamiliar with the reef fishery, but a number of other techniques are also popular along the reef line. Know a few tactics and you can always pull a few fish from the reef.

A little deeper, past the bar and east or west of Sand Key, any time of the year, you can jig for mutton snappers, grouper, kings, and wahoo in depths of 120 to 200 feet. Ledges run parallel to the reef at various depths where a variety of species find protection and forage, and where sailfish often turn up in the wintertime looking for a meal. In the cooler months, migrating cobia and kingfish lurk in the depths and occasionally surface to feed on schools of passing baitfish. By the late spring, right in these same waters, dolphin will

Capt. Brice Barr intercepts a winter sailfish off Key West.

appear in their Technicolor best, all of this while still in sight of Key West.

Wrecks in the vicinity hold many other species, including black, scamp, and red grouper, amberjack, African pompano, blackfin tuna, and a whole lot of other surprises. Feel like wrestling with a dinosaur? Try hooking up with one of the wreck's resident goliath groupers, which can top out at 500 pounds or more.

Beyond Sand Key, blue water and the Gulf Stream beckon anglers in search of pelagics, including billfish. The exact location of the Gulf Stream varies from day to day, and its edge might be found at some distance between five and fifty miles from Key West as it meanders between the Keys and Cuba on its way northward. Most anglers troll these blue waters to cover the greatest territory. A few other locations, such as the End of the Bar, draw anglers who anchor and chum with live pilchards in hopes of luring blackfin and yellowfin tuna and other species to their stern. For wahoo, kings, and cobia, troll live baits along the edge of the bar out to 200 to 250 feet and near Eastern and Western Dry Rocks. Most big fish will tail into the current along any color change or, if it's murky, in the powder. Keep watch for a cobia or a king, or the black back of a sailfish or a tuna rising near your boat. Dolphin show, too, in winter, especially when the water warms, but because they're migrating in that season they're less likely to hang around your boat than they are in the summer. In winter, go past the bar and look for dolphin fifteen to twenty miles either east or west in about 300 feet. In summer, head either southwest or southeast from the bar, into slightly deeper waters.

Along with trolling, other winter-fishing techniques for bluewater species include chumming, live-lining pilchards, and kite-fishing. Famous angling locations include the legendary Woods Wall, which runs eastward and westward and drops from 900 feet to depths of 1,600 feet in various locations and draws plenty of billfish, including marlin.

Match the right baits and tactics to the color of water that you're facing, and you'll improve your odds out past the bar. Blue water

Since Captain Tony's days in '58, conservation has become a bigger concern for local anglers. Photo courtesy of Monroe County Library, Key West.

means tuna and sails, maybe dolphin. In green, look for cobia, kings, the reef species, and snappers. Then follow the usual signs— the current, the birds, the popping baitfish. Work the bait, the color change, and the currents, and be aware of the influence of the Gulf Stream, which adds another element of excitement when it brings the big fish in close.

Go west from Sand Key more than fifteen miles, and you are in wild territory. The Marquesas, Dry Tortugas, and Rebecca Shoals all lie to the west, which explains another big draw to Key West along with the variety of fishing: its relative isolation. For anglers, that means less fishing pressure, more and bigger fish, and, if the fisherman desires one, a better chance at a world record. The islands and patch reefs out there are absolutely gorgeous, and the potential for discovering great new spots is high.

As plentiful as these possibilities are, it's still only a fraction of what Key West offers to anglers.

Turn northward out of the harbor and you'll come to some of the greatest flats for bonefish and permit in the world. Tarpon, sharks, and cobia come up to these flats and haunt the channels that cut through them, and a flats boat, either your own or a hired one, will be your way into that magical maze.

Key West is the Madison Square Garden of flats fishing. The sport was born here in the sixties, pioneered by a handful of now legendary figures, and anglers come from around the world to test themselves. The Lower Keys are the best place in North America for a chance at a flats slam—catching and landing a permit, bonefish, and tarpon all in the same day, one of the toughest challenges in angling on spinning gear and an even greater triumph on a fly.

Tower Flats, Seven Sisters, Cottrell Key, Content Pass, and Bluefish Channel all offer good fishing and are all less than thirty minutes from the docks. The shallow banks all the way to Boca Grande are riffled with basins and channels that fish call home. The sight of a school of tarpon swimming toward you along a flat or the edge of a wave, their dorsal fins camouflaged on the wave crest, will not soon leave your memory. If you can cast to the one you choose among that school, you know that you've achieved a measure of calm in life.

On either side of winter, permit and bonefish action can be strong. But when the winds come and the water temperatures drop, those fish move deeper, and you can expect sharks and barracudas on the flats, both extremely sporty quarry. Be prepared though: Bull sharks are known for fighting back and attacking boats. Redfish and snook haunt secret backcountry spots as well, as do sea trout. Each of the three species are more regularly associated with mainland Florida but are evident in the Lower Keys too. Juvenile tarpon and mutton snappers lurk around the mouths of channels year-round.

Keep going northward through the backcountry into the Gulf of Mexico, and you'll find wrecks and towers that hold seasonal populations of permit, cobia, and kingfish, as well as resident snappers and groupers. Trolling bucktail jigs or live bait scores fish north and west of Ellis Rock, north of Boca Grande channel, around wrecks to the west, and southwest of Smith Shoal Light. Even party boats catch cobia and kings on their Gulf trips.

For simply fun fishing, there's really no need to even leave the Key West harbor. The harbor itself and nearby Northwest Channel can be hot locations for tarpon, cobia, snappers, and mixed-bag fishing, and it's a haven during inclement weather. The patch reefs close to Key West, which are marked on charts and visible to the eye, offer easy-going family-style fishing, but watch for big coral heads. Big fish, such as cobia and mackerel, also frequent Hawk Channel, between the island and the reef.

~~~~~~~~~~~~~~

"Key West has it all," says longtime local charter captain Richard Houde. "A lot of different fisheries come together right here: light tackle in the Gulf—both wrecks and patch reefs, the blue water, and the flats and backcountry. And everything is so close. Guys are surprised that they're going after big fish within sight of land.

"Of course," Houde says, "you never know what you're going to come across no matter where you are. I've seen sails in the Northwest Channel."

On the flats, in the Gulf, and on open water, boater access and the best action will depend on the winter winds and the weather they bring. The chill that turns on the kings and sailfish slows fishing action on the flats, so it's a day-to-day necessity to strategize and have a back-up plan. Almost any north wind will allow you to get out for some kind of fishing to the southward or leeward side of the Gulf islands, but if conditions are rough because of north winds greater than 15 knots, there are rock piles inside the reef sheltered by Key West itself. If it's howling from the south, go northward to the Gulf wrecks and reefs. If you're in no mood for a rough ride at all, you might stay in the harbor and plug for tarpon or present live bait to cobia and muttons. On a calm day, the hardest decision will be which way to turn once you're out of the harbor.

Charts such as the *Florida Sportsman Fishing* Chart No. 11 for Key West reveal several GPS numbers for wrecks and artificial reefs. Anglers in their own boats in pursuit of bluewater species may also want to scan the captains' conversations on channel 08 and 78 on the VHF radio. You might learn that tunas are attacking bait near Pelican Shoal or that sailfish are showing in 190 feet off Rock Key. If you do chase down that action, remember to keep a polite distance from boats that are on fish.

"There's an etiquette out there just as there is on the flats, and there's fish for all of us," says Captain Houde.

If you don't live in the Keys, you can still do plenty to prepare for a trip down to the islands, whether you plan to bring your own boat, stay for a few weeks and charter captains, or visit for only one or two charter trips. With proper knowledge of the fishery and good planning, you'll be able to make your time on the water productive. That may mean chasing big, migrating dolphin fish during their peak season in the spring, going for a grand slam on the flats in the spring or fall, or targeting black grouper on the bottom offshore almost any time of year. Only your time and, on occasion, the weather, will limit your possibilities.

The following chart highlights the best times of year to cross paths with the most popular game species in the Lower Keys.

Species by Month for Flats, Inshore, and Offshore

Species	Jan	Feb	Mar	Ap	May	Jun	Jul	Aug	Sep	Oct	Nov	Dec
Amberjack	F	F	B	B	B	G	F	F	G	G	G	F
Blackfin Tuna	B	G	G	B	B	G	G			G	B	B
Black Grouper	B	B	B	G	G	G	G	F	F	G	G	B
Bluefish and Ladyfish	B	B	B	G	F							G
Blue Marlin	F	F	B	G	F	G	B	G	F	B	G	F
Bonefish	F	F	F	G	B	B	B	G	G	B	G	F
Bonito	G	G	G	G	G	F	F	F	F	G	G	G
Cero Mackerel	B	B	B	B	G	G	F	F	F	G	G	B
Cobia	G	B	B	B	G	F					G	G
Cobia, flats	G	B	B	B								
Dolphin	F	F	G	B	B	B	G	F	F	G	F	F
Jacks	B	B	B	G	G	G	G	G	G	B	B	B
Kingfish	B	B	B	G	G	G	F	F	F	G	G	B
Mangrove	B	G	G	G	B	B	B	G	G	G	G	B
Mutton Snapper	G	G	G	B	B	B	B	G	G	B	B	G
Permit, flats	F	G	B	B	G	B	B	G	F	G	G	F
Permit, wrecks and reef		G	G	B	B	G			G	G	G	G	G
Pompano	B	B	F									F
Red Grouper	B	B	B	G	G	G	F	F	F	G	B	B
Sailfish	B	B	B	G	F	F	F	G	F	F	G	B
Sharks and 'Cudas, flats	G	B	B	G							G	G
Skipjack Tuna	F	F			G	G	G	G	F			F
Snook, Sea Trout, and Redfish	B	B	B	G	F	F	F	F	F	F	F	G
Spanish Mackerel	B	B	G	G	F					F	G	G
Swordfish	F	F	F	F	G	G	B	B	B	B	G	F
Tarpon	F	G	B	B	B	B	G	G	F	F	F	F
Tarpon, night			G	G	B	B	B	B				
Wahoo	G	G	F	G	F	G	B	G	F	G	G	B
Yellowfin Tuna												F
Yellowtail	G	G	G	B	B	B	B	B	B	B	G	G

Notes: F = Fair; G = Good; B = Best; empty cell = negligible chances.

Whether you plan your trip to Key West around the fishing, or around other vacation options, take a look at the chart in advance of your visit. Decide when you'll have the best chances to catch the species that you're after, or else determine what's running strong given your travel dates, and you'll get a good idea of how to arrange your days on the water. If you're chartering a captain, remember that the best ones get booked for hot bites sometimes months in advance. If your chosen captain is already booked, ask him for references. If you're towing your own boat down, call tackle shops in advance to check the conditions and get specific advice.

Booking Charter Captains

Key West and other towns up and down the Keys are home to some of the best charter captains in the world, and the very best are as good with people as they are with fish.

Chartering a good captain can be expensive, but it is money well-spent. The price buys the best chance at catching good fish and gaining an experience that would otherwise be unattainable for anglers and their friends and family. Most captains are extremely generous with their knowledge, and a good trip can also provide a wealth of knowledge that anglers can put to their own use. Even very good anglers who live in the Keys will charter captains to learn more about a particular fishery. And if you're visiting the Keys, chartering a captain may be the only way to get out on the water.

On the other hand, a bad trip with the wrong captain can be a disaster. So use every means possible to learn about your captain before you arrive. Check their Web sites, ask for references, post requests on message boards asking for opinions, and most of all, have a conversation with the captain you plan to hire.

You should always feel comfortable discussing your possible fishing options, hopes, and ambitions for the trip with the captain during the planning stages, and if he makes you uncomfortable, take it as a sign that he might not be the right one for you. But on the day of the trip, let the captain make the ultimate judgment on the best possible strategy for your time on the water, because you're paying them for that expertise. Rest assured that the captain will do everything in his or her power to give you the best day, because he wants you to come back. Repeat customers are the best kind for charter captains. In return, if an angler can build a working relationship with a charter captain, over time that captain will assist them in every way possible, from calling them about a hot bite, to coaching them on techniques, to holding open dates.

Also, it's very important to discuss with the captain what you'll do with all fish caught, whether you want them released, or how many or how much you want to keep. In the Keys, it's customary for the client to keep the fish that they catch, but many anglers don't need or want as much fish as they can catch, and the captains can sell extra fish to enhance their income in a very tough business. Sharing the fish equally with the captain seems like a good deal for everyone, and gives the captain and crew more incentive to catch fish, but whatever you plan to do, discuss it in advance with the captain, preferably at the time you book the trip—so no disagreements, ill feelings, regrets—or worse—come up at the dock.

Also, customarily, the crew gets tipped twenty percent of the charter price, and captains on small craft without crew get twenty percent tips too. Believe it or not, profit margins in their business are very slim and shrinking, and tips make a big difference to their operations, especially in a resort town such as Key West, where business is seasonal.

The Weather

Except for hurricane days, you can count on being able to fish near Key West every day of the year. But other than the type of boat you or your captain run, weather conditions primarily determine where you can go and what you might catch. Good days for fishing in Key West mean that winds are out of the north, east, or south from 10 to 15 knots or less. Westward winds are less than favorable and very rare.

In the winter, rougher weather prevails, and anglers see about two calm days out of seven to run to the destination of their choice. Those rough winter days keep anglers close to the islands or in the harbor. Fair weather days increase in the spring, when your opportunities improve to roughly three or four days out of seven to go wherever you like. By summer, when calmer winds prevail, good conditions run as high as six out of seven days, allowing for periodic thunderstorms or hurricanes passing by. Fall sees about three good days out of seven.

Good knowledge of the fishery allows you to strategize to find a way to fish safely even when rougher conditions prevail. There is no doubt though that the best strategy depends on knowing exactly what's been happening in days preceding your planned trip and taking advantage of the best bite given the weather conditions. In other words, act as opportunistically as possible on that information, seize the chance, and you'll catch fish.

No-Fishing Zones

Anglers are reminded that there are certain reefs south of Key West where fishing and spearfishing are prohibited. The Florida Keys National Marine Sanctuary has designated Sand Key, Rock Key, and Eastern Dry Rocks as Sanctuary Preservation Areas (SPAs). These reefs are marked by 30-inch round yellow buoys. Similar buoys mark the Western Sambos Ecological Reserves, another no-take area from the shoreline at Boca Chica to the outer reef. The Eastern Sambos Special Use Area, also marked, is closed to everyone but scientists. For more information, contact the Lower Region office of FKNMS at (305) 292-0311, or visit the Web site at www.nos.noaa. gov.

2

~~~~~~ ~~~~~~ ~~~~~~

The Harbor

24° 33.81'N 81° 48.42'W

"There used to be an old wooden dock at the end of Duval Street, what was called Porter's Dock, and they used to pull four hundred–pound Jewfish out of there. There was a lot of lobster back then too. We could drop net for lobster there and get a hundred pounds in a night. Or you could walk out in the shallows and pick up conchs and stone crabs and lobsters. In the forties and fifties, all that side of the island was nothing but fishing fleets and shrimp boats, and most of the local conchs had small boats with live wells, and Peter's fish market had these big wells made of wood slats where they'd keep the fish alive, and you'd pick the one you wanted and they'd net it for you.

"As teenagers we made money by unloading the turtle boats and heading shrimp. I remember when I unloaded the turtle boats and after we got through I'd see thousands of eggs on the deck and even as a kid I used to say, you know what pretty soon there aren't going to be any turtles if we keep doing this. A lot of the fish from the party boats, they used to throw away into the garbage cans. Some people would come by and pick them up. Maybe that's when we should have taken care, you know.

"Anyway, those were the days that Key West was *Cayo Hueso*. This was a real paradise then. You didn't have to go home for lunch. You could catch a conch right on the beach. Fruit trees all over the place. And we didn't have any crime. No one would steal anything. You didn't have to lock your doors or your bike." ⋖═◄

—Native Conch Armando Parro about his youth in Key West in the forties

Aerial photographs, such as this one of Key West from the U.S. Geological Survey, give anglers a bird's-eye view of waterways. From the USGS Project NAPP. Roll 6953-Frame 67.

Whether you charter a trip, live locally, or bring your own boat, Key West's harbor, officially called Truman Harbor, is the center of the action. As strategic a place for fishing as it is for boating, learning the harbor's ins-and-outs gives you the home-field advantage in Key West's entire angling game.

The harbor leads to primary routes of passage to all of Key West's varied fisheries. Like spokes off a wheel, Calda Channel goes to the backcountry, the Northwest Channel to the Gulf, the Lakes Passage to the Marquesas and the west, and the Southwest Channel and Main Ship Channel lead south to the reef and offshore grounds. All those waterways also lead fish to the harbor, where they find shelter from seasonal temperature extremes in its deep water, the deepest inshore water in the Lower Keys.

In summer, the harbor has some of the coolest water around, and in winter, some of the warmest, depending on the tide. For that reason, the harbor offers a spectacular winter–spring season for cobia, kings, tarpon, permit, and snapper. It also offers a dependable twelve-month fishery easily accessible from all nearby marinas, with good protection during rough weather and comfortable fishing at night in the lights of Key West.

The harbor's surrounding channels, flats, and mangrove islands give the flats boat anglers a year-round shot at permit, bonefish, tar-

Capt. Phil Thompson releases a tarpon in sight of Key West.

pon, and other species. In good weather, that's where flats skiffs will go, and even during extreme weather conditions in the summer and winter, the flats can be productive at the right times of day. In bad conditions, flats anglers will find places in the harbor and protected positions by mangrove keys to fish.

On those rough, windy winter days, not only flats anglers, but also light-tackle fishermen will take refuge in the harbor. The sure thing is to anchor in the Northwest Channel, start chumming and bottom-bouncing ¾-ounce jigs tipped with cut bait,or shrimp. Rods will bend with resident muttons, snappers, seasonal cobia, yellow jacks, and mackerel. Live shrimp are also readily available from local marinas in the winter and make surefire baits either freelined or bottom-fished weighted with split shot or a slip-sinker. If live shrimp are scarce, bring a handful of D.O.A. weighted shrimp artificials in root beer and white, and drift them back and bounce them along the bottom. Other good and protected spots for anchoring in the harbor include Sailboat Basin, right up against Key West, and Calda Channel. Those spots always offer a quick fix of fishing, no matter the weather, and with live bait, there's no telling what you'll catch.

Many captains consider the winter the best time of the year in the harbor because the fishing heats up—there's also little boat traffic, fewer jet skis, and fewer parasails. The height of the harbor fishery begins in late February, when you'll find plenty of boats prospecting for tarpon using thick chum lines of shrimp trash—the famous harbor fishery for big tarpon, probably one of the best in all Florida. Those days you'll see plenty of boats lined up and hooking up. You can crowd among them, or for more of a challenge and more space, find your own spot along the Northwest Channel by checking charts or watching your depth finder for sudden drop-offs and bottom depressions. Even a slight depression of a few feet on your depth finder can be a worthwhile place to try, especially if baitfish hover around it.

Also in the winter, you can get good action for tarpon, permit, cobia, snapper, and blacktip sharks around Pearl Basin just north

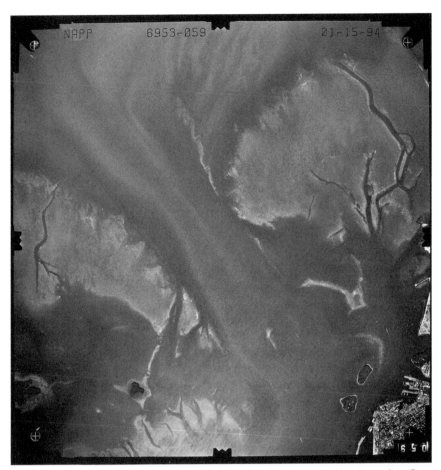

NAPP   6953-059   01-15-94

The Northwest Channel (from the top left of the frame to the island), surrounding flats, and harbor area hold plenty of spots fishable even in rough weather. From the USGS Project NAPP. Roll 6953-Frame 59.

of the harbor. In April and May, the fish move and filter into the Fleming Key area and to the tip of Key West near the mouth of the harbor, on their annual migration pattern. Then you have to search around for them in Jack Channel, around Sunset Key, and Calda Channel, until you find them.

Putting seasonal strategies aside, sometimes when you're in Key West you just want to fish for a couple hours, and the harbor is the convenient place to go for short trips. Many of the harbor's cuts and channels well-known for holding tarpon and permit are less than a mile from local marinas, including the most popular put-in for anglers towing boats, City Marina. Right along the channel parallel to Fleming Key, anchoring and chumming produces good catches of mangrove and lane snapper year-round. To know where to anchor, simply motor slowly over the channel's edge and watch your depth finder for congregations of fish marking below. Sometime chum will draw fish to your stern, but it's always better to start with fish below to get a good bite going.

Year-round, the many patch reefs throughout the harbor area teem with snappers and groupers that will give kids the fight of their lives, and it can't be beat for a day of fun fishing. *Florida Sportsman* Chart No. 11 marks numerous wrecks and patch reefs within minutes of local marinas, making the harbor a great destination for family fishing with a minimum of fuss.

Massive amounts of water pour through the northern side of the harbor from the Gulf and the harbor is open at both ends, which ensures constant water movement that cleanses and revitalizes the harbor with new bait and fresh activity on a tidal timetable. From the mouth of the harbor to Fleming Key at its back, there's about an hour and a half to two hours difference in the tide change. That means you have plenty of time to pick and choose your spots depending on your preference for tidal movement—incoming, high, slack, or outgoing.

All that water pouring into the harbor also means that high waves can build at its mouth during tidal flows, especially if the winds go against the tide, and with all the boat traffic around there, navigation can get tricky, fast. Don't be surprised to suddenly see six-foot waves at the harbor mouth when the surrounding seas might be only a foot or two.

In rough weather, anglers headed westward often take the nearby Lakes Passage to the west for protected and less crowded grounds. The Lakes Passage is a shallow, protected cove averaging four-feet deep that separates the Gulf and the Atlantic on the harbor's west-

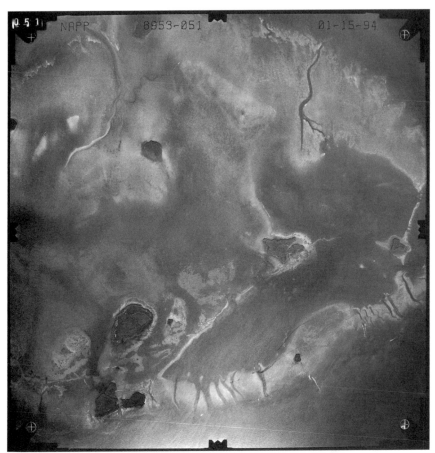

The Lakes Passage offers the calmest route between Key West and the Marquesas, and plenty of good fishing along the way. From the USGS Project NAPP. Roll 6953-Frame 51.

ern side by the Northwest Channel. Its waters often remain clear even when water everywhere else has turned muddy, so the Lakes offers flats anglers fishing of a last resort. The Lakes Passage also provides smaller boats protection from rough seas all the way to Boca Grande Channel. From there you need to know what's ahead. Boca Grande Channel, a major outlet for Gulf waters into the Atlantic, can be wicked, and coral heads south of the Marquesas stand less than a foot from the surface at low tide, so exercise caution.

However, for all boats, entrance to the passage is precise; the channel is surrounded by flats so shallow they become exposed at low tide. Near the mouth of the harbor, between those high flats that often strand unwary boaters, a couple of stakes, barely visible, mark a series of quick S turns into the Lakes. Boaters should consult charts before trying the entrance and go slowly if unfamiliar with the grounds.

Aside from all its angling opportunities, the harbor plays another important role in the fishery. It's one of the main places to catch many baits. The harbor and its markers yield all manner of baits for the fleet of charter boats and recreational anglers that head out of Key West on an almost daily basis, year-round. Many local captains start their day by pulling up to channel markers and catching their baits on sabiki rigs. Blue-runners, pilchards, threadfin herring, ballyhoo, mahua, pinfish, and other species all flourish in the harbor and its seagrass environs, which attests to its value as a nursery, shelter, and foraging ground for the entire surrounding fishery.

From the harbor, to the east and west you can see the backcountry keys and their channels and flats, one of the legendary shallow-water fisheries in the world.

3

The Flats

One of the World's Famous Fisheries for Tarpon, Bonefish, and Permit

On the flats with Phil Thompson on a late summer day, no less than a thousand juvenile gray snapper swarmed under us in the space of a minute's drift down a channel behind Cottrell Key, along with schools of baby barracudas, sharks, and countless pinfish, which flashed like dimes against the seagrass beds. Phil scanned the flat for the school of large permit he'd been seeing there, with tails so big "they were flopping over like the dorsals of killer whales," he said.

If that was a slight exaggeration, I knew what Phil meant. In the intricate world of the flats, even subtle signs of life feel huge, even awesome. That's why it's so electrifying to watch a big permit turn for your bait or fly in clear shallow water and why it's so staggering to witness a seven-foot bull shark attack a fly on the flats.

The Lower Keys fishery stretches from Big Pine to Key West to the Marquesas, across backcountry keys such as Content, Sawyer, and the Muds, over to the oceanside, including seagrass shallows off Bahia Honda, Sugarloaf, Big Coppitt, and many other keys. Chief among its game fish species, but far from the only ones, are tarpon, the silver king; bonefish, the gray ghost; and permit, a fish so wily and skittish on the flats that no one has yet successfully given it a nickname.

Capt. Phil Thompson never gets lonely in his backyard flats.

Anglers from around the world come to these waters in May and June for the annual tarpon migration, for bonefish in the fall, and for permit in the late spring and summer. Of course, the possibility of a flats slam—catching all three species in the same day—exists all year. Flats fishing as we know it developed here back in the sixties and seventies, and that historic appeal and the good quality of the fishing today, make the Lower Keys not only a popular destination, but also a proving grounds for flats anglers.

Some of these backcountry keys and their flats stand less than a 20-minute ride from Key West marinas. To the west, lie Archer and the Man and Woman Keys, and to the east, lie the Bay, Harbor, and Mud Keys. There are even a number of places along U.S. 1 where you can park your car and fish excellent flats—on the eastern side of Sunshine Key near Bahia Honda, and even in Key West, on the island's southern side, along Smather's Beach.

Though the flats may be the most easily visible, and other than the harbor itself, the most accessible fishery, they are by no means the most easily understood. Their mysteries, secrets, and sport are generally revealed only to those with patience, cunning, concentration and the kind of will to fish that can endure baking in sun on a slow-moving skiff for hours.

Some knowledge of the flats ecosystem helps to understand how fish behave when they're on and around the flats. As the main island chain of the Keys is built primarily upon what's left of an exposed reef, created and destroyed by intermittent rising and falling of sea levels over the last few hundred thousands of years, so too are the backcountry keys and their flats products of those same geological processes. As these reef tracts grew and were exposed by rising and receding seas, shifting sands formed shoals around them, and most recently, the backcountry islands that we see grew up on these shoal areas, attracting plant, mangrove, tree, and animal life. Next, the biological process of growth and decay developed the islands over thousands of years, a process that we can more or less observe as it happens around us today, in the way those tiny mangrove shoots grow to a stand of a few trees over a couple years, and then one day, into a small island. The cuts and channels around the flats and backcountry keys may change drastically with the passing of a single hurricane.

Because that shelf over which the backcountry keys stand is approximately one to twelve feet under the sea's surface and protected from wave action, the tidal flats that form can remain relatively undisturbed. With the region's average tides of one to three feet, some of those flats get exposed at low tide, while others remain at least minimally submerged. The effect is to create a gentle, yet dynamic tidal zone that attracts and supports a variety of benthic communities of underwater life, including seagrass beds, hard bottom structure, patchy coral formations, and bare substrate—the flats where many fish species forage.

Tarpon cruising in the face of a wave breaking over a flat on a windy morning, a permit tailing near the shoreline of a white-sand island, or a school of bonefish hunting through blades of green turtle grass in waters slick as glass are a few of the sights that strike the nerves of observant anglers. Even aside from those appearances by the big game fish, the entire experience of being on the flats is amazingly visual. A skiff can take you on a magic carpet ride over clear, shallow waters into another world.

The mazes of deep channels and cuts that border the flats not only carry Gulf and Atlantic waters in and out of the islands, but also hold a variety of species—fish, turtles, rays, birds among them. The animals use these channels and cuts for shelter and travel areas when they're not up on the flats hunting their favorite tidal cycle for prey.

The flats are important foraging grounds for a variety of species, and they are a vital and intricate link in the entire island chain's fishery for other reasons. They serve as a nursery grounds for a wide variety of game fish, including snapper and grouper that migrate offshore when they mature. The flats are also prime habitat for many of the Lower Keys most important baitfish, including pilchards, pinfish, mullet, and mahua, and you'll find many anglers on the flats stalking baits with cast nets early in the mornings.

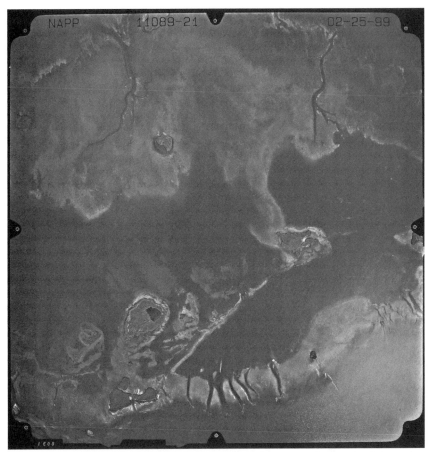

This aerial photograph shows the Seven Sisters Channels, to the south of the Lakes Passage, in broad contrast to the surrounding flats. From the USGS Project NAPP. Roll 11089-Frame 21.

Conditions, Tides, and Quarry

There are a lot of really good flats close to Key West—Tower flats, Seven Sisters, Cottrell Keys, and along Bluefish and Calda channels, Archer Key, Man and Woman Keys, Boca Grande. If an angler— guided or unguided—comes down to them with the single-minded purpose of catching a tarpon, bonefish, or permit on the flats, then he might get frustrated. If he comes down ready to catch fish and willing to learn more about the flats, then he'll have a good time.

Hiring a guide can be a worthwhile investment for a serious angler, whether or not the angler has his own boat. A good guide knows the waters, the baits to use, the tides, and what's running and biting in recent days. He'll also be able to pole you across the flats while you concentrate on fishing. Guides will also share a lot of information and expertise that their clients can later put to their own use.

Beginning with understanding the importance of tidal movements, there are a few tactics that can improve anyone's chances in these waters. Tidal flow governs the flood and fall of water and the movement of game fish on and off the flats and, just as importantly to anglers, determines whether your boat or skiff might be able to navigate a particular flat without getting grounded. Tidal changes range from a few feet during strong spring tides of the new and full moon, to less than a foot during mild neap tides. In practice, that means that at high tide, some flats might be fishable from center consoles with drafts of twelve inches or more, but as the tide recedes, the angler behind the wheel better be watching for a quick escape route or risk being grounded until the next high tide. With careful and observant navigation, the nearby channels can be fished in bigger bay boats and center consoles, but in general, the flats are the realm of skiffs, poled by guides and local anglers who either know the maze of waters and the intricacies of their tidal flows fairly well, or else are willing to learn by experience. Bigger boats get grounded quite easily, and remember that on the flats, time is measured not so much by hours but by rising and falling tides. Also, keep in mind that fines levied by the marine patrol for tearing up seagrass habitat are measured by the linear foot of damage.

To fish the flats in and out and up and down, you'll really want a boat that can get you into six inches of water or less, and running the flats requires practiced knowledge of how to read the water. Because of the clarity of the water in the Lower Keys, for the most part a boater can navigate the flats by sight, using the old saying,

"Blue, blue, sail on through, green, green, nice and clean, white, white, you just might, brown, brown, run aground." Still, be exceedingly careful of changing conditions. Even if the sun slips behind a cloud it can obscure your light in the instant that you need to find the curve of the narrow channel you're running. Twilight sneaks up like a thief. There are coral heads on turtle grass flats that can rip out your lower unit, and recent hurricanes have left a few wrecks that you don't want to discover by surprise.

It's essential to know—or at least have an accurate estimation—of the departures in time, plus or minus minutes or sometimes hours, for high and low tides for the locations you'll be fishing compared to the tides at known locations as stated in the area tide charts. Departures in tide times are not easy to map, and the more area-specific information you can gather before a trip, the better, considering what's at stake is not only the fishing, but also the chances of getting grounded. Anglers can usually obtain a good tide chart for their general fishing area—either Key West, Sugarloaf, Big Pine, on up the keys—from a nearby tackle shop and then either map out or ask about the time differentials for the specific flats areas that they'll be fishing. With all the channels and cuts and islands between the backcountry and the ocean side, less than a mile's distance between two places can easily mean a couple hours' difference in the time it takes a tide to arrive at the second location. If you know the flats really well, that means you can keep fishing the same tide stage at different flats, if you like, by moving along to them at the right intervals.

For the fishing, the effect of the tide, whether rising or falling, really depends on a particular flat. Guides say that they see bonefish on some flats only on a rising tide and only on a falling tide at other flats. Many flats, especially in the Marquesas, will find permit on the falling tide, trying to nose up crabs, whereas closer to Key West, permit come up on flats around Archer Key on flood tides.

After the tide, the most important factor on the fishing will be the water's temperature. (That is, the most important factor that we can reasonably determine, because the most important factor of all, of course, is the prevalence of food—the reason the fish are even on the flats in the first place. But the movements, abundance and hatchings of worms and fish and other creatures that flats species eat are fairly unpredictable.) So, finding the fish on the flats requires knowing not only where to look for them at their favored locations, but also knowing when to look for them given their comfort zones for temperature.

You can consider the water's temperature according to the season in order to judge how likely a certain species is to be on the flats. Tarpon enjoy a comfort zone around 74 degrees, the springtime temperature. Permit and bonefish like water in the 70s, but they can stand it a little warmer, about 76 to 82 degrees, which are the cooler water temperatures for the flats in the summer. Some guides say that tarpon are the most tolerant of the heat, and that you'll find them on the flats even as the water temperature approaches 90 degrees and goes higher. Permit have a hotter range than bonefish, but not as high as tarpon. Higher than 85 degrees, the water feels pretty hot to most species, including humans, and bones and permit don't hang around in it long.

However, because water on the flats is so shallow, it warms and cools quickly, and slight but significant temperature fluctuations occur not only seasonally, but also daily and even hourly. That means that with a period of warm weather in the winter, bonefish might move up on a favorite flat to comfortably feed before returning to their deeper, warmer haunts in the channels and elsewhere. In the summer, the permit and bonefish will get up on the flats in the mornings and late afternoons and, in the meantime, keep cool in deeper water. In the middles of those summer days, you'd be more likely to want to jump in the water than fish it.

As in blue water, on the flats it's difficult for the untrained eye to even see the fish, but sharpening your vision on the flats is probably the skill most necessary for improving your fishing. If you're relatively new to the flats, you can increase your chances of seeing movement by spending more time watching the white-sand patches where bonefish and permit show more easily than they do against the turtle grass. The fish won't stay over that sand long, but they'll travel the edges of it and give you a chance to see them. Against the grass, you might not see a permit until he's spooked and moving or unless you see it tailing in the distance and differentiate that tail from a piece of uprooted turtle grass. You'll also learn to read the surface of the water for any shimmering or ripples or wakes working against the current, or even disturbing the surface in the least. Also, always watch for the little puffs of mud from the bottom that might be created by a bonefish or a permit feeding, and check around rays, especially when they're feeding and mudding, because often they're trailed by other fish looking to pick up a quick bite of food.

Those anglers who are good at seeing fish know the difference between sight and vision, and they develop their vision, no matter how good their sight. One reason guides are so uncannily able to see fish is that they spend so much time watching the water when no fish are present at all that they can easily pick out the slightest difference in the normal scene—that mark or movement that turns out to be a fish. That ability says a lot about the patience it takes to fish on the flats.

Staking Out and Poling

Once you're out where you want to be when you want to be there, knowing the environment comes into play. Flats fishing is a lot like hunting. You stalk them, sight them, and take your shot. If you don't see a lot of life on the flat you're fishing, be prepared to move on, because most often, a lot will happen on a flat once it becomes alive with the proper conditions and tidal flow. Depending on the season, a number of species will appear on the flat together, including sharks, rays, tarpon, permit, snapper, baitfish, and all their various prey. Watch along the edges of the flats, at the channels, where tarpon and permit will sometimes hover waiting for prey to wash off

Capt. Phil Thompson scans and poles, looking for the tell-tale signs of flat-out action.

the flat in a falling tide, and always know what tide, and its strength, you're facing. The big three species are each affected by tides but will be influenced by different tidal movements at different locations.

Anglers have two choices on the flats: They can either stake out by planting their pushpole in the sandy bottom at a likely point of intercept and tying it to their platform or off their stern to hold the boat in place, or they can pole across flats to cover more territory. For anglers exploring the waters on their own, especially when fly-fishing, a little of both is recommended to get the best chance to learn the area and to get a few calm shots at fish.

An ideal situation for the angler is to be able to stake out along the edge of a flat where you know, by experience, that the tarpon or permit will come from a certain direction. That way, you can get set in the right direction, considering the wind, to make the casts as the fish approach. That's especially important when fly-fishing. One of the big advantages to staking out is that you'll be ready when the fish show, with little risk of spooking them when they approach. If the fish don't come when you expect them, you might have to risk moving to find them. Even on good days, there will be lulls, fifteen to twenty minutes, maybe an hour, and they have to be endured with patience to preserve the advantage of a silent position when fish draw near. In some hard-bottom areas, anglers can even get out and wade for an even stealthier presentation to cruising fish. Both tactics work, but one may be preferred depending on the angler's level of patience. Staking out requires considerable knowledge of a flat, experience with its fish, and confidence in that knowledge, while poling can get very tiring and takes practice to learn.

General consensus says that more and bigger bonefish are available in the Middle and Lower Keys, whereas more permit are available around Key West and westward, especially around the Marquesas. Tarpon run throughout the Middle and Lower Keys, and the spring migration during May and June sees the highest numbers of them present. The Seven Mile Bridge and Bahia Honda Bridge are

Capt. Tim Carlile, of Sugarloaf, with a prized backcountry bonefish, about average size for the region.

favorite places to anchor and bait-fish for tarpon on spring nights. The year-round resident tarpon of the Lower Keys are much warier than the migrants, and summer nights are the best time to go for them.

Flats and Backcountry Strategy

The next area that we'll visit on the tour of the fishery, in a bit, the backcountry, actually contains the flats within it, at least north of Key West. To the west, the Marquesas flats aren't in the backcountry, but in the Marquesas. It's a bit of local directional terminology, but the import of it is simple. Close to Key West, the flats generally get separated out from the backcountry because they're each such specific terrain that the same species will behave differently on the flats than they do in backcountry channels, and they require different techniques. Yet it's easy to fish the flats and those backcountry islands together in the same day. Most anglers do at least prepare to fish both types of water, in case the flats are quiet, and to increase their chances of hookups with multiple species.

Anglers should map a route in advance of likely hot spots on flats and backcountry terrain, and the time that they'll spend fishing each. The best routes will depend on the activity of the season, of course, so each quarter of the year will produce a different, though typical daily routine.

For instance, in winter, flats anglers might pole a couple of flats looking for permit, then by mid-day when the water warms, look for barracudas and sharks sunning themselves in shallow flats. Finally, they might finish the afternoon by hooking up to food and fun fish such as redfish, jacks, and snappers around backcountry keys. They might also find a few pompano, sea trout, and snook in the backcountry channels in the winter months too, especially if they head eastward up toward the Mud Keys and Sawyer Keys.

In the spring, the flats–backcountry routine can be tailored to include a pass on the flats for big keeper cobia and trailing mudding rays or shots at tarpon and mackerel in the channels. In the summer, fish early in the morning and late in the afternoon, and take a break at the hottest part of the day. The fall in the Lower Keys may be the best time for anglers to pursue a grand slam on the flats.

Whatever the season, plan a series of spots to check in your search for tarpon, bonefish, and permit between the flats and the channels, and you'll create a memorable trip for yourself. At any time of the year, a number of other species, such as mutton snappers, kingfish, mackerel, and bluefish, can appear by surprise on the flats and backcountry channels. If you can safely navigate these different waters in your boat, then the fishing can be quite varied from the flats to the backcountry key channels, even though they're literally side by side.

Now, onto the flats' surrounding terrain, called "the backcountry" in Key West.

4

The Backcountry and the Gulf of Mexico

Targeting Structure to the North

The backcountry in the Lower Keys refers to the waters and the islands between the main island chain and the mud banks bordering the open Gulf. That includes all the keys, flats, channels, and basins in between.

The backcountry islands and channels can be fished in the spring and summer, especially for mangrove snapper and small tarpon, and up the Keys, for redfish and sea trout, but for the most part in those seasons, anglers will concentrate on finding the flats species in and around the backcountry—with one exception in summer's second half: spiny lobsters. The backcountry basins, ledges, holes in hardbottom terrain, and rockpiles are havens for lobsters and they see their share of divers all during the lobster season. Plenty of spots no deeper than fifteen feet give shallow-going snorkelers good chances to bag some bugs.

The backcountry fishery changes dramatically every thirty miles or so as you move farther up the Keys, due to the differences in water temperature and salinity levels. Year-round, anglers find more redfish, snook, and sea trout toward the Middle Keys than around Key West, though the populations of snook and redfish near Key West seem to be increasing in the last few years, perhaps due to the rebound of baitfish stocks, thanks to the state's net ban implemented in 1995. Those same nets, of course, also killed plenty of reds, snook,

Prospecting backcountry channels turns up numerous species of game fish.

and other gamefish, so the benefits of the net ban to fisheries and to the environment are broad, complex, and profoundly important.

In the winter, Key West's backcountry really comes to life as a fun fishery. During those cooler months, many fish normally associated with inshore mainland Florida waters make their way down through the Gulf to the backcountry islands and channels—species such as redfish, bluefish, sea trout, ladyfish, Spanish mackerel, and the magnificent pompano. To catch these species on their seasonal migrations makes for great thrills and, especially in the case of pompano, great dinners. Big mangrove snappers also take up residence around backcountry islands for the heat that the mangrove root systems hold.

Around the Mud Keys and Harbor Keys, drifting through channels and bouncing jigs tipped with fresh shrimp along the bottom will turn up fish on almost every cast. In December and January,

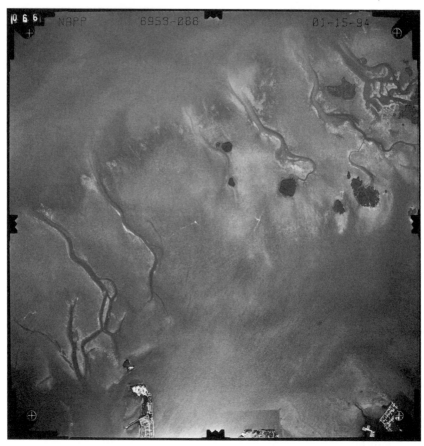

The backcountry, such as this swath directly north of Key West, stretches all the way up the island chain. It includes varying terrain and borders the open Gulf to the north (top of frame). From the USGS Project NAPP. Roll 6953-Frame 66.

speckled trout (live shrimp under popping corks) frequent the backcountry grass flats around Turkey Basin, the Contents, and Sawyer Key, just north of Big Pine and Sunshine Key, and the Upper Harbor Keys. All the grass flats in four to eight feet of water are prime grounds to see schools of these fish cruising by, and what's more, the lee sides of backcountry islands provide protection for smaller boats from the frequent blustery winds that blow this time of year.

On some of the hard-bottom flats in the fall and winter, you can even wade around looking for redfish and snook. Snook, like the mangrove snappers, will also hang around the root systems of many of the backcountry islands, happy to ambush live baits or sometimes even topwater lures and flies. Snook can be found down in the Marquesas too.

The close proximity of so many backcountry islands affords quick, though not easy, navigation among them. The flats between them offer treachery to boaters unfamiliar with their waters.

Not a bad way to spend a January afternoon, chasing pompano in the backcountry channels.

Often, anglers will start the day in the backcountry by cast-netting a few dozen pilchards from some of the deeper channels where they're usually plentiful in the cooler months. Then they'll take those baits and cast them along the banks of the Harbor Keys or Bay Keys for mangrove and snook, and maybe try jigs bounced along the bottom in the channels. If you can't get live baits or if you prefer artificials, always bring some D.O.A. TerrorEyz, D.O.A. shrimp, maybe some Gulp! for the jigs, and any other of your favorite lures.

In rough winter weather, the backcountry channels and basins offer about the only refuge, and those days you'll see center console boats anchored in the channels chumming up snappers and whatever else they can manage. The Northwest Channel is a favored spot to do this, but sometimes, with a north wind, even that gets too rough. On those days, stick close to the main islands, even between them. As a last ditch effort in bad weather, you can fish the channel directly north of Key West along Fleming Key, and anchor anywhere you mark fish, usually about a hundred yards from shore.

For the best results, look for somewhat clean water in the channel, and try to mark fish before you drop anchor and start chumming. You can pick up pinfish on a sabiki in that channel and drop them down on a knocker rig for the larger mangroves and possibly cobia lurking down deep. That channel, as well as nearby Calda and Bluefish Channel, run between ten and thirty feet deep, and in the winter, they hold plenty of fish, including tarpon and permit and lane snapper, and cero and Spanish mackerel. The mangrove snapper in this area are plentiful and usually range from barely legal to up to two pounds—not great but pretty good for a day when fishing would be impossible in most other locations.

The navigation is tricky in these waters, especially in a bigger boat with murky conditions that obscure the boundaries between the safer channels and the dangerous flats. If you're in a boat that draws a foot or more, be careful navigating through these channels, and always look ahead for markers to give a general indication of direction.

A little farther to the north, accessible to center consoles, are the small wrecks, rock piles, and patch reefs (many marked on maps) along the border of the backcountry and the open Gulf. North out Calda Channel, to the north of the Bay, Harbor, and Mud Keys, the shallow banks slowly give to the sloping floor of the Gulf. In those ten- to twenty-foot depths are the rock piles and patch reefs that hold snapper, grouper, redfish, and kingfish and cobia, as well as plenty of sharks, including blacktips. You can anchor in a position twenty to sixty feet off the patch reef and start chumming. These can be very good spots right after one of the frequent winter cold fronts that blow down from the north in January and February, because the backcountry fish retreat to these depths in the chill. It's possible that those winter fronts, with their winds, stir up the shrimp that live in the Gulf grounds and backcountry flats, and that the fish gather at the rock piles to rest between forays looking for shrimp.

These spots can be a great place to set up for a few hours of fun fishing, and they're only a twenty- to thirty-minute ride from local marinas. For tackle, 12-pound line on spinning gear with a fluoro-carbon leader does the job, and jigs tipped with shrimp or live baits work well. D.O.A. Bait Busters pull in plenty of fish, and redfish and jacks and snapper all love the D.O.A. weighted shrimp. You can also use a bare hook weighted with a split shot to keep it down as you drift it back with the current. Remember to anchor far enough away from the mark so that hooked fish can't run right back and cut you off in the rocks or wreck, or at least not every time.

Redfish, a great winter and spring catch in the backcountry channels around the Harbor, Mud and Content Keys, and Gulf rock piles, are known for their sense of scent. Many anglers believe that redfish rely primarily on scent, maybe because as inshore feeders, they frequently encounter murky water, or because their prey, shrimps and crabs, can hide their bodies but not their scent. Redfish certainly are not blind, and when they're in the relatively clear waters of the Lower Keys, they're reluctant to take anything but the most delicately, cleanly presented baits, even live baits. They can't be easily fooled with cut bait on heavy bottom rigs as they can elsewhere. They prefer a live shrimp or pinfish or pilchard on a light fluoro or mono leader, and they'll strike a bucktail jig worked along the bottom.

While those near-shore waters of the Gulf at the edge of the backcountry can often be clear even in the winter, a spate of windy weather can churn up the waters enough to discourage the bite from most species, but not sharks. Some anglers say that they do better on an incoming tide from the Atlantic on those patch reefs and wrecks because it sweeps the baits out of the backcountry channels and off the flats into the deeper water, and whether on an incoming our outgoing, you'll definitely want some moving current to get your chum flowing to the fish.

The Florida Keys National Marine Sanctuary

Nearly the entire backcountry and flats fisheries are covered by the Florida Keys National Wildlife Refuges and subject to their rules and regulations. Many anglers who travel hundreds, even thousands of miles to that tiny corner of Florida for a chance at a flats grand slam may not even know that they're fishing in waters mandated by Congress and sanctioned by the state primarily for wildlife preservation.

Three refuges cover the Lower Keys backcountry from Bahia Honda west to the Marquesas—The Key West Refuge, established in 1908; the Great White Heron Refuge, in 1938; and the Key Deer Refuge, in 1957. Their territories overlap significantly, and they are managed as one unit. Like all of the 542 refuges nationwide, they were established by Congress to protect endangered species and their habitat. The National Wildlife Refuge System began in Florida with the establishment of Pelican Island in 1903 to protect shore and migratory birds from being hunted for their plumage used in ladies' hats.

In the Lower Keys, the refuges' ecosystems provide habitat for those threatened and endangered species, including goliath grouper, who use the backcountry shallows as a nursery ground before moving out to deeper waters in the Gulf and Atlantic as adults. Three species of endangered sea turtles live in refuge waters, and a fourth moves through the area. The waters are an important rest and refuel area for birds migrating between the northern and southern hemispheres. Resident bird species include ibises, bald eagles, frigates, egrets, ospreys, herons, plovers, pelicans, and cranes. The biggest population of great white herons anywhere nests there in the winter, and ospreys nest in the branches of mangroves alongside winding creeks.

The refuge includes no-motor zones to protect nesting areas of birds, including frigates, and no-entry zones by craft of any kind. The no-entry zones give the fish a place to rest, with no pressure, and you might see fish schooling there, even if you can't go after them. All no-motor and no-entry zones are marked by signs and buoys. These and other actions regulated and enforced by refuge authorities benefit the fishing, including the jet-ski ban in back-country waters implemented in the early nineties.

The Fish and Wildlife Service, an agency of the Department of the Interior, owns the lands of the refuges. In most areas, the refuges overlap with the Florida Keys National Marine Sanctuary, an agency of NOAA and the Department of Commerce, which was created in 1990 to help protect the reef and the marine environment from Key Largo down to the Tortugas. The sanctuary's rules for safe navigation benefit the refuges, of course, and sanctuary officials handle all boat groundings and infractions, like plowing through seagrass and anchoring on coral.

Neither agency manages the fishery. The refuge can close areas to protect wildlife, and the sanctuary can close areas to protect the reef and build fish stocks, but the state retains the rights to fisheries management. Refuge and sanctuary officials enforce those regulations by citing and ticketing violators.

The refuges, and the system that manages them, are both designed to enact the will of the people to protect those waters—our waters.

The Gulf of Mexico

North of the backcountry keys, the Gulf's floor is mostly hard and flat, without much cover. It slowly slopes away from the islands, dropping only to about 80 feet at its deepest within range of Key West. It's like a desert for migrating fish, and any structure attracts fish as an oasis does a traveler. It's not that hospitable to anglers either, unless they know the terrain. But those wrecks, patch reefs, towers and shoals in the Lower Gulf of Mexico offer good fishing for a number of prized species.

For the greater part of the year, both mangrove and yellowtail, amberjack, bonito, red, black and goliath grouper, and king and cero mackerel, among other resident species, can be found around the various wrecks located between fifteen to forty miles north of Key West. In the springtime and summer, for those anglers willing to make the trip, a hot fishery develops behind the traveling shrimp boats in the Gulf, and blackfin tuna are the main quarry.

Different species seem to dominate different locations. For instance, on the Craig wreck, you'll often find yellowtail. Another popular spot is the Sturtevant Wreck, in sixty-five feet of water, at seventeen miles (#16 on *Florida Sportsman's* chart for Key West), where permit gather in the spring. The string of U.S. Department of Defense towers that run from Southwest Florida out to the Tortugas and hold cobia and snapper and grouper, among other species, are also marked on charts. Of them, the closest to Key West is the V Tower, in shallower water just east of the New Grounds, thirty-two miles west–northwest of Key West. The P Tower is north of Key West at forty miles, and the S Tower northwest of Key West at fifty-six miles.

These and dozens of other locations like the Grouper Bar, Smith Shoals, Edmund Lowe Shoals, Ellis Rock, and the New Grounds, and numerous wrecks, some marked on maps and others too new to make it into print, provide good fishing year-round.

For productivity in the Gulf, no time of the year can match the heights of the spring season, when permit, cobia, kingfish, and

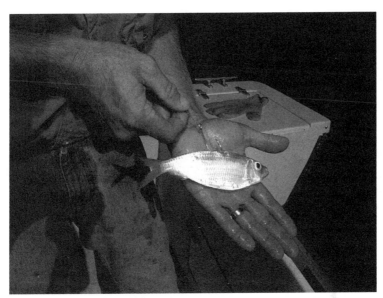

Big pilchard rigged for Gulf kingfish.

blackfin tuna all pass through the Lower Gulf on their seasonal migrations. Each of these species is often available at different locations within miles of each other, and often more than one of them inhabits the same location.

Not only cobia, but also Gulf kings gather at wrecks to rest and feed before moving northward with the warming temperatures, and spawning permit school at wrecks in the vicinity too. Bonito and blackfin tuna also swarm in the Gulf north of Key West to feed alongside shrimp boats, where they take advantage of the by-catch thrown overboard by shrimpers every morning.

By late April, the permit spawn has peaked, and water temperatures in the Gulf begin to rise into the mid to high 70s, which prompts the cobia to begin their migration north. Once the waters reach the high 70s, most of the bigger, non-resident cobia will be gone. The tuna hang around the shrimp boats well into May and June.

But for those March and April weeks when all species of fish I've mentioned are present, it's hard to turn away from a trip into

Bonito make great sport on all tackle but must be released quickly if they are to survive.

the Gulf. Conditions for these trips are especially good on the first calm day after a hard stretch of southerly wind. The fish are often bunched around the wrecks and towers after rough weather, whether pushed there by the wind or hovering there for food and protection. Being the first anglers there after windy stretches usually brings good results.

For fishing the wrecks and towers with live bait, try pinfish to satisfy the cobia, a few blue runners and pilchards for kings, and live crabs for permit. It's best to start the run northward across the Gulf's pale slate waters as early as possible in the a.m.

Everyone wants to be first on a spot, but whatever your position, it's important to observe guide's etiquette at towers and wrecks and respect everyone's right to fish. Go upwind and upcurrent and drift down in your turn, and you might even ask what's happening before starting to fish.

Before anchoring, pull up over a wreck to see which way the wind and tide push your drift. That prepares you for setting the anchor and getting the wreck downcurrent so chum pulls the fish off the wreck. Block chum and chopped-up fresh mojarra work fine, though any kind of cut fish works to put more substance in the chum. The average depth of wrecks out there is about sixty feet.

Sometimes you'll find schools of bonito, blackfin, kings, or smaller mackerel feeding on bait schools in open water, and it's fun to corral them. But if you really want to find blackfin, you have to go to the shrimp boats, and involvement with the shrimpers themselves can be one of the most elaborately involved and interesting of all Keys fishing trips. The fishing can be so hot anglers can get their fill before noon.

It is by no means impossible for out-of-town anglers to try the Lower Gulf trip in their own boats, but it takes advance work to plan the list of wrecks that you'll visit and time to get the baits.

Joel Day prospecting at the V Tower. Nearby wrecks hold amberjack such as this one landed by Capt. Ralph Delph.

The Gulf is out of cell-phone range, and the ride out to those Gulf wrecks, towers, and shrimp boats can be long and costly. Because of the distances involved, it's really the province of a handful of Lower Keys captains, most of whom have been fishing there for many years. And, if the temperamental spring weather blows up on your chosen day, you'll have to change plans. For both wrecks and towers, an early start and good numbers and charts are essential. Once you're out on those waters, it's a long way between the wrecks. You don't want to waste time, or gas, hunting for spots. It's easy to cover 100 miles in a day, even 150, especially if you're going after tuna behind the shrimp boats. The relative inaccessibility of these locations makes the trip difficult, productive, and worth every bit of effort.

GPS coordinates for towers closest to Key West:

V Tower—32 miles from Key West—24-40.84'N/82-17.21'W
P Tower—40 miles from Key West—25-07.0'N/82-00.0'W
S Tower—56 miles from Key West—25-02.0'N/82-22.0'W

5

Into the Atlantic

Patch Reefs, the Reef, the Bar, and Offshore

Throughout the Lower Gulf, you can find rock piles and patch reefs that produce good fishing year-round with a seasonal rotation of species. Similar small aggregations of coral heads, sea fans, sponges, and other creatures that attract fish can be found even closer to Key West, near the harbor and on the Atlantic side, throughout Hawk's channel, which borders the southern side of the islands down from Islamorada.

By offshore anglers, Hawk's Channel is considered a border to cross on the way to the wide open Atlantic, but the zone is a good fishery in its own right, especially for anglers visiting the area or on smaller boats. Even rock piles in there hold fish. The nearest Hawk's Channel patch reefs lie in less than fifteen feet of water, within swimming distance of the island. Others stand thirty- to sixty-feet deep, closer to the reef. In size, they range from small, low-profile stretches of coral and structure only a foot high, less than thirty yards long and twenty yards wide, to 100-yard tracts of big, high, old coral heads interspersed with other marine growth. Generally, these patch reefs are dominated by soft coral congregations and sea fans and sponges, while the main reef tract has hard corals. All types of corals are extremely susceptible to damage from anchors, chains, and hands.

Patch reefs may be one of the best-kept public secrets in all Key West fishing, and the anglers who do quite well on them are grateful to the majority of other anglers who completely overlook them.

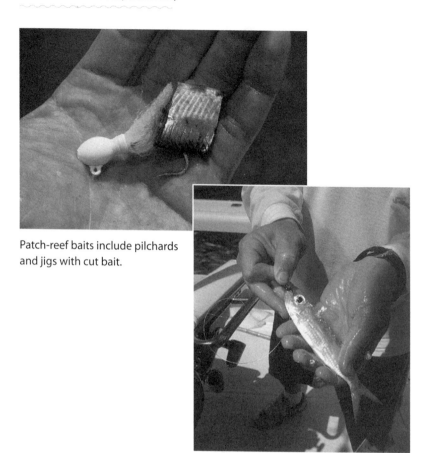

Patch-reef baits include pilchards and jigs with cut bait.

Quite a variety of snapper and grouper live around them, and more visit in their foraging journeys. Year-round it's common to see good size mutton snappers, hogfish, lobster, plenty of yellowtail, resident cero mackerel, and at least one big grouper if you're diving, even on shallow reefs. Other species come and go with the seasons, and seasonal visitors include cobia, Spanish mackerel, and tarpon, plus much bigger grouper and snapper.

Standard technique for fishing patch reefs involves anchoring upcurrent from the structure and chumming. Jigging, live-baiting, drifting cut baits, trolling, and even throwing plugs all bring fish to the boat. The technique you use depends on the time and bait you want to spend at the patch reef and the species you're after.

To catch a mixed-bag, anchor in a position upcurrent of the patch reef that lets your chum line flow toward the structure, but be careful not to anchor in the middle of the few nearshore channels that larger boats use to reach island docks. Anchor far enough away so that you'll get the fish off the rocks, but not so far that fish won't respond to your chum. In most conditions, forty to sixty feet is a good measure. Most anglers like long fluorocarbon leaders and use jigs tipped with cut ballyhoo or fresh mackerel strips. Bonito and squid strips work well too, especially for yellowtail. Live baits, including ballyhoo, shrimp, pinfish, and pilchards work like a charm.

As on the flats, tide phase plays a big role in the angling action at patch reefs. Offshore, more complex forces govern currents, but inshore at the patches, the tidal currents will dominate water flow, and you can therefore time your fishing to coincide with your desired conditions. A good, but not ripping current suits fishing in these waters, and after about an hour you'll see a change in the flow, either increasing or decreasing. Rest assured that the fishing may change with it, and if it drops off, consider moving to another spot.

The patch reefs are also a great place to stop and chum up live ballyhoo to use as baits offshore, and often you can catch them and use them for bait at the same patch reef, especially for big cero mackerel that cruise these waters. Once the ballyhoo gather in the chum slick behind your boat, immediately throw a cast net on them quickly or pick them off with a sabiki rig tipped with tiny bits of bait, because oftentimes they'll disappear as quickly as they arrive, run off by their predators, barracuda and cero mackerel.

The patch reefs really are hidden treasures in the local fishery. Many anglers run right by them on their way to the reef, only to catch the very same species. It's true that the yellowtail may not be the big flags that you can catch down at the End of the Bar, but keepers are plentiful, and a lot less time and fuel to reach. Many are also accessible by kayak.

The patch reefs even have their seasonal times when they turn into hot spots. Hawk's Channel can be an excellent place to look for cobia in the winter and early spring. In mid-summer, big mangrove snapper are migrating from the Gulf to the reef to spawn, and they stop at patch reefs, and again in August on their return. After that, at summer's end through the fall, fairly big mutton snappers come in from deeper water to hunt shrimp and baitfish that begin to reappear in the cooling shallow waters. Mutton snapper tend to prowl around the edges of patch reefs, often over sandy bottom or where the sand meets a grass edge. This is true of muttons out past the reef as well. They like the sandy hard terrain near rocky and coral structure, though they won't be hiding in the rocks as grouper will.

And for most of lobster season, the patch reefs on the Atlantic—from the Lower Keys all the way down to the Marquesas—are favorite spots for divers in small boats to anchor and catch lobster and spear fish in ten- to twenty-foot depths.

In the colder months, December through March, bigger black and red grouper move from the depths to the patch reefs in the warmer shallow waters. Trolling diving plugs and feathers with strip baits over, around, and alongside patch reefs is one favorite technique for landing them. These are fairly big black grouper, often greater than twenty pounds, not commonly associated with such shallow water. The technique requires fairly strong tackle and a stiff rod to hold and fight them, too, because once the fish attack the trolled lures, it's necessary to keep the boat moving forward to help draw the grouper from their holes. Otherwise, they'll turn and run right back inside and cut the lines against the rocks and coral heads. Use a wire shock tippet and a heavy, long fluorocarbon or monofilament leader, and get the plug or lure down deep enough, about fifteen feet down, or five or ten feet off the bottom, to entice the grouper to chase it.

The big patch reefs in Hawk's Channel are easily accessible and clearly marked on fishing charts, and once you spend a little time out there, you'll find plenty of others. The size of the patch reef doesn't necessarily correlate to the size and number of fish on it either, and a very small patch is worth checking for fish. Try not to hit any of the patches too hard, or too often, or you'll risk wiping it out and ruining it for other fish and other anglers. Take a few fish from a patch reef and move to another one. They're especially valuable locations to those anglers with smaller boats who can't make it out past the reef very often at all.

The patch reefs grow on the slowly deepening sea floor of sand and seagrasses between twenty and forty feet. The sea floor rises to the main reef about seven miles from the harbor, clearly marked by Sand Key Light—a great destination itself and a landmark for so much offshore action.

The Reef

The Florida Keys reef tract is the third largest living coral reef in the world, after Australia's Great Barrier Reef and Belize's Meso-American Reef. The Keys reef runs about 220 miles, from Key Biscayne down to the Tortugas, at a distance between four and eight miles from shore, pretty much parallel to the island chain. Staghorn, elkhorn, and brain coral are dominant hard coral species, but many other species of hard and soft corals and sea fans live along the reef in its incredibly diverse ecosystem.

These species of coral need sunlight to grow, unlike deepwater corals, and in some locations the reef almost reaches the surface, creating potential disasters for unwary boaters. In many places near Key West, the reef rises ten to twenty feet off the bottom in forty-foot depths, though there are walls along the edge where the reef drops off to fifty- and sixty-foot depths. Many canyons, where fish and lobster roam, cut through the reef like a maze.

The reef's history is intricately linked to Key West's. In the 1800s wreckers and salvagers of ships on the reef earned so much money that Key West became one of the wealthiest cities in the country, and the reef fishery has long helped to support the area's commercial and recreational fisheries. Today, the Keys' reef gets more divers and anglers than any other reef in the world, because of its ease of accessibility, the density of the population nearby and the highly developed tourist industry.

Coupled with the additional stressors of runoff pollution and warming sea temperatures, the naturally fragile reef has been struggling lately. Whether or not the tract near Key West will even survive in the near future remains to be seen. Portions closer to the Tortugas appear to be healthier. Everybody knows about the trouble and that damage from anchors and groundings kill coral immediately, and no one needs the troubles and fines these mishaps bring. Some anglers are even concerned about the amount of sand that gets dumped around the reef by people chumming with sandballs, an old-fashioned technique whose time may now be passed. Always know the rules for reef use created by the Florida Keys Marine Sanctuary, including its numerous no-take, preserve, and mooring ball anchorage-only zones, and abide by them. A brain coral takes 50 years to grow two feet tall, and can be wiped out by the swipe of an anchor.

On very slow days, charter boats take their clients to the reef to troll up a barracuda, an almost guaranteed catch. In winter, expect cero and Spanish mackerel and yellowtail on top of the reef, grouper and muttons on bottom, and blacktip, lemons and spinner sharks anywhere. When water temps rise to the mid 70s in the early spring, permit might hit jigs and live crabs where they spawn at certain reef locations. All along the reef, anglers troll for grouper with #20 or #30 diving Rapalas with a 50-pound-test leader. If you have a downrigger, try a ballyhoo and pink or green skirt for muttons and grouper (remember to monitor your depths and run the downrigger accordingly). If it's too weedy to troll, fish the bottom with half a ballyhoo on a heavy deep-jig. You can easily combine a half day fishing near the reef with a half day snorkeling. The sights and snorkeling are especially good in the Sanctuary's no-fishing zones, and boaters can easily tie off at the big white mooring buoys provided by the Sanctuary.

South of the reef, we're into blue water, but first we have to make a stop at another nearby offshore landmark: the Bar.

The Bar

From the reef, depths drop steeply to sixty to 100 feet before rising quickly to the Bar, which is completely submerged but an important feature of the offshore fishery. Also known as the Intermediate Reef, the Bar is a dead reef just south, about one-eighth mile away and parallel to the living reef. It had its heyday when sea levels were a bit lower than they are today. Wherever it runs—more consistently in the Upper and Lower Keys than in the Middle Keys—the Bar forms a trough between itself and the reef, and this trough dips to forty- to sixty-foot depths. The Bar itself rises to within twenty and thirty feet of the surface—various depths at various places as it runs. That trough between the Bar and the reef provides plenty of habitat for reef fish, baitfish, and the fish that forage on them, including pelagics.

Right on top of the Bar itself is prime yellowtail snapper habitat, and the first place anglers look for those fish on their depth finders. Given the right conditions, yellowtail might be found schooling at a steep drop-off in the Bar, or on the oceanside of the Bar, where the ocean floor begins its descent. Those depths past the Bar of 100, 150, and 200, are all extremely significant readings in the fishery. By those depths, anglers mark their positions past the reef, and many of the depths are associated with prime grounds for certain species. For instance, ninety to 120 feet is prime yellowtail territory; ninety to 200 feet, mutton and black grouper; 150 feet, sailfish; 500 feet, snowy grouper, 2,000 feet, swordfish and marlin.

For most species, the favored depths change with the seasons. For example, dolphin in the spring will be found in 200 to 600 feet, but in the summer, more often in 600 to 2,000 feet. At all times, local anglers will mark and call their catches by those depths, and familiarization with the depths and even the terrain past the reef is the key to understanding where to catch various species, and also how to listen and talk about the offshore fishery.

Approximately fifteen miles southwest of Key West, nearly south of Boca Grande Key, the Bar's sixty-foot face abruptly ends in 100

African pompano visit Atlantic wrecks, but their brief migratory appearances make them tough to target reliably.

feet of water, creating a steep drop-off appropriately known as the End of the Bar. The radical drop causes currents to swirl, catching baitfish in rippling waters and drawing pelagic predators—and anglers. The End of the Bar is another hot spot and a landmark feature in the fishery by which local anglers indicate their positions relative to currents, color changes, weeds, birds, and schooling fish and baitfish, basically everything important to offshore action. In its own right, the End of the Bar is probably the premier destination for live-baiting trips out of Key West for blackfin tuna and wahoo. Many nearby wrecks, such as the Sub, are favorite spots, and they're all marked on *Florida Sportsman's* Chart number 11. Big flag yellowtail, dolphin, kingfish, grouper, porgies, muttons—almost all game fish in the area visit the End of the Bar at some time of the year.

The End of the Bar also marks the gateway to "down west," all the locations that remain relatively untouched due to Key West's isolation. Tail End Buoy, Cosgrove Light, Coalbin Rocks, the offshore region between the Marquesas and the Tortugas—these locations account for much of Key West's reputation as an offshore mecca. Rebecca Shoals and Tail End Buoy are tournament kingfish locations, and those anglers who have the numbers for bottom spots down here catch fish every outing. Often, they'll visit spots untouched since their own previous visit. The cold months bring great trolling in nearby shallow waters, and by the spring that bottom fishing heats up in depths more than 100 feet. Numerous wrecks in the vicinity hold amberjack and red snapper, and in the winter, cobia too. These locations mark the westernmost limits of a day's round trip from Key West, though no one says you can't go down to the Dry Tortugas and stay a few nights.

South of the Bar, you're in open water, ninety miles to Cuba across the Straits of Florida. Compared to some other well-known fisheries such as Kona, Hawaii, and Andros Island, Bahamas, which have steep drop-offs to thousands of feet of blue water close by, the continental shelf south of Key West descends fairly gradually south of the reef. But compared to the rest of Florida, where the drop-off is even more gradual, Key West offers a steep decline to great depths. At every depth, there are productive habitats and wrecks for bottom fish. Let's emphasize—there are *a lot* of wrecks off the reef in Key West—far more than any other area in the Keys. Check charts for them.

Most recreational anglers in center console boats troll between the reef and Wood's Wall, 2,000 feet deep, about eighteen miles south of the reef, where the continental shelf finally drops off. Generally, only bigger sportfishers and charter boats range beyond 2,000 feet.

Wood's Wall is probably the most important feature of the offshore fishery in Key West. It is named for Norman Wood, who along with his fishing partner Wayne Hunt, explored and rediscovered the potential for offshore fishing in Key West in the seventies and eighties. Especially for blue marlin fishing, the Wall still provides the best year-round location for offshore action. Dolphin

Slammer dolphin can be found close to the reef in spring and farther offshore in summer.

in the spring, summer and fall, tuna in the summer, swordfish in the summer, marlin in the summer and fall, sailfish in the summer, wahoo almost any time of year—all show up around the Wall. It's usually the first destination of anglers fishing in Key West marlin tournaments.

In addition to the Wall's steep drop-off, plunging from about 800 feet down to 1,200 and quickly thereafter to 2,000 feet, three major cracks in the Wall also attract action, and they're the primary destinations for anglers. They're known as the West, Middle, and East Cracks.

These are their coordinates and headings from Key West:

Lat/Long number, Miles, and Heading from Key West
West Crack: 24° 15.37'N 81° 50.06'W, 13nm, 193 degrees
Middle Crack: 24° 14.76'N 81° 47.01'W, 14nm, 181 degrees
East Crack: 24° 14.20'N 81° 35.38'W, 18nm, 146 degrees

These are the places where Hemingway found marlin on his trips over to Cuba, though it's not certain whether or not he knew what structure attracted the fish there.

Other good hot spots on the way to the Wall include the jagged sea floor peaks between 600 and 700 feet known as the Ups and Downs, which also hold good deep bottom fishing and produce ripping surface currents that can attract baitfish and pelagics. These are good areas to begin to troll if you're headed out to deeper water. The Ups and Downs numbers are:

Ups and Downs East: 24° 27.90'N 81° 10.60'W
Ups and Downs Middle: 24° 25.10'N 81° 21.40'W
Ups and Downs West: 24° 22.50'N 81° 30.70'W

Most Keys anglers keep a variety of outfits handy for the innumerable opportunities in nearby waters.

Beyond the Wall, the ocean floor drops off. You're not likely to encounter too much traffic except freighters, Coast Guard vessels, commercial fishing vessels, the occasional big yacht on its way down to Mexico or Central America, and even occasionally, especially in the spring and summer, crafts carrying Cubans escaping to the States. Out there, you're halfway to Havana, and you're on your own.

At night, the oceans out past Wood's Wall are the territory of cargo freighters and very alert captains. Were we there in the late afternoon, we would likely go back to Key West for the night, before heading down west for the next leg of our tour, unless we were on a big sportfisher with at least one very wide-awake and dependable captain. From Key West, it's about an hour-and-a-half ride in a fast boat down to the Tortugas, Key West's fishing frontier.

6

The Marquesas and the Dry Tortugas

Adventure Destinations within a Day's Range

The days and nights that I have spent west of Key West, in the Marquesas and the Tortugas, have been some of the most memorable outdoors trips of my life. If you can, I recommend going to that corner of the earth as soon as possible. Not only will you find wild fishing, but also sights and experiences that you've never had and will find only there—especially if you stay overnight.

At twenty-five miles west of Key West, the Marquesas offer pristine flats and shallow water fishing, and many deep water options close by. These islands are entirely remote, yet accessible in a flats boat within an hour of Key West marinas. With no facilities, and beyond the range of most cell phones, the Marquesas still belong to the wild.

Simply a ring of small mangrove islands and beaches that shelter shallow Mooney Bay on the shelf between the Gulf and the Atlantic, the Marquesas are the only atoll in the continental United States. Unlike most atolls, geologists suspect that the Marquesas weren't formed by an underlying volcano, but rather by the slow accumulation of sands on the old reef (no camping allowed).

Along with shallow flats for permit, bonefish, and tarpon, mangrove-lined channels with snapper, snook, and sharks, the Marquesas offer old target wrecks nearby that hold cobia and

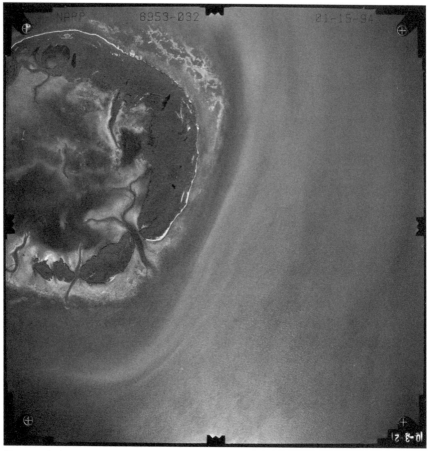

This aerial photograph of the Marquesas shows the deep channel at the southeastern portion of the atoll where big boats can anchor, while flats craft and kayaks can enter Mooney harbor, seen inside the ring. From the USGS Project NAPP. Roll 6953-Frame 32.

grouper, and offshore spots such as Cosgrove Light a few miles to the south. You can even dive for lobster in the shallows.

You can run out there for a day trip and catch a chosen tide, but the Marquesas also make an outstanding overnight destination for Florida boaters. After the worst threat of summer hurricanes has passed, and before the big winter winds blow, the autumn brings great weather and overnighters to the Marquesas. Big boats require careful navigation around the Marquesas' channels, but they offer the mothership option of carrying and towing other craft to explore all the Marquesas varied environs. Ideally, if you can tow a flats boat and carry a kayak on your deck, you can get to every nook and cranny of the Marquesas. Smaller craft can take the Lakes Passage to Boca Grande, but bigger boats take the oceanside route. Either way, little more than an hour after leaving Key West, the Marquesas' low profile will rise up on the horizon.

A bent stake barely a foot above the water marks the southeastern channel entrance, and big boats need high tide to get in there. Another stake fifty yards farther indicates the narrow course to safe anchorage. The southwestern channel provides slightly deeper passage. Most channels and islands in the Marquesas don't even have names.

Mullet, pilchards, mahua, pinfish, and ballyhoo are all readily available in the area by cast net, but be sure to bring crabs or crab imitations: Few places in the world provide a better opportunity to catch permit on crabs or on a fly than the Marquesas.

In a kayak, you can get so high on a flat that the fish come to you, and you can cover a lot of territory fairly easily and other areas that might be too mucky to wade. If you're kayaking the Marquesas, unsuspecting fish might not even know you're around.

It takes about an afternoon to kayak through the channel east of Gull Key and around Mooney Harbor, where juvenile tarpon and good size mangrove snapper swirl under you at the channel's edges. It's about a two-hour paddle from the western side of the Marquesas back to the eastern side.

Inshore anglers might want to check the inside mangrove banks, especially around small channel mouths, for mangrove snapper and snook on the feed. A surprising number of snook live in the Marquesas, possibly with underwater springs as their freshwater source. Look for tarpon in the channels on the falling tide.

"When the spring migration comes through here, you can see a thousand tarpon at once," says Phil Thompson, veteran of many Marquesas overnighters. "Their bodies are silver and blue from the

A mothership vessel offers comfort, and with a kayak and flats boat in tow, gives complete access to all Marquesas waters.

clear Caribbean waters, unlike the green shade of local Key West tarpon. In the summer, you come out here and at night the tarpon are popping so hard it sounds like somebody's throwing handfuls of lit M-80s all around."

Even in the fall, many tarpon and very big sharks roam through the deeper channels at night, and the sharks love live-lined mullet, so much that they'll cut through heavy wire leaders to get them.

In the mornings, snook feed again and wait among those roots for the ambush, and those mangrove banks make a great place to toss a fly for juvenile tarpon. On a rising tide, look for bigger tarpon on the inside of Mooney Harbor, and in the winter and spring, keep an eye out for big bull sharks and lemon sharks roaming the Marquesas flats looking for tarpon lunches.

Out in the Marquesas, it's easy to slip into the rhythms of local life, which move to the rising and setting of the sun, and the moon and tides. It isn't hard at all to reach a happy state of mind where you forget the date, and even the day of the week.

South of the Marquesas, Cosgrove Light offers good shots at blackfins and other pelagics, and fishing the outer reef excels for bottom fish and yellowtail. To the northwest of the Marquesas, target wrecks hold good-size yellowtail, mutton and mangrove snapper, jacks, sharks, and plenty of cobia, especially in late fall through spring. The two target wrecks, named for the Navy's former habit of taking bombing practice on them, sit only a few miles from the Marquesas. They're marked on charts, and there are plenty of smaller wrecks in the vicinity also marked on charts and rarely visited by anglers. They're all good places to chum up fish and cast for them on fly. You'll run a good chance of limiting out on snapper, especially with live shrimp. If the cobia don't show on the surface, try dropping a jig down to the bottom baited with a ballyhoo, but try to hold the fish before it gets back to the wreck.

Capt. Ralph Delph weighs an average-size mutton down-west.

In the Marquesas, the world seems reduced to its simplest elements. If you have any interest in flats fishing, go there for at least one day, and if possible, consider arranging an overnight stay either on your own, or with the help of a charter captain.

The Dry Tortugas

In 1846, the United States started construction of Fort Jefferson on the biggest island in the Dry Tortugas, 21-acre Garden Key, to protect Gulf trade routes and the coastline. The fort is one of the largest brick structures in the Western Hemisphere, and though no battles were ever fought there, it still holds original armaments. Today, the fort is part of the Dry Tortugas National Park, which encompasses 100-square miles, most of that water. There are great diving sites throughout, including the *Windjammer* Wreck, a tall sailing ship that sank in 1907 less than a mile from Loggerhead Key in twenty feet of water.

The Dry Tortugas also make a dream destination for Keys anglers, and for that matter, anglers worldwide. The waters around Fort Jefferson and the Dry Tortugas National Park offer some of the best offshore fishing in North America, for both bottom species and pelagics. The mooring and camping facilities available within the park's boundaries make overnight trips manageable, and the old fort and the surrounding keys add unforgettable tropical scenery to the adventure. Only a handful of charter captains have permits to fish within the park's waters, but everyone has the right to anchor in the harbor, and recreational anglers can fish in the park subject to its regulations. Spearing and lobstering are prohibited within the park's bounds.

In early 2007, a no-fishing zone, or Research and Natural Area (RNA), was established in the park. The RNA comprises 46 acres, but anglers are still permitted to fish in approximately half of the 100-square-mile park and within a one-mile radius of the fort. Within that one mile radius—a good range for days of kayak fishing—lie plenty of fishable wrecks, ledges, and bottom structures that hold sizeable yellowtail, mangroves, amberjack, black, red and goliath grouper. The area also provides cover for occasional hogfish, tarpon, and small mackerel, among other species.

Most of the park's visitors book passage on one of the two public modes of transport—seaplane or ferry from Key West, seventy miles away. The ferries cost about $130 round-trip per person, including a breakfast on board and picnic lunch on site, plus a $35 flat fee for camping, and a $35 fee to bring a kayak. Two ferry companies make round-trips each day, while the sea planes zip people in and out for half- and full-day visits. Nothing but clean air, tropical water, and

Capt. Bill Delph finds productive fishing in sight of Fort Jefferson, in the Dry Tortugas.

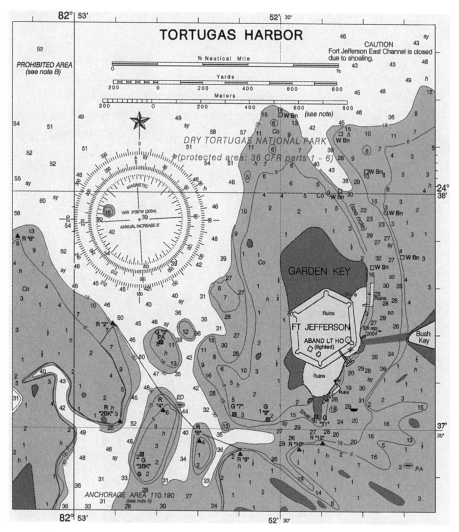

Maptech Dry Tortugas. Web sites such as Maptech's feature a searchable index to topo maps that give anglers a chance to preview bottom structure and contours complete with corresponding GPS coordinates. Image courtesy of Maptech (www.maptech.com).

a beach camp is available at the park, so make sure to triple-check your supplies if you go camping.

The natural harbor at Garden Key offers protection and mooring for recreational anglers lucky enough to make it there under their own power or with a charter captain for an overnight stay. If you happen to be there on your own when the visitors leave, you'll quickly discover the Dry Tortugas and Garden Key transformed into a remote, quiet, subtropical outpost.

Waters around the Dry Tortugas hold big black grouper, mutton snapper, red grouper, hogfish, yellowtail, and all the other species available around Key West, only in more abundance. For these and any waters far from home, nautical and bathymetric charts give visiting anglers a valuable look at bottom contours in advance of their arrival. By studying these charts and toting up GPS numbers, anglers can map out a route of spots worth fishing or at least worth investigating. Maptech Mapserver's online site (www.maptech.com) even gives GPS coordinates with its nautical chart, an invaluable tool for investigating any area beforehand, especially one like the Tortugas where your time at the location will be limited.

The sample on page 68 comes from Maptech's site, and it gives a good idea of the general depths, wrecks, and dropoffs near the fort, all within fishing territory. As you scroll over the visual on the site, the location's GPS coordinates appear in the "Latitude" and "Longitude" boxes at the left.

If they are well-prepared and ready to explore new waters, private anglers who can make it down to the Dry Tortugas on their own will find their own private hotspots in short order.

Even if you don't have a boat, or don't want to take it all the way to the Dry Tortugas, you can still fish those waters either by chartering a captain for a private trip, or boarding a long-range head boat. Hard-core, overnight head-boat trips are run by four operators out of Key West—Andy Griffiths charters, the Yankee Captains, Florida Fishfinders Boats, and Dry Tortugas Fishing Adventures. These trips are popular among hard-fishing fanatics who are happy to sleep in bunks and eat with strangers to get a chance to fish in the

Dry Tortugas, and given good weather, they are all productive with yellowtail, red and black grouper, mutton snapper, and often many more species.

Sunny Days Catamarans, (305) 292-6100, www.drytortugasferry.com.
Yankee Freedom II, (305) 294-7009, www.yankeefreedom.com.
Seaplanes of Key West, (305) 294-0709, www.seaplanesofkeywest.com.

7

Shorebound, Kayak, and Bridge Fishing

Boatless, but Not Hopeless

Gone, at least for our lifetimes, are the days when people routinely caught big mutton snapper and grouper off the docks at Mallory Square. Gone too, at least for now, are Depression-era days when locals fished to make dinners of grits and grunts. But even nowadays you can still catch dinner and good game fish in Key West waters without getting into a boat.

At the top of the land-bound fishing circuit must be the winter redfish run at White Street Pier. When the waters cool, reds show up this far south, and they have the good grace to visit White Street Pier, usually in the early mornings and evenings. The local redfish are sensitive. To ensure their survival they've learned to detect a tourist-rigged line easily, so rig yours lightly with a slip-sinker and a small hook with one of the silvery pilchards that sometimes school around the pier. If the pilchards aren't there, scare-up some live shrimp. Reds can also be taken by jigging bucktails close to the bottom. Their strike at your jig might feel like a snag on a rock at first, until that snag starts moving.

If it's not happening at White Street Pier, there's Fort Zachary Taylor. Fishing is only allowed at the far right of the park as you enter, on the rocks along the Key West Channel, which just happens to be one of the premier tarpon spots for people with boats or money to hire boats. Out in open water you can often see tarpon feeding and rolling—their silver bodies lazy and impressive—or jumping when hooked by the fishers in the boats.

Every inshore fish in Key West, including grouper, snook, mutton snapper, yellowtail, and mackerel, passes by that rock point at some point in the year. But whatever you do, don't use a small-size yellowtail as bait for some of the huge grouper there. That's strictly illegal. Instead, you might hang a shrimp from a popping cork for tarpon or bottom-fish for snapper. When you hook-up to a good fish, the barracudas on patrol will be waiting. Anything is possible at Fort Zach. It's also a good place to bring the kids for snorkeling and for watching the sunset.

The bridges along U.S. 1 provide more chances at big fish and sharks for the shore-bound angler, but to be productive, success requires a little knowledge of the tides and an indifference to 60 mph traffic at your back. There are bridges on quiet back roads, including those on Big Coppitt, that offer grey snapper and tarpon fishing with a minimum of hassle. When you catch the right current, around sunset you can freeline a live shrimp or a piece of squid down into the mangroves and hook-up to sizable snappers that you'll have to fight to keep out of the mangrove roots. When it's a little darker and the stars salt the sky overhead, the juvenile tarpon slide in. You hear them making popping-sounds as they gulp prey. Shine a flashlight into those narrow, shallow channels and the tarpons' eyes will glow like big orange marbles. Use either a live shrimp or a pinfish, and hang on, because even these young tarpon can put up a stunning fight. Bring mosquito-repellant.

Some good wade fishing, either by casting plugs, jigs, or flies, can be had on the southern side of the island off Smathers Beach. In winter months, tarpon, snook, redfish, and at times, occasional bonefish appear in these shallow waters. The sand-spits that jut into the water from Smathers Beach are fine places to cast for cruising jack crevalle and who knows what else. You can also wade off Dog Beach, near the Southernmost Point, and go westward toward the Navy Base, looking for snook and tarpon.

Kayak Fishing

The booming popularity of kayak fishing in the rest of the country somehow hasn't really spread to the Lower Keys, which is great news for those who do it. For out-of-towners, a kayak can make for some relatively carefree and economical fishing, since kayaks properly rigged for fishing can get you on good fish close to the island, on almost every side. If you want to go all the way out, you can also make arrangements to take your kayak on one of the ferries for camping at Dry Tortugas National Park—a dream trip for kayak anglers.

On Key West, not far off the southern side, patch reefs hold good yellowtail, lane and mangrove snapper all year, and for their proximity and productivity, they are a great place for kayak fishing. In winter, grouper and small mackerel also provide good action and eating with only a short paddle from shore. Your kayak needs proper equipment though, including an anchor and a proven chumming system.

The same method of anchoring and chumming from a kayak can also catch good fish on the westernmost tip of the island, outside the swim boundaries of Fort Zachary Taylor. You can put in from the park's boundaries. There are also patch reefs a mile off the island's western side, but these are slightly more exposed to the prevailing winds most of the year.

On the northern side, the harbor and its deep water offer anglers the best chance at big fish, including tarpon and big mutton snapper and cobia, but the boat traffic and the seas in the harbor can both get pretty rough for kayaking, so the right equipment, skills, and experience are required for this trip. To get access to the harbor, you can put in at Fort Zach, though that requires a gutsy paddle across the mouth of the harbor. Easier entrance to the middle of the harbor can be had from the public ramp or beach at the end of Simonton Street.

Also on the northern side, intrepid kayakers can reach the backcountry channels or even the flats, though this is a day trip and not for weak paddlers. Cayo Agua is one of the nearest backcountry Keys and takes about an hour and a half of paddling to reach. The best put-ins for that trip are the parking lot of the Florida Keys Community College dive-training facility on Stock Island, the road's end at the northernmost tip of Boca Chica Key, and the public ramp on Big Coppitt. To reach the backcountry or the channels between the islands, it's also easy to run up the Keys a bit and launch from public ramps along both sides of U.S. Highway 1 or from marinas on Sugarloaf or Big Pine. As long as you bring chum in bags, a rope or an anchor to hold you in place in the channels, and an awareness of the ways of the tides running through those channels, it's very easy to have a great day catching snapper from a kayak.

Roads and Bridges

When it comes to fishing bridges in the Keys, timing isn't everything; it's the only thing. The massive amount of water that rushes between the Gulf and the Atlantic under the bridges during tidal flows makes fishing extremely difficult even on heavy tackle, and when the tide's not running at all, offerings will go nowhere in the slack water. Plan your trips to coincide with the ending and beginning tide phases at your chosen bridges, and even plan to run to a few different bridges to catch the right phases there. Anglers who fish the bridges successfully possess good knowledge of tides at their favorite bridges, and as many tricks of their trade as any angler offshore.

Along with good decisions about where to catch the right tide, bridge fishing requires style choices. Can you take fishing on a sidewalk with your back to traffic, as is often the case at small bridges? Or will you stand at one of the dedicated fishing bridges alongside U.S. 1, fifteen to fifty feet over the water? Or, do you want to climb down the banks, where possible, to reach the waterline? Each of those positions allows anglers to employ different tackle and techniques—from freelining live baits on light tackle, to soaking cut bait on the bottom, to casting soft plastics and top water lures.

Seven Mile Bridge offers shore-bound anglers a shot at decent fish year-round.

Despite its inconveniences, bridge fishing is popular because it gives people, many who would not otherwise have a chance, water access and a chance to hook, and possibly land, a great fish.

Little bridges such as those on Big Coppitt's Boca Chica road are characteristic of ones you'll find all up and down the Keys, just off the main roads, where you stand on sidewalks with your back to traffic. The waters can be thick with snappers, and often hold tarpon and snook, among other species. With less water flow than bridges on U.S. 1, a good tide (moving in the right direction) will take your live baits back to the fish hiding along the banks. These smaller bridges offer closer water access and quieter fishing, but they are lonely, local roads—true secret spots. These are not the big bridges that comfortably host all comers.

At most locations, live baits, such as shrimps, crabs, and pinfish, make the best offerings. Though cut baits—mullet, ballyhoo, and squid—pull in fish too.

The first real prospect for bridge fishing on the way down U.S. 1 is Tea Table Bridge (MM 79). Off southbound U.S. 1, a gravel side road ends near the bridge, and from there, a short path leads to the water. It's a perfect place to shoot top water plugs and soft plastic lures such as D.O.A. shrimp and swimbaits such as a Storm Wild-Eye Shad or a Curl Tail Minnow around the pilings for snook and snapper.

In the Upper Keys, Lignumvitae Channel Bridge (MM 77), Channel Two Bridge (MM 73), Channel Five Bridge (MM 71), Long Key Bridge (MM 65), Tom's Harbor Cut (MM 63), and Tom's Channel (MM 60), each have separate fishing bridges alongside U.S. 1. These bridges allow you to fish over both sides and between the pilings of both bridges, so that you can fish on either an incoming or outgoing tide. Many anglers fish on Channel Two Bridge for snook on the full moon with shrimp on a one- to two-ounce jig head, depending on the current, and for tarpon in the evenings. Crabs on egg sinkers down near the bridge pilings draw permit and tarpon, and mangrove snapper go for freelined shrimp. Redfish and snook show at Tom's Harbor Cut, sheepshead at Tom's Channel, and tarpon at Long Key Bridge.

Both Anne's Beach (MM 73) in Islamorada and an unnamed ocean side flat (MM 75), offer roadside access to wade fishing for permit and bonefish.

The common practice at bridges is to drop baits—cut mullet, ballyhoo or squid, or live shrimp or pinfish—down along those bridge pilings, with however much weight is necessary to keep the bait down with the current. The strong tidal movements around bridges will blow light-tackle gear away. Even moderate current flows will take one- to three-ounce slip-sinker rigs and rock them up constantly. Many anglers use stout rods, 50-pound test, and heavy terminal tackle with drop weights rigged for the bottom.

If you actually want to land your catch from one of the higher bridges, bring a bridge landing net on a long rope. Trying to land and hoist a big fish, either a snook, redfish, small tarpon, or a big snapper, from the fixed position of a bridge is not only sporty, but also invites heartbreak.

That's the appeal of bridge fishing though. It takes great faith to play, and it's almost impossible to win the jackpot. It's the lotto of angling. David Still, owner of the Tackle Box in Marathon, suggests a few general bridge fishing principles that hold true all up and down the Keys.

"The best fishing is early in the day and around the magic hours—an hour before and after the sunset," Still says. "Tide is a matter of preference, but it's good to have some current running for sure. Fish the shadows of the bridges during daylight hours, where the fish hide from the sun, and generally, use a sliding sinker, sixteen-inch leader, and a one-ought hook for snapper and a three-ought hook for grouper."

Chumming also works to bring fish around, either with block chum in a bag hung from a long rope tied to the railing or with a chum mix balled up and dropped in the water.

Vaca Cut (MM 53), near Marathon, is easily accessible and good for mangrove snapper, mutton snapper, and tarpon around slack tide and when the tide just picks up. A short road on the northbound side of U.S. 1 lets you drive right down to the water. You can get right down to the water line and cast close to the bridge pilings on both sides of the cut, but when the flow picks up it really rips.

If you're using live shrimp, keep the bucket shaded with a wet towel, and make sure you don't get any sunscreen from your hands into their water—it's instant death to the bait. Also, throw a little ice in there to keep them cool, and put a few rocks on the bottom to let them rest and not wear themselves out during their travels. The shrimp cling easier to the rocks than the slick plastic bucket.

Seven Mile (MM 46.5) and Bahia Honda (MM 37) are the two popular prospects in the Middle Keys. In May and June, you might get lucky with a hogfish if you put a live shrimp right in front of its face. Also look for big, 7- and 8-pound mangrove snapper on live mullet and shrimp, or keeper grouper and good-size lane snapper.

Of course, jack crevalle, barracuda, grunts, needlefish, and remoras also love these bridges. The tarpon bite moves around from night to night in the Middle and Lower Keys, and it's unpredictable, but in the spring, it's a good bet you'll see a number of tarpon and a number of boats fishing for them at the bridges.

~~~~~~~~~~~~~~~~

In the Lower Keys, numerous dedicated fishing bridges offer close access to the water and chances at tarpon, sharks, snappers, and permit. Especially in the winter, look for schools of pilchards along the banks to cast-net for bait. A few bridges span water too shallow to fish at low tide, so go for those over deeper channels. Opportunities include Little Duck Missouri Channel (MM 40), Ohio Missouri Channel (MM 39), Ohio Bahia Honda Channel (MM 38), and two bridges at Bahia Honda (MM 37), U.S. 1 and the old U.S. 1 bridge in Bahia Honda state park. No Name Key Bridge, off U.S. 1 between Big Pine and No Name Key, has a deep middle channel, and less fishing pressure than others. If you head there, first check in with Jig's Bait and Tackle (MM 30.3 Gulfside) in Cudjoe to find out what's biting.

Spanish Harbor Channel (MM 33), a dedicated fishing bridge, holds plenty of snappers but has strong currents when the tide picks up. On light tackle, you're at the mercy of those flows, and it's hard not to get rocked—the curse of bridge angling. Both Niles (MM 26) and Kemp (MM 24) are tarpon hot spots in the spring and summer, and Bow Channel (MM 21), a.k.a. the K.O.A. bridge, a forty-foot high fishing bridge over water ten to twenty feet deep, holds good-size gray snapper around its pilings. Snapper action wanes when the tide slacks off.

Closer to Key West, the Saddlebunch Bridges between MM 16 and 19 are over fairly shallow water, but aptly named Shark Key Channel (MM 15) has a good, deep channel. Hammerheads occasionally munch tarpon there. Boca Chica Bridge (MM 13) is the last big bridge before Key West.

At Boca Chica, ballyhoo and snappers swarm chum lines off the bridge embankments, and if you can get live pilchards from the beach around Key West this is a good place to take them. There's always a surprise big fish or two waiting around Boca Chica, probably right now, for anyone who wants to try their luck.

part 2

Techniques

8

Deep Jigging and Butterfly Jigging

Get Down

By the afternoon of our trip for muttons, the wind had flickered out, the seas had calmed, and our drift had slowed. I decided to add more action by jigging harder and keeping the bait close to the bottom.

Before I knew it, I was into a fight, but the drag was a touch light, so I failed to get the fish far off the bottom in the crucial opening moments. After a few minutes, I feared the worst: rocked.

Rather than suffering the sinking feeling of a break-off, I handed the rod to Joel Day (that's an admission you won't hear often). Perhaps the fish ran from its rock the instant I released pressure to pass the rod, I don't know, but Day had it on the way up immediately.

That's when Day's rod at the stern bent double. At the same time, the flat-line drag screamed, and Day yelled, "Sailfish!"

I took my rod back to finish landing the fish. At one point, I turned around and saw Day holding a rod in each hand as the sailfish leapt with alarming frequency. A few moments of comic choreography followed, then we boated two nice red groupers and had the sail coming to the boat.

"These aren't even great jigging conditions," he said. "It's so calm."

"I love it when we have these bad conditions," I said.

After the orientation to local waters and a rundown of the general fishing prospects at every compass point, you'll have an idea of where you need to spend your time to get the fish you want to target. Next you'll need to know a number of classic offshore techniques, all with certain variations in tackle that give them even more specific applications to Key West waters. After that, get your numbers off charts, or from friends, for a few good locations to start fishing and you're ready to go.

Three techniques, all with variations, target bottom-fish—jigging, live-baiting, and trolling reef edges and patch reefs with diving lures. (A fourth—spearfishing—is another game entirely.) Versatile anglers know each, because one method might be more suited than another to given conditions, locations, and angler preferences. And knowing all three is great, because each can be worked simultaneously with other tactics. For example, live-baiting on the bottom works together with yellowtailing, deep-jigging with drifting live or dead surface baits for pelagics, and quick-trolling an area works while in transit to other destinations. Sometimes, whether you jig with dead bait or live bait might simply depend on whether or not you can get any live bait.

The first elemental technique would be jigging, an old and reliable way to catch fish in almost all depths. Before live baits became popular among South Florida's offshore crowd, simpler tactics such as jigging caught plenty of fish and involved less preparation. For the variety of fish that light-tackle jigging produces and the range of options it provides, the technique still belongs in every offshore angler's playbook—right next to live-baiting and trolling.

Most anglers are familiar with some version of jigging in shallower water for redfish or speckled trout, but for Key West, they'll want to know about deep jigging, which picks up a whole different variety of species, including, snapper, grouper, and pelagics.

"I call it nymphing at two-hundred feet," says Joel Day, alluding to the skill and understanding it takes to properly scout a deep-jigging spot. Day, a maestro of the style and a world-class angler,

Muttons and red grouper take jigs side by side over the same bottom territory.

knows that anglers might be on to newer techniques, but the fish
haven't changed.

So many reef and bluewater fish yield to the charms of a jig:
Mutton snapper, yellowtail, and grouper on the bottom; pelagics
like wahoo, tuna, sails, and kings; and even cobia, jacks, and sharks.
That's because the technique covers the entire water column. When
properly baited and presented, jigs can be as effective as depth finders for discovering what fish lurk below.

For a day of jigging, we'll load a few blocks of chum to draw bait into our drift, packs of dead ballyhoo for the jigs, and head past the reef line. Starting in depths of ninety feet, we'll look for water that shines a rich cobalt blue over the broken bottom of rocks and sand. Though fish such as cobia, sailfish, and kings take jigs in off-color water, mutton snapper and grouper prefer dark, clear, clean water over structure. Clear water turns on the bite, maybe because the water clarity better allows bottom fish to sight feed. Think of the blue water as the equivalent of clean, fresh-air for people at a picnic. Currents will often push that clear water in closer to the reef farther to the west, toward Western Dry Rocks and the End of the Bar, and if the blue water isn't over our planned fishing spots when we get there, we'll keep moving west in search of it.

Sometimes, you'll easily be able to see the color change snaking along at some depths, and that can be a productive place to check for pelagics. If that color change is right over your bottom spot, that can make for very good conditions, because schools of fish feeding near the surface create scraps of bait that sink to the bottom, which will compel the bottom fish to start feeding.

Six- to 12-pound test monofilament line on spinning tackle or light conventional gear is all you want to cover the territory below. It might surprise some anglers to know they can catch 20- and 30-pound grouper, 50-pound kings, and 30-pound tuna on 12-pound line or less, when bottom fishermen commonly use 30-pound test and greater to haul fish from their rocky hiding places. And, in fact, you *do* need much heavier tackle when anchored and jigging around wrecks, reefs, or rock piles. But that's not the case when you're drifting. As you drift, the bottom fish swim up, away from their hideouts, lured by your passing baits. When they strike, they can't run and rock you as easily because they're away from home, so you wind up fighting the fish, not rocks and coral heads.

Light-tackle battles demand strategy over force. If a fast-striking grouper does get its head against bottom in a defensive move, you can loosen your line to encourage it to run. Let sprinters such as

Before releasing this 'cuda, Joel Day carefully documents it for the Key West Fishing Tournament. Records from sportsmen help scientists to track species' populations and overall catches.

muttons tire before you rein them in. And for hefty pelagics, pick up lines and give chase since you won't be anchored.

Position the boat to drift over good bottom territory and break out the baits. A variety of jig types and weights can be used, but depending on the amount of weight needed to get down and stay down against the current, we'll use the lightest jig possible. If the current runs stronger than three knots, jigging can be tough with any amount of weight. Generally, we'll use anything from one-ounce pilchard-shaped jigs (also called Uppermans) with a white head that's long and flat to heavy six-ounce bullet-shaped jigs. Bait

the jigs with whole fresh dead ballyhoo or even thawed frozen ballyhoo (see rigging details at end). Off the bow and stern, we'll toss
our jigs thirty feet into the boat's drift. Casting upcurrent allows the
jig to sink faster and gives you a headstart in getting deep to keep
it down longer and make the most of each drift. As the boat drifts
with its sides to the current, then a few anglers can fish comfortably
on one side, as long as everyone watches that their lines don't pick
up off the bottom and tangle.

While anglers jig off the stern and the bow, you can send out one
or two baits for fish that feed higher in the water column, either on
a very light jig or on a freeline. With any sea at all, you can put the
jigging rods in holders and let the boat's rocking motion work the
bait, so a drifting boat with two or three anglers might have six or
more lines in the water, from the surface to the bottom. It's a good
system for covering the full depth of the water column.

On the drop of the jig, be ready for a strike, but once the jig hits
bottom, crank up a turn or two to take out extra slack, and make
sure you can feel the jig bouncing along the bottom within a short
lift of your rod tip. You can set the rod in the holder, but it's important not to set the drag too tightly, or the line will easily break
with a good strike. As a rule, set drags at twenty-five percent of the
line test. That means that with 12-pound test line, the drag would
hold against three pounds of pressure. That's not much drag, which
means the fight becomes less about brute force and more a matter
of wearing the fish out with steady pressure.

Jigging Strategy

Where you jig and how depend on conditions and the quarry. When
targeting snapper and grouper, wind and current determine how
quickly—if at all—jigs find the bottom as your boat drifts. That's
why light line can be crucial. Six- to 20-pound-test lines, especially
braided lines, drop quickly and stay down when heavier lines can't
sink through the current. Light lines also draw more strikes because

they're less visible to picky bottom dwellers and pelagics with X-ray eyes.

Generally, monofilament performs well up to depths of 200 feet, beyond which you'll need braided line. Some anglers like monofilament's stretch, which absorbs some of the shock when a big fish hits or an overeager angler sets the hook too hard. In fact, the best tactic for setting the hook for each line type, when the fish don't hook themselves on the take, is to simply reel tight to the fish, and when you feel a solid close connection, give a couple short, sharp strikes. Lifting and sweeping upwards with the rod immediately after the strike will likely only pull the slack out of the line or the stretch out of mono, and alert the fish to drop the bait if it's not already hooked.

If the current runs too hard to keep your jig working near the bottom, you can still drop a light jig to catch pelagics, which feed throughout the water column. A lot of times, if you're in 150 to 200 feet of water, you'll see marks on your depth finder 100 feet down, and it could be tunas, sails, kings, or cobia, depending on the season. A one or two-ounce pilchard-head jig drifts along with the current at that mid-water depth, and a lot of times, pelagics will follow the jig as they see it dropping.

When you mark fish off the bottom or you want to prospect an area, cover the entire water column and entice bites with a moving jig. Let your jig hit bottom and crank it up to the surface, occasionally pumping the rod from waist to shoulder for added animation, then let it drop back down. If you don't get hit, let it drop again, and repeat the jigging with varying retrieve speeds until you find fish. Tuna, bonito, kings, wahoo, and sailfish will follow jigs and strike as close as ten feet from your boat—be prepared.

If you're working the bottom for muttons and groupers, bring it up fifteen, twenty, or thirty feet and drop it again. Muttons come thirty and forty feet off the bottom for a jig. Kingfish, on the other hand, have those keen eyes, and they'll see a jig from some distance and slam it anywhere in the water column.

When wind and seas calm, move that jig continually. That can mean a lot of work during a six-hour trip, but it pays off with bites from fish that wouldn't touch a motionless bait.

For the most part, anglers jig bottom structure between 125 and 200 feet deep for snapper and grouper, though these tactics work in shallower depths, too. But don't let that rule of thumb stop you from targeting other fish in deeper water using relatively new, super-deep jigging techniques.

For that matter, if you find yourself in 2,000 feet of water and find a board, weed line, or debris, drop down a jig to find the fish. "I have jigged for dolphin," Joel Day says. "Sometimes you come across floating structure, such as weeds or debris, which has obviously been hit hard by anglers that day, but you might be marking fish. What happens is, the fish get pretty beat up and they retreat deep for a while, but they still might pick up a jig down there. Also, jigging around deepwater floating structure can be deadly for wahoo."

The analogy to nymphing applies not only to the ocean as a river but to the tackle as well. Day uses his boat, rods and reels as complementary tactics to nab the fish, the way a fly-fisher drifting a river matches fly patterns and presentations to the habits of the fish. As his boat drifts, Day's jig bounces along the ocean floor as a fly-fisherman would bounce a nymph along a streambed.

Once a fish gets hooked, changes in its rate of acceleration or direction create force; both are fighting tactics of pelagics. Bottom fish, like jiu-jitsu grapplers, take the fight to the floor and try to pin you. The aim of the game is to try to get their heads coming up, and coming steadily, before they sever the line by the force of their strikes, or by rubbing it against the rocks and coral of their neighborhoods. On light tackle, it's necessary to play the fish with steady increments of pressure, applied either by holding the line against the rod handle with a single finger to add tension to turn or bring in the fish, palming the spool gently ready to unhand it instantly when the fish bolts on a run, or by a skilled manipulation of the drag system. Generally, muttons will make a mad dash or two, but won't

Both monofilament and braided lines work well with jigs on light-tackle gear.

rock you up. Groupers, especially the big ones, will rock you up, at least once, and you might need to run your boat to them, and give them slack line to trick them into leaving their hole, but whatever you do, don't try to stop these big fish from running on your light tackle. You'll lose them for sure. Work them with steady pressure.

Inevitably, you'll lose some fish on light tackle, but the trade off is that you'll get your baits down to where they live, and you'll cover more territory, so you'll get more strikes.

Jig Tackle

A sturdy but sensitive rod will animate the jig and aid in fighting sounding fish. Use a strong 6½-foot rod rated for 20-pound test when fishing 6- to 12-pound line. That rod will help lift and hold bottom fish and take pressure off the light line. The length will allow casting accuracy and maneuverability aboard the boat if you have to chase a speedy pelagic. Offshore Angler makes line-class rods specifically built for this style of angling. You can use spinning reels, level-winds, and lighter conventional reels, but conventionals offer a tremendous advantage with larger quarry, because as you fight fish with a spinning reel and crank against the drag, you're going to end up with twist that weakens the line's strength. Level-winds and conventional reels don't twist lines, but on a spinning rod, with 8-pound test, stressed line might really end up with a weakened, 4-pound test capacity because of the twist.

You can usually remove the twist by cutting off the jig and trailing a few dozen yards of line behind the moving boat. But sometimes, the line's memory retains twist no matter what you do.

Drag systems become a primary concern with reels used for light-tackle jigging. Penn 4500 spinning reels are durable, dependable, and feature good line capacity. Shimano, Daiwa, and Penn International model reels currently top the list for conventionals. Always spool reels to full capacity to accommodate long runs by big, pelagic speedsters.

As for the jigs themselves, the arrowheads are good for the bottomfish, but there's no question that the pilchard-heads are the best, by far, for the pelagics. The normal bullet-heads are good all-around jigs. Mylar flash seems to help, and colors do make a difference. Jig colors range from white to neon shades with sparkle finishes. The formula of a lighter pattern on lighter days, darker patterns on darker days, tends to hold true. At times, certain species seem to prefer certain colors, so it's good to have a few back-ups on hand in case your target species shows a preference.

A few of the best nationally distributed jigs come from Carolina Lures and Bagley, and most Key West tackle shops sell good jigs made by local angler Jim Cass. If you prefer to make your own jigs, supplies including molds and materials can be purchased from Cabela's (www.cabelas.com).

Because jigs can cost $2.50 to $8 apiece, protect against cut-offs from kings, barracudas, and sharks by tying about a foot of 30- to 45-pound multi-strand wire from jig to leader.

Use an Albright knot to join the wire to a length of 50-pound mono leader to protect against abrasion. Tie another Albright from the leader to the line, which should be doubled using a Bimini twist. If you fish by IGFA rules and use 20-pound line or lighter, remember that the maximum length of your double line and leader can't exceed twenty feet (including any hook or lure length). Neither double line nor leader can exceed fifteen feet on its own. The flash of metal swivels sometimes attracts strikes that would sever the mono, so we use knot connections. This setup should provide 100 percent line strength to the leader.

The bounce of a bright jig moving along the bottom attracts big muttons, such as this twenty-plus pounder.

While pelagic fish key on the jig's action, bottom fish often prefer natural-looking, fresh whole baits dressing the jig. Whole ballyhoo makes a prime offering, but you can also bait jigs with chunks of fresh or frozen fish. Kingfish and bonito (little tunny) belly strips create a strong scent and remain tough on the hook. With long baits such as ballyhoo, adding one or two trailing hooks to the jig helps hold the bait and reduces short strikes.

If bait becomes unavailable, or if you prefer a purely artificial presentation, add a six-inch plastic worm to the jig. The worm's fluid swimming motion in the current attracts strikes.

Bottom fish that haven't blown their swim bladder on their way up will dive right down if they come unhooked, so use a gaff just in case.

Constantly read the depthfinder to learn the underwater terrain. On each trip, even during every drift, pay attention to the direction and speed of the boat to determine whether or not it will take you over the rocky foraging grounds of muttons and grouper below. Sometimes, considering the effects of the wind and current, you may need to reposition your boat for a better drift over the spots, or the ledges.

Rig to Jig

You can jig "pure" with a rubber worm on a jig's single hook or use a ballyhoo-baited jig, with or without trailing hooks. But remember: Each link in your rig affords a chance for failure, so trailing hooks become a measured risk.

To add one trailing hook, use heavy pliers or the side cutters on good pliers to pry open the hook eye (or buy hooks with open eyes). Slip in a barrel swivel, close the eye, and clamp the swivel's other end onto the jig's hook point and down onto the hook shank. The trailer hook should be loose enough to move but not detach.

To add bait to a two-hook rig, snip a ballyhoo's beak short so it doesn't interfere with the jig. Run the point of the trailing hook under the ballyhoo's gill plate. Push that hook into the body, cupping the bait in your hand to bend it as you slide the hook in so that the point emerges from the belly. The jig's hook should then enter beneath the bait's mouth and emerge, hook point forward, from the top of its head.

Three-hook rigs—a jig with two trailing hooks—can be especially effective on kingfish and other notorious short-strikers. Some clubs and tournaments prohibit three-hook rigs, so check the rules if you're fishing for records or standings. With this rig, you bury the points of both trailing hooks into the bait's belly from the outside. This three-hooked bait can improve hookup rates but may turn off finicky bottom dwellers because of the excessive hardware.

Butterfly Jigging

In 2005, the Shimano company introduced a new line of "butterfly" jigs along with rods and reels to accompany them, and the new technique afforded by this tackle has created a lot of discussion and debate. The slim-shaped metal jigs drop quickly to the bottom for wreck and structure fishing, and their erratic, fluttering action on a steady retrieve seems to entice bites from a variety of fish, from grouper and snapper to kingfish and tuna. While some anglers point out the similarities of these jigs to diamond jigs and iron jigs used for deep-water bottom fishing for decades, the technique as currently presented definitely capitalizes on the newer technologies of braided lines, high-speed reels, and strong lightweight rods. That alone makes it worth investigating. While other manufacturers are now introducing their own versions of these jigs, and other makes of rods and reels can be used in this technique, there's no doubt that the Shimano company has done a lot of the legwork to introduce and popularize this technique to North Americans.

The basic difference between this technique and standard deep jigging involves the retrieve, which is faster and more constant than bumping a jig along the bottom or giving it a sweeping upward motion and letting it fall back. The action of the new-style jigs supposedly entices bites out of aggression or instinct, if not out of hunger. To produce that action, anglers need to lift the rod with short upward thrusts, steadily and quickly, while simultaneously retrieving line. The newer graphite rods are limber and strong, and most important, lightweight, a feature that enables anglers to work these jigs constantly without tiring out. The rods also have long butts that extend beneath the armpit when jigging to provide the angler a fulcrum to lift the rod more easily. The high-speed, lightweight reels provide quick enough line retrieve to keep the jig coming. The braided lines offer no stretch, thin diameter, and strength, to give anglers the feel of the jig fluttering, and the fish striking, and a heavy fluorocarbon leader provides shock resistance. A Bimini twist in the braided line tied to the leader with a Yucatán knot, a

Angler Ron Glinski and Capt. Rob Delph send butterfly jigs deep for snowy groupers.

variation of the Albright, is becoming the popular line to leader connection. The assist hooks are attached by split rings to the jig with heavy braided line.

Of course, the speed and style of the retrieve of the jig is up to the angler and his or her experimentations, but generally, because the jig's action elicits the strikes, the jig must be kept moving to be effective. Also, whether you fish these jigs closer to the bottom or higher in the water column might determine what you'll catch.

There are plenty of pros and cons with this new style of jigging, and as yet, probably because of the equipment's expense, it hasn't become terrifically popular. But then, neither is traditional jigging, and the use of braided line offshore is only slowly catching on. While some of these jigs run from $15 to $25, other companies offer comparable jigs for half the price, which is still pricey considering the hooks cost at least a few dollars more, and a kingfish can cut the whole deal off on the first drop. Some anglers use a short, six-inch length of wire to prevent that loss. The assist hooks also require manipulation by pliers to be rigged up, and special pliers are available for the job. For that matter, a special carrying case to hold the jigs is also sold separately.

In practice, the style requires serious, steady physical effort, which might be a drawback to some and a thrill to others. In results, some anglers in the Keys say that especially around wrecks, kings and amberjack attack these jigs so quickly that it becomes hard to get the jigs to the bottom fish that they're after, and kings and amberjack can readily be caught with other tackle anyway. At least so far, there's no consensus that these jigs beat out live baits for catching grouper and snapper, but that may be a function of their relative lack of popularity so far.

On the plus side, you don't need bait, live or dead, at all with these jigs, and they do produce action. Even if it's a fairly indiscriminate bite that they produce, they keep anglers busy with whatever fish are in the vicinity. Also, the method can introduce anglers to a lot of advances in lines and tackle in the last few years, and in that way, produce revelations about what's possible offshore using high-speed reels and braided lines—super-deep jigging, for one.

9

Super-Deep Jigging

Testing Limits

How deep can you jig? What about 300, 500, 700 feet deep? Super-deep jigging, especially around Key West, lets you get to one of the most exciting fisheries being explored today—the bottom species way, way out there.

Anglers familiar with jigging for sea trout in twenty feet or muttons in 120 may be skeptical about the prospects of working a jig along the bottom in 300 to 1,000 feet for snowy and yellowedge grouper, rosefish, barrelfish, tilefish, and other species, all on conventional rods and reels. Certainly it takes the right combination of tackle, conditions, spots, and presentation to be successful, but the principles are the same as drifting and jigging in that shallower water. Super-deep jigging, or as the legendary Capt. Ralph Delph calls it, "deep pulling," takes the same technique, and our equipment and our expectations, to their known limits.

Where most guys troll for dolphin, says Delph, there's a rich bottom fishery, one that stays consistent through the year, even during the doldrums of summer, because nothing much changes down there. At 600 feet, the water temperature is in the low 50s. At 300 feet, there's a lot of available light. Down deeper, however, there's probably not much light, and the fish are used to that. Even the moon's phase, according to Delph, isn't so much of an influence in deep water as in shallow—meaning 200 to 300—where tidal flows are felt throughout the water column. Plus, there's not much pressure on the spots, especially not compared to the pressure fish nearer to the reef face week-to-week, year-round.

Delph and his sons Rob, Bill, and Mike, who are also captains in Key West, have been super-deep jigging in these waters for nearly twenty years now. Ralph first discovered the super-deep techniques on his forays to fish in New England, where "jigging for cod in three hundred fifty feet is standard," he says. Decades ago he brought these tactics home and adapted them to the local fishery.

The essential, in fact absolutely necessary element to jigging deeper than 300 feet is the use of low, 8- to 15-pound-test braided line, better known by its brand names, Spiderwire, Fireline, and Power Pro, among others. With its small diameter, the line cuts through water and current to allow jigs to hit and hold bottom, even in windy conditions when boats drift quickly. It has a higher breaking point than similarly rated mono, and more of the braided line fits on the reel's spool to reach the depths. The line also, importantly, has no stretch compared to monofilament. That means your six-inch high lift on your rod pulls the jig six inches, even at 500 feet and more, so that you can set the hook accurately when you feel the hit. Monofilament has about twenty feet of stretch per 100 feet of line when you're fighting a fish. So, at hundreds of feet, the angler with mono is only taking the stretch out of the line for the first crucial seconds of the fight, not even fighting the fish. By that time, you can imagine that the grouper has wrapped you twice around nearby structure, run back to his hole, and fallen asleep. Delph, along with his sons, and John Ahern and other local anglers pioneered the use of braided line in Key West in the '80s, even before it was introduced to the market.

"There's no way you could fish at these depths with regular mono," Ralph says, "It's out of the question. With the braided line, you'll feel the bottom at six hundred feet and more, no problem."

Since the lines don't stretch, you need to team them with rods that give and flex to prevent line breakage and not to place the entire force of the fight on the reel's drag. Fifteen- to 20-pound class rods with level-wind, conventional, or spinning reels absorb the shock of the fish's dives and allow the angler to pull the fish up without putting too much pressure on the line.

The Delphs and other super-deep jiggers drift over their chosen grounds—what were shorelines in ancient times, during Ice Ages, and are now ledges—and take passes over wrecks not only because it's out of the question to anchor in such depths, but because a drifting boat has the advantage of luring the groupers away from their home structure as they chase the moving bait. Once they're hooked, groupers will still bury their heads against any ledge or spot that they can reach, and big ones, over 30 pounds, might do it a number of times. When they do, you can't lift them off the bottom, you can only take the pressure off and trick them into running again. Work your boat around the fish until it runs, and once it does, try to get its head coming up steadily.

As you're drifting, watch the fish on the screen and "when he's at his pinnacle, you drop," Ralph says, "because that's as close as you'll get to him, and he'll be farthest from his holes."

Use six-ounce jigs up to 400 feet deep and nine-ounce jigs beyond that, not only for their quick-sink action, but because the heavy jig pulls down quickly to animate the plastic worm's tail into lifelike swimming action. Lighter jigs, even if they could hit bottom, would float down, not pull, and leave the plastic tail still and less like a fluttering, wounded baitfish to a predator. Use a 50-pound mono leader to the jig. Generally, anglers tie a Bimini twist or spider hitch into their main line of braid and use one of a variety of connections to join the monofilament leader—a Uniknot combined with a clinch knot, an Albright knot, or the Stren knot created by angler Dave Justice. You don't need to use a Bimini twist or spider hitch in your main line if you can tie the complicated midnight knot to join main line and leader.

One of the complaints from anglers who've used braided line is that it tangles with itself on the spool. That's because braided line is so thin that it can slip underneath itself on the spool, and even cut itself when subject to pressure, if it's not packed down on top of the spool tightly. To remedy the problem, keep strong tension on it to

Super-deep jigging catches a variety of species including tilefish (*left*) and rosefish (*right*).

pack it onto your spool, and always retrieve it onto your spool with tension on it as well.

Other than jigs, anglers can bait up and drop weighted bottom rigs, often with multiple hooks on a single rig in order to catch a few fish at a time. Such a configuration is handy, because it allows a fisherman to avoid having to reel up 500 feet of line after missing a bite on a single hook rig. These rigs can be purchased pre-made, or for savings, made yourself by tying dropper loops in the leader material. Some anglers also connect lights on deep drop rigs. Anglers who practice the technique called deep dropping, becoming more popular all the time, take the lead from commercial anglers and use electric reels on heavy rods with strong lines, multi-hook rigs and five- or ten-pound sash weights. Deep dropping takes the manual work, and some say, also the sport, out of the fishing, but it produces fish. By 2007, smaller but very powerful electric reels for recreational anglers were being introduced to the market by Daiwa.

Standard jigging methods apply for presenting jigs, whether baited with strips of squid, belly, or glow worms. Work the lure once or twice as it drops, before it hits bottom, which might take a few minutes in 600 feet. If it gets a steady pull, kick it into gear and reel tight. Ninety percent of the hits come on the bottom.

"You don't have to jig up and down so hard to get the attention of these fish as you do when you're using pure artificials for muttons and black groupers," Ralph says. That's why he calls the technique deep pulling rather than jigging.

"You want to present the bait over and over at the right depth. If you don't get hit on the first drop, raise it and let it fall again. They'll take it into their mouth to investigate it, and that's when you strike. With Dacron and other braided lines, you can feel the fish beating its tail even with 300 yards out."

"Once you get them coming up," he adds, "you need to keep pulling steadily, hard, all the way to the boat, because the heavy jig exerts downward pressure which might help it dislodge from the fish's mouth."

Unbaited jigs have a lot of advantages: less mess, more sporty, and they don't attract bites from sharks, which rely on scent to feed and are attracted by jigs with cut or whole bait. Bill Delph, however, pointed out to me the best advantage to unbaited jigs when he said, "With pure jig, you won't wipe out the stock of fish down there. The fish bite, but then catch on, and they'll quit, and you'll have to move on. They don't stop hitting baited jigs, and that way anglers can easily damage the populations."

Snowy groupers in the area range from few pounds up to 45. Check bag limits; they change frequently as this fishery becomes more popular. The snowies average about 8 pounds, and they have the delectability of other cold-water species, such as halibut, that range farther north.

Drop-offs and wrecks in 300 to 500 feet hold yellowedge and snowy grouper, tilefish, and even some yelloweye snapper. In 500 and 600 feet of water there are fish-filled ledges with 50-foot drop-offs, and swaths of productive hard bottom holding a good variety of species including snowies, Nassau and yellowedge grouper, varieties of tilefish, barrelfish and rosefish, a member of the ocean perch family, which are also well-known for their food value. At those depths, with much current, even a 20-pound braided line might not hit bottom, which illustrates the difference a minor increase in line diameter makes in the ability to fish these depths and how access to the fishery can be limited by wind and current conditions. But that's good, because it will keep the fish protected naturally. After a few tries, anglers know what conditions make good days for super-deep jigging. Once you've added it to your arsenal of techniques and rigged for it, you can always give it a try, even for a break during dolphin fishing.

Ralph Delph agrees that the speed of the current can be a limiting factor for the technique. A 1.0- to 1.2-knot current or more makes the jigging awfully hard, he says, and to do it then you'd have to set up your drift along ledges that run the same direction as the current. A half-knot current can be perfect, because it allows you to cover bottom territory on your drift while not running so hard to make dropping even narrow diameter lines difficult.

While you're drifting out there, don't be too surprised if sailfish, wahoo, tuna, and dolphin come along as you're fishing.

One of the many mysteries of super-deep jigging which the Delphs revealed to me was why more anglers don't pursue these fish. Rob pointed out that most anglers aren't familiar with techniques and tackle for jigging in depths of 200 feet, much less 600. Billy suggested that the time to learn the electronic systems necessary to "see" the terrain at such depths can be prohibitive and so can their cost, and no doubt that's true. Ralph Delph agreed with both observations but pointed out that many anglers simply won't take the time to experiment with new techniques or even explore new terrain, both pursuits which make fishing exciting and challenging to him, even after nearly fifty years on the scene.

He added, "People have a mental barrier to jigging in depths beyond 300 feet, but as you see, it's easy to do. A little child could do it, with a little supervision. Then people will say, why do I want to work so hard to bring the fish up so far? But isn't that fun? And when you can get a fish with almost every drop, isn't that worth it? Even if catching fish tires you out, isn't that worth it?"

10

Bottom Fishing for Grouper and Snapper

Live Baits, Carolina Rigs, and Grouper Diggers

Many Key West fishermen devote themselves to the pursuit of snapper and grouper simply for the sporting and table qualities of the fish. They'd probably say that live baits definitely have the reputation of being able to seal the deal with big grouper and snappers, but still they try to learn all the possible techniques so that they have no end of tricks to show finicky fish.

Not only black grouper and mutton snapper, but gag, scamp, and red grouper, big porgies, white (or Cuban) snappers, kingfish, amberjack, almaco jack, African pompano, and almost every other species that prowls the rocky bottoms and wrecks offshore will be your targets with live baits on the bottom. Of course, you never know what you might hook fishing along the bottom, and species from sharks and sailfish to cobia and tuna are potential game when you're using these tactics, because most fish, including pelagics, feed from the bottom to the top of the water column. Inside the reef, targeting patch reefs, plenty of yellowtail and black grouper show up, along with mackerel, muttons, red grouper, and occasionally in winter and spring, cobia.

A word about GPS (or Loran) numbers: These techniques are essential, but without knowing where to fish for the species, even the techniques won't help much. Bottom fish congregate around relatively small areas of structure in a giant range of ocean, and it can be frustrating searching around for them on a featureless surface of sea. Good bottom fishing absolutely depends on having good GPS numbers to productive fishing spots. Watching your depth finder while under way reveals plenty of good bottom structure worth investigating.

Western Dry Rocks, Eastern Dry Rocks, EyeGlass Light, Middle Sambo, Pelican Shoal, American Shoal, Ten Fathom Ledge, the Rubble Pile, and wrecks—the Sub, the Airplane, the Curb, the *Wilkes Barre*, the *Adolphus Busch*—are all marked on charts such *Florida Sportsman* Chart Number 11, and all and plenty more are quickly accessible from Lower Keys marinas. Though you'll need to be aware that crossing the reef can be treacherous, even in daylight if you don't know the waters. Past the bar, the prospecting begins, and good rockpiles and drop-offs hold great bottom fishing.

It's basic to say that certain habitats host certain species, and that black grouper live around rocky ledges and coral formations, and muttons prefer sand-bottom slopes near rocks and ledges, and amberjack school near wrecks. But simple as that is, having that basic knowledge of the sea floor and its depths beyond the reef, and knowing what fish live at what depths and near what structure, provides the start of your hunt for GPS (or Loran) numbers. Once you explore the fishing grounds using these techniques, keep a constant eye open for productive bottom features via depth finders, with assist from bottom charts. You won't need anyone else's numbers, because through trial and error, you'll find your own and begin to develop of circuit of favorite spots. Of course, when you're in new waters, you can always start by fishing those numerous wrecks and drop-offs marked on charts.

It's amazing to discover how the same spots can hold the same species season after season and still be productive over the years. However, hitting a spot too hard can certainly wipe it out and end the fishing there for some time. According to the Delphs, overfishing a spot first takes away the big grouper, and then the mid-range grouper, and then the muttons are removed, and by then, the sharks have taken over the spot.

A big mutton snapper or black grouper might turn up their nose at a live threadfin dancing in front of them on a weighted bottom rig and prefer to strike a jig, but those cases are rare. Even good, fresh-cut baits such as ballyhoo plugs, whole squid, and bonito strips draw good fish. At locations near wrecks, rock piles, ledges, the reef, and along the bar, anglers anchored and chumming will need heavy tackle to lift groupers from the bottom, while anglers drifting can try to pull fish off the spots with lighter tackle.

Bottom Rigs

The main rig used for bottom fishing is a variation of the Carolina rig. The primary variations involve placing the sliding egg sinker above or below the knot—or swivel—connecting your double line with your leader. The traditional and still very effective method is to place the egg sinker above the swivel, threaded onto the doubled mainline. But whether anglers connect the double line to the leader with a swivel or a knot, many Keys anglers put the weight below that connection and let it slide all the way down to the hook, which allows for easier boat-side handling of the rig and easier casting. This variation is generally called a knocker rig.

The rig starts by doubling the main line into a Bimini twist or spider hitch, though for extremely heavy line, greater than 80-pound test, that's not necessary. The double line can be tied to a swivel, or directly to the leader with an Albright knot. For the knocker-rig variation, thread your three- to six-ounce egg sinker onto the leader of two- to ten-feet length. The knot or swivel keeps the sinker from moving too far up the line, though if you use a swivel be careful of reeling it in against the rod's tip and damaging the guide. Some people put a bead above the swivel to protect the knot and top guide, but these rigs get lost pretty quickly to sharks, other fish, cut offs, and rock abrasions, and that bead just becomes another piece of lost tackle. For the leader, use at least a 30-pound mono (most anglers use 50-pound) or heavy fluorocarbon leader, which has added abrasion resistance. Some anglers also believe fluorocarbon is less visible than mono, and for that reason, some fishermen even prefer to tie their doubled-up mainline directly to the hook rather than use a heavy mono leader. Many anglers use at least five feet of leader to keep the bait away from the weight because they believe the fish are shy and sharp-sighted. The hook of preference on bottom rigs is often a circle hook, not only because they tend to hook fast-hitting fish effectively, but also because they offer good chances of a clean release on undersize fish.

As in jigging, the least amount of weight necessary to hit and hold bottom is the best, because it gives the bait the lightest, liveliest presentation. Basically, you must rig for the conditions, especially the current, so some anglers won't tie on terminal tackle until they're out on location and can surmise the current. Optimally, you'll want a moving current but not so strong that it makes holding the bottom a problem. Too strong a current will also blow out your top game by spreading your chum too quickly and preventing a chum slick from forming. Too dead of a current is just as much a curse on fishing.

There are plenty of other basic rigs—chicken rigs, three-way rigs with dropper weights, breakaway rigs, and fishfinder rigs. A primary variation of the popular Carolina rig uses heavy braided line on the mainline, and that requires a longer mono or fluoro leader, usually about ten feet, to ensure that anglers handle the leader and not the braided line, which can cut fingers and be difficult to manage, especially if it is connected to a hot fish. Many anglers believe heavy-test braided line helps them lift fish faster and, because of its lack of stretch, minimizes a grouper's chance to get rocked and hidden. Others say it helps get fish up faster and away from sharks who do their fair share of damage to bottom fish on the hook. Either way, it's a matter of preference and practice how well braided lines work for bottom fishing, and for backcountry and flats fishing for that matter too.

The light-tackle version of this rig uses 20-pound test or less with an egg weight threaded on the mainline, which is tied straight to the hook. Alternately, 12-pound test can be tied into a Bimini twist and a 20-pound leader can be attached, and it's the angler's choice to place the sliding weight above or below the line–leader connection. If the tag end of the connecting knot between main and leader is left long, it will stop the egg weight from moving up and down the line. This is a very light bottom rig and can be used not only for snappers, but also for a variety of fish in a variety of situations, such as patch reefs and in channels.

Also for light tackle anglers, 8-pound braided line with a 50-pound leader can be a good choice for live-baiting to muttons and groupers between eighty and 200 feet while on the drift over the spots. The line gets down and helps the weight to stay down, and the eight-pound braid is strong enough to hold very big fish.

Bottom Baits

Now, the live baits might include threadfin, pinfish, grunts, pilchards, blue runners, even ballyhoo, and mangrove, mullet, lane, or yellowtail snapper. Usually, your choice of baits will depend more on what you can get at markers or in the cast net, or even while fishing, rather than on what you'd like to use. Sacrificing a lively legal yellowtail or mangrove to bottom fishing sometimes makes the day. Grunts are almost always available at inshore rockpiles.

Bring plenty of chum, at least a few blocks for every hour of fishing, and maybe even a chum mixture to drop to the bottom in a ball once in a while. Remember, whatever bait you're using on your hook, throw some into the chum line. Bottom fishermen will almost always, in some manner, be chumming as soon as they drop anchor. Some of them chum with cases, not boxes, of chum.

Anchoring

When you're dealing with the rocky bottom past the reef, rigging your anchor with a breakaway cord can save a lot of trouble, maybe even the anchor. Everyone who anchors near the reef will get their anchor hard in the rocks once in awhile, but it will be easier to extricate if you tie the anchor chain to the anchor shaft with a break-off cord of plastic cinch or light nylon twine, giving it a few wraps to secure it before you knot it or cinch it. If your anchor gets stuck, use your boat to pull it from a variety of directions, which will exert pressure on the chain until that binding cord snaps. When it does, the released chain will pull from the opposite direction (top) at the anchor and snatch it out of its crevice.

Also, using an anchor buoy to help lift the anchor saves a lot of work, but the procedure takes practice and extreme care each time. Boaters must be watchful not to let the rope wrap around the prop, which can happen easily. If it does, unwrap it immediately, and even be prepared to cut the rope and lose the anchor. You don't want to run the risk of getting swamped by the ocean as your anchor rope pulls your stern down into the water while the current gushes in over your transom. Have a knife ready to cut the rope! For the same reason, *never* anchor off the stern but always from the bow.

11

Nighttime Snappers

Cool Relief at the Reef

Put those bottom fishing techniques to use on a trip just past the reef late in the afternoon some spring or summer day, and you'll get a different view of Key West and its fishery. With the right preparation and precaution, a night trip to the reef can get you some hot fishing. Even locations along the reef that take heavy fishing pressure in the day can be entirely different places at night when the daily cycle of fish feeding reaches its secondary peak. Chances are you'll need to bring a few friends so you don't limit out too quickly. The allure of night fishing not only includes the chance at that hot bite out of the heat, but also the thrill of seeing familiar places transformed under the moon.

The reef in the Keys makes an excellent night trip because it has high populations of resident fish at precisely marked locations within a close range of local marinas. Out of Key West, take dead aim on Sand Key, seven miles from the harbor, and go northeast or southwest to spots along the reef from there. Western Dry Rocks, Eastern Dry Rocks, Eyeglass Light, Middle Sambo, Ten Fathom Ledge, Toppino Buoy, and countless other spots are all easily accessed for anchoring up. The primary quarries at these spots is a trio of snappers—mangrove, yellowtail, and mutton.

Three and 4-pound yellowtails, 10-pound muttons, and a variety of other species are pretty common around Eastern and Western Dry Rocks, close to Key West. Big muttons can come along too, at any moon phase, though conventional wisdom dictates that those

Capt. Pepe Gonzalez with a night mutton and yellowtail caught on drifted cut-bait.

fine fish bite best nearer full moons. In the summer, especially in July and August, big mangrove snappers, up to 5 and 8 pounds add to the mix. Cubera snappers also can be targeted, especially by using frozen lobster heads as bait, and they get big, up to 40 and 50 pounds. Cuberas are also known to carry the ciguetara toxin in the area, so no one would recommend eating them.

The same techniques that work for the snapper trio during the day work at night too, only better. Cover the water column from top to bottom. To do this, for each angler, Capt. Pepe Gonzalez, who grew up fishing the Key West reef, sets up a Carolina rig on bottom and puts it in the rod holder while the angler freelines a bait on a hook or light jig off the stern. For the freelined bait, Gonzalez likes a fluorocarbon leader and a small, sharp 2/0 hook or small lead-head jigs, especially bright ones. Keep feeding the line out to keep it in the current; if you stop feeding it out, it'll come up to the surface and away from the fish.

As always while bottom fishing, once a fish hits, get on it fast. If you're on anchor, you're going to have to get the fish's head coming up as soon as possible. After that, keep the fish coming and don't give it any breathing room. That might mean pressing your tackle—reel, rod, line, and knots—to the limit, and you have to know those limits. Muttons won't hole you up as groupers will, but they will hold against rocks on the bottom, and even press themselves against the seafloor with all their considerable strength. In those situations, and even on their runs, lines can be shredded against rocks and coral.

Around Eyeglass Light, Eastern Dry Rocks, and Western Dry Rocks, all favorite mutton spots, big groups of blacktips, lemons, and other sharks wait, and the loss rate to the sharks can be so bad at times that there's no point in continuing to fish. That can be especially so at night, when the sharks hunt more fiercely. Forty- and 50-pound braided lines let anglers hoist muttons as quickly as possible after their initial runs, but sometimes, no matter how fast you fish, the sharks win. The last thing anglers want to do is train sharks to wait there for an easy meal, though that may already be happening.

The fishing continues along the same reef lines in the Middle and Upper Keys. Here, however, anglers have an even shorter ride to the reef, about four miles to hot spots such as Alligator Reef, Tennessee Reef, and Davis Reef, among others.

If the productivity of night fishing for snapper increases, so does the level of care and preparation involved. Following a few rules of procedure helps to ensure safety and enjoyment in the darkness.

First and foremost, always check the forecast on the NOAA Web site (www.srh.noaa.gov/key/) or its radio channel. Even if it looks clear, check the local radar on the local noaa.gov Web site before going out. Many nights, trips will be called off due to a serious threat, much less the presence, of thunderstorms.

Next, keep trips simple. Know your destinations in advance, and if possible, travel to the first spot in daylight, at least once before fishing there at night. Plan a good time frame for the trip. As wade fishers like sunrises in the surf, snapper anglers like sunsets at the reef, so try to get away from the dock in daylight and set up for fishing by sunset.

Check your safety equipment. Charter captains, whose livelihoods depend on the safety of their clients, are accustomed to the daily routine of checking all their electrical systems, lights, pumps, rescue equipment, and everything else that maintains safety standards on board our boats. Before a night trip, double-check that all the equipment required by the Coast Guard works, including boat lights. Captain Gonzalez suggests buying life jackets with LED lights that can be spotted in the dark. If your boat doesn't have plenty of deck lighting, remember to bring flashlights to aid in tying hooks. Headlamps work well also.

Night navigation also presents its own sets of challenges, none to be taken lightly. Navigation by experience, aided by sight, and plenty of care, is the best combination to ensure a safe trip.

"Always have on your GPS, the whole time, so that if you do get lost, you can retrace your route from the start and get back home," Gonzalez suggests. "Also, it's not a bad idea to go out with a friend on another boat to have someone to help and to give it in case they need it. File a float plan and route with someone who can be reached easily, and you can also schedule routine check-times if you'll be within cell phone range.

"Basically," Gonzalez urges, "you should never run farther at night than you can see. If it's a bright moon, that may mean that you can get on plane, if you and everyone aboard carefully watch the waters ahead. If it's in deep darkness or if there are mists or haze, it might mean that you must idle home."

Dim your electronics before the run back to shore to help your eyes adjust to the darkness. Otherwise, if electronics on the dash remain bright, the pupils of your eyes will take longer to adjust to the darkness beyond your boat, and that split-second could be the difference in arriving home safely should a critical moment arise.

12

~~~~~~~~~~~~~

Get the Drift

Drifting Live and Dead Baits

Once you've got the bottom basics covered, move up to mid-water- and upper-water-column bait presentations. Drifting baits along with the current has to be one of the most basic yet one of the most-often overlooked techniques. Silent and effective, drifting also happens to be economical on fuel. Its variations are really prime ways to catch most of the pelagics, including tuna, dolphin, kingfish, and swordfish.

The drift technique can be applied so many ways. Drifting over wrecks, while watching the fish finder to know when to drop, lets everyone, including the captain, fish without the hassle of anchoring. Offshore, wherever it looks fishy, pull upcurrent of the location, shut off your motor, set baits down current, and let the current take you there. On a hot day in the summer offshore, instead of running all day looking for weeds, consider choosing a fishy spot along one good weedline and setting yourself up with chum for a good drift right there. Give yourself a couple hours there, with steady chumming to draw fish in the vicinity to your boat. Before you know it, you might have schools of dolphin cruising by, tripletail, a wahoo or two, and maybe even a marlin.

While you're drifting, experiment with turning your engines into the current to help control your drift. On outboards, the engines' lower units act as rudders to steer the boat in the current, so understanding how they control your boat's direction helps you to

This cow dolphin took a dead ballyhoo drifted in 200 feet off Sand Key

get the best position depending on where you want to fish from the boat. Wherever and whenever you're drifting, keep your eye on your depth finder's screen and you might discover some good new bottom territory.

Simple as it is, drifting opens up a whole new avenue of attack on species that anglers might primarily go after first by anchoring or trolling.

Drifting Live Baits

Drifting live baits, one of the stealthiest and simplest techniques for catching pelagics offshore, is basically the upper water-column equivalent of live-baiting on the bottom for snapper and grouper. Drifting baits near the surface, coupled with a good chum line and especially with live chumming, entices pelagics from the depths and from distances. Once you've rigged the lines and caught your baits, there's nothing more to it than running to your chosen location and setting up the drift. In fact, for many anglers, acquiring the live baits might be the toughest part.

Drifting live baits is especially successful for tuna and sailfish. Both of these species are not particularly attracted to the sound and action of running motors, and often, they're put down by them. Drifting baits, along with kite-fishing, are the preferred methods for sailfish in the Keys during tournaments, and drifting live baits and chumming with live pilchards on anchor top the list for tuna on the Atlantic side of the Keys. Wahoo, kingfish, marlin, and dolphin also snatch live baits on the drift.

As in bottom fishing for grouper and snapper, knowing the right location plays a big role in meeting success with drifting live baits. While you're likely to encounter various pelagics year-round in waters deeper than 200 feet, some fish have their favored seasons, and some their locations. South of Sand Key to Western Dry Rocks sees

Blackfin tuna, such as this one caught by Ron Glinski, take silently drifted threadfin and other baits.

plenty of sailfish, while the End of the Bar and Tail End Buoy become tuna hot spots in the late fall and again in the spring. Marlin are only occasional but by no means unknown visitors to shallow waters, especially in the springtime.

While most of the depths between 100 and 300 can yield fish on the drift, anglers rarely use the technique in waters much deeper, except for swordfish. Beyond 300 feet, where coverage of territory becomes more important, most troll, while inside 300, bottom structure gives rise to surface conditions that make favorable fishing. Schools of pelagics will frequent the same areas for days if there's a productive rip or current break collecting baitfish. Livebait drifting also produces along color changes.

Conventional reels and bait runners are the first choices to hold the serious pelagics you're targeting with drifted live baits. Baitrunners give the added advantage of letting a fish run with a bait in freespool, a very important feature for sailfish, which often hit, hold, and run before taking the bait into their mouths. Tuna often will hook themselves on their strikes, but send the hook home once you're firmly to the fish. To give a pelagic room to play with its prey, set the drag light on a conventional when fishing it in the rod holder.

Most of the time, the baits will tip you off moments in advance of a strike by acting nervous, and when one does, you can pick up a rod from the holder—without pulling the bait away—and lessen the drag a little, especially if you're targeting sailfish.

Even spinning reels can be rigged with a rubber band or a wire clip to hold the line until the fish strikes and the line freespools. To use a rubber band to hold the line, first remove the reel from the rod and wrap a rubber band tight around the upper rod grip. Replace the reel, and after the bait has been deployed, slip a loop of line under the rubber band. Line will pull out as the fish strikes. To use a length of copper rigging wire, wrap it around the rod grip above the reel, and fashion a hook or clip with the wire to hold the line. The strike pulls the line out of the wire clip and the fish takes off with no drag.

Most anglers will target sails and tuna with 15- or 20-pound test, but a 25-pound tuna on 8-pound test challenges an angler's skills and tackle equally and fairly. Use a five- to eight-foot length of fluoro or mono leader, and a circle hook or live-bait J hook. Where to hook the bait depends on the species and how you want it to move, but just behind the dorsal works for many rounder-bodied species. You can also hook the fish through the top of their eye sockets. Lip-hooked fish won't last as long.

Threadfins make great drift baits. They're hardier than ballyhoo, active, and flashy, and they don't constantly attempt to dive as blue runners do. But go with whatever you can get—whether that may be big Sand Key pilchards, goggle eyes, or even live mullet.

To keep those diving blue runners on the surface, some anglers slip-knot an inflated toy balloon onto the double line between the knot connecting the leader and the Bimini twist's wrap, so that the knots keep it from sliding to the hook, or up the main line. Keep the hooked bait in the livewell as you tie on the balloon. Once the rig drifts out, the balloon also makes a handy visual marker for the bait, which helps in seas of a couple of feet or more.

Let the baits out to a distance of seventy to 100 feet as the boat drifts side-to the waves. A few lines can be let out, increasing the likelihood of action and a Chinese fire drill if a school of tuna hits.

While drifting, don't hesitate to drop a jig down to the bottom to see if it produces. Oftentimes, a good surface bite turns on bottom fish, and you might just discover a good bottom spot by surprise.

Sea Anchors

Some anglers use a sea anchor or a drift sock while drifting live baits. Both devices act like parachutes in the water to keep the boat's drift constant with the current. They catch the force of the current in their breadth of fabric, more or less anchoring the boat to drift with the current, negating the effects of wind on the craft's drift. But there's a big difference between sea anchors and drift socks, otherwise known as drogues or boat brakes. Sea anchors are much bigger, stronger, and more costly than drift socks because they're meant to be safety equipment, designed to be deployed in emergency situations (such as loss of power or captain's fatigue or illness) to stabilize the craft and keep the boat's bow into the waves to prevent capsizing in rough seas. In comparison, a drift sock has a minimal effect. It can help stabilize the boat, catch the current, and depending on where it is tied off on the boat, fix the boat's position against the current. It will slow the boat's drift but will not work in very rough conditions.

For fishing purposes, drift socks and sea anchors are most often used while kite-fishing to slow the drift in windy weather, but they can be used while drifting baits too. By slowing the drift, they also lessen the drag on your presentation, which often extends the bait's life on the hook. Tie the sea anchor off your bow or to a side cleat, depending on how you want to position the boat against the drift and where you want to fish on the boat.

In general, drifting live baits can be a terrific tactic when you know or strongly suspect that good fish are nearby. It makes a fairly natural presentation of baits easy. Though it might not be as flawless a presentation as kite-fishing, which suspends the entire leader out of the water, unseen by fish, drifting baits entails none of the rigging and maneuvering of kite-fishing either. When it's more important to cover territory to find fish, skip the drift and slow troll baits until you find the right area.

Drifting Dead Baits

An even easier technique than drifting live baits, drifting dead baits still catches plenty of pelagics, especially kingfish and tuna when they're around. Frozen baits—ballyhoo, threadfins, and goggle eyes—thawed in a bucket of saltwater work perfectly well as drifted baits. For convenience, nothing beats picking up baits at the marina minutes before your trip, and on the water, dead baits never tangle lines, swim around the props, hide under the boat, or die too quickly on the hook. No one would suggest that a tournament

Drifting a dead ballyhoo fooled a fifty-plus pound king for Joel Day.

angler drift dead baits, but for a day of recreational fishing, the time they save might be better spent looking for the fish.

Longtime Keys angler Joel Day has perfected a system of jigging the bottom structure combined with drifting dead baits on the surface that has a high yield for a relatively low investment in time and money. With the dual tactics, Day covers the entire water column with baits and connects to a wide variety of fish—exactly what most recreational anglers want. The system also allows a few people to fish comfortably off the stern, side, and bow of a twenty-five-foot center console.

Besides its convenience, another brilliant aspect to the technique is its reliance on the very dependable predatorial practices of game fish. They roam ceaselessly, far and wide, and they're not too picky when they're hungry. If they're in the vicinity, chances are they'll find that dead ballyhoo that's drifting out there, eighty feet from your boat. The tactic turns their strengths of predation to the angler's advantage. Let them come to you. It also saves on fuel burned trolling.

Start with 6- to 15-pound test and tie on a Bimini. Use an Albright knot to add a six-foot length of leader to the double line, and a foot's length of 30- to 45-pound Steelon leader to protect against king, wahoo, and barracuda cut-offs. For the terminal tackle, connect a trailer hook to a 5/0 or 6/0 short-shank bait hook with a swivel. The trailer hook goes behind the whole ballyhoo's gill plate, down through its stomach, and the short shank comes up through the hard part of the bally's head, between its eyes. Break the bally's beak to lessen its drag in the water and keep the beak from fouling on the hook.

It won't hurt to put out chum bags. If you're out on a weedline in the summer for dolphin and have the chum bags out already, try a dead bait drifted on a flatline. That wahoo prowling around the scene might just pick it up.

You could even run one or two kites downwind to cover the territory around and below your drifting boat, but many lines in the water might create problems when the fish strike. If it turns out to be a big fish, you might have to chase it with the boat, and minutes lost early in that fight often weigh heavily in the outcome.

Recreational anglers who pair the dead-drift technique with effective coverage of the lower water column by jigging can gain good results with a relatively low investment.

13

Trolling

Number 1 in the Offshore Playbook

Offshore trolling can be a roller-coaster ride physically, up and down with the ocean's movements, and figuratively, riding crests of enthusiasm and expectation but sliding down banks of dejection and disappointment. Each wave that brings you up either drops you down farther than the one before to a place of terrible stillness in your heart, or brings you to a new place of expectations satisfied, maybe even of joy, where you never grow tired. The pursuit can lead to deep depressions and glorious highs, and when it does both in the same cycle of trolling, you feel as if you've lived well, at least for that day. After that, you always want more.

Trolling is not all about fate or chance. Before and after your baits get set out, you're constantly looking, scanning, trying to decipher the seas and the horizons for weeds, debris of any kind, rips and currents in the water, and for birds. It's an indication of the harshness of the marine environment that a small piece of wood or a piece of plastic trash can provide protection for small fish and so harbor game fish underneath it.

You might see a bird skimming low and fast over the waves, but more than likely it was doing what you were doing, looking around. Even one bird wheeling back, circling and diving, possibly means a large school of fish. So it becomes important to learn about bird behavior. Sometimes those fast-flying birds were headed to a feeding, and you just knew it and wished you could follow them there fast enough.

As many places as there are to troll, whether along the weeds, near diving birds, past turtles, around floating structure, along the reef, over bottom structure such as the Wall, or in the blue of the open sea, there are as many ways to present baits and trolled lures, depending on your level of skill and ambition with trolling, your boat's design and equipment, and the species targeted. What, where, and how to troll, most of all, depends on that last variable: the species you're after. Trolling is a fairly species-specific tactic.

That said, even without downriggers, outriggers, dredges, kites, planers, or even release clips, recreational anglers can get in the game with a minimum of rigging and relatively easy trolling pattern. Two rods with conventional lever drag reels, one on each side of the boat, baited with a dead "naked" ballyhoo, trolled at equal distances back, about fifty to seventy feet, will get you in action for dolphin, tuna, kings, and sails off Key West. You can add another heavier setup in the middle of them, trolling a bigger lure, positioned from the leaning post. Then you can experiment with adding other lines set even farther back, positioned from the holders overhead on T-tops. For the trolled bait rigs, you can use 12- to 50-pound test with a Bimini twist attached to a big swivel (either a barrel or the stronger ball-bearing swivel) with a cat's-paw knot (offshore swivel knot). From the swivel, add a 50-pound mono leader with a cat's-paw knot, and then use an Albright knot to attach a short, four- to six-inch length of 30- to 40-pound wire leader to a size 6 live bait hook. Alternately, you can use an Albright knot to attach your doubled main line to a mono leader, and then tie that to a barrel or ball-bearing swivel to connect to a short length of wire. *The placement of the swivel between leader and wire depends greatly on how attracted you suspect any kingfish or wahoo might be to it; the closer the swivel is to your bait, the greater the chances that these toothy predators will cut off your line.*

You can also add a trailer hook with a swivel onto the bait to catch short-striking fish. Hook up the ballyhoo with the trailer-hook point aiming down, out the body, and the front-hook point

You've found the fish. Now how to approach them?

up, pointing forward from the head, and set them out about seventy feet back.

This trolling spread requires minimal rigging and can be managed easily with two anglers—quick deployment and quick line retrieval. It's good for smaller, fast boats, and it allows you to cover territory in search of fish—the run-and-gun style of trolling. To keep it quick and simple, you can buy frozen packs of the bigger ballyhoo at marinas, even pre-rigged, if you so choose. Or, with the extra effort for the bang of live baits, you can easily catch live ballyhoo at the reef. If you're strictly targeting bigger dolphin, you can use Panama strips, dead rigged bonito, or even live bonito on a harness, or a rigged flying fish, which is the premier prey for dolphin, though sometimes hard for anglers to find at baitshops. Each species has its own favorite baits and specific tackle strength requirements.

Line-to-leader connections (knots, swivels, or snap swivels), and shock leader choices (heavy mono or wire) depend not only on the species targeted and terminal tackle used, but also on the angler's familiarity and skill with rigging options. Heavy mono leaders might get more strikes and hook sets from dolphin and tuna, but they're more likely to get cut off by wahoo and kingfish. In general, a single-strand wire leader attached to your lures or baits with a haywire twist at the terminal end and attached via haywire twist to a snap swivel at the end of the leader, suffices for smaller game fish such as cero and Spanish mackerel and small kingfish and dolphin.

But if you're trolling for bigger game, such as dolphin and tuna, use barrel and ball-bearing swivels and knots or crimps to make your connections. Some anglers believe that a more lithe presentation with the swivel connected to the mainline and only a short, four- or six-inch length of wire Albright-knotted to the heavy mono leader will significantly improve the number of bites that trolled baits attract. Heavy-duty snap swivels often come into service for quick change of pre-rigged looped-up leaders with trolling lures and skirted baits.

Terminal tackle choices include an ever-increasing range of lures, such as Billy Baits and Turbo Rattlers, Islander lures and spoons, skirts for natural baits, chuggers and diving lures, and plugs.

The arrangement and deployment of trolling spreads increase dramatically with the addition of outriggers and downriggers, flatline release clips, and planers. Each requires its own brand of knowledge for rigging the attendant tackle, clips, baits, and lures, and all together, these techniques amount to a vast field of study. To learn much more about how to rig swimming baits with lead weights and live-baits with harnesses, using teasers and dredgers, release clips, tag lines, kites, and many other tools of the trolling trade, a basic rigging book, such as Vic Dunaway's *Baits, Rigs and Tackle* (Florida Sportsman Books) gives good specific instructions.

For anglers who want to amplify their trolling spread to increase strikes, the first consideration might be to add trolled lures and baits to cover the entire water column, including the lower and middle columns, as well as the surface. Increasing the number of trolled baits and lures in your spread not only requires more rigging and preparation but more care and line maintenance while trolling, though it certainly raises the odds of hookups by increasing the variety and depths of baits in your presentation. It also increases the chances of hooking a fish that misses a bait on its first strike by giving it other choices, and bigger spreads may also serve to attract and even raise fish from the depths.

Generally, anglers find their comfort level with a trolling spread for their boats and that particular spread's rigging demands, and unless they push themselves to learn new techniques, they'll stick with their favorite routine. Remember that any fish, from a dolphin to a marlin, might strike one of your lures or baits while it's being trolled, and you'll have a tough time landing that fish unless your line, connections, and tackle, are properly matched to it. That's one of the greatest arguments for keeping at least one rod appropriately rigged, if not baited, ready to drop back to a big sailfish, wahoo, tuna or marlin, at least for a fighting chance at that fish. In the same vein, having a few live baits handy seriously increases your options should a surprise pelagic show up.

Where to Troll

Trolling speed and direction primarily depend on conditions. If seas are rough, help keep the baits in the water by trolling down sea. If conditions are good, trolling three to seven knots presents baits at a good speed for dolphin and most other local species.

Dolphin, and the birds that follow them, are known to generally move east to west in the Keys, along current lines, whereas tuna generally travel north to south. Trolling with or against the prevailing current may make a difference in how quickly you encounter debris carried by the Gulf Stream coming from the west. Eddies also spin off the stream and alter the direction of the current in a localized area, so it's best to know the stream's position at all times and be on the lookout for divergent currents. But all that doesn't seem quite so important when fishing for dolphin as finding the fish at their

Weeds and dolphin often go together, but scattered weeds make trolling tough.

depths that day, which might depend more on bait, current rips, or debris, because they'll be where the bait is. So that means, head southward and keep going until you find fish or hear reports on the radio of the depths the fish are running. Once they find fish, many anglers troll across the current, believing that the biggest dolphin travel into the current, looking for baits carried to them. Trolling across the current also increases your likelihood of finding a fish in that area by covering more of the moving water. Consequently, many anglers end up zig-zagging through the seas they think will be holding fish. They zig-zag to increase their chances of finding the fish, and the chances of finding the big fish that might be moving into the current. Zig-zagging is a good compromise strategy when the fish really could be anywhere in the vicinity. You can also devise your own trolling pattern, of course. The important matter is to have some kind of pattern to follow to cover the area.

A good strategy for most trolling days, depending on the season and its corresponding water temperatures, is to start your search at 150 feet. From there, watch for birds and weeds, and head toward the southeast or southwest, depending on your overall day's plan, where you want to end up in the afternoon, and how far from home. Listen to captains' channels 08 and 78 on the VHF radio. Search for birds, even with binoculars. Sometimes only a couple of birds feeding over a spot, almost holding steady, can indicate a big dolphin working baitfish or a school of tuna. Even if you see a single frigate bird close to the water's surface, it's worth investigating. Generally, birds working over dolphin will be moving east to west with the current lines, and birds over tuna might be flying and diving more erratically to follow the impetuous school of skipjack and blackfin that are likely to be around the Lower Keys. Don't work too close to other boats that are trolling.

Turning and running along weedlines without tangling baits in the weeds or the lines with each other, and trolling near structure accurately, is also crucial to hooking fish. Always look for the cleaner side of the weedline with less stray weeds and troll along it. If you can see birds working along weeds, you also have the choice of a quiet approach by slowly idling over and casting spinning tackle to the fish. The best approach may depend on whether or not you have the fish to yourself and can take your time, or whether or not other boats might be heading there too. While it's always an advantage to get to a bite first, it's an absolute imperative not to crowd anglers already fishing a feeding school, or even worse, cross someone's trolled lines or chum slick, and a neck-and-neck race with another boat to a bite will not pay off for either crew. There will be other schools in the area, and a fight between anglers and the bad blood that comes of it can ruin the day.

In the end, the direction that you troll for the greater part of your time on the water will depend on your overall strategy for that day, and you might include more than one technique. A whole day of trolling for dolphin, for instance, might cost plenty in fuel and might not even be necessary, unless you're tournament fishing. Often, hitting a couple or three schools of fish produces plenty of catch.

One important consideration about trolling direction involves the time of day you get to the debris in your locale, a concern that becomes crucial during tournament fishing. The depth and direction of the offshore current will affect what direction the structure and the fish will be moving. So it's a smart move, especially on busy weekends in the summer and in tournaments, to position yourself to be among the first anglers to find the fish-holding debris in the morning. Whether that means getting out early or running some distance westward from Key West to be among the first anglers to greet the debris pushed eastward by the Gulf Stream current and its offshoots and eddies. It's a small price to pay, but being the first anglers to a good floating structure can make the difference between a good day and a great day on the water. Finding a floating bucket in the morning with a couple tripletail on it and chumming there can turn into a few hours of fun and fishing when dolphin, wahoo, or even a sail or a marlin turn up.

No matter what else though, to consistently troll effectively, anglers must understand how ocean currents operate in their waters.

14

Ocean Currents and Eddies

Follow the Cues to Pelagics

The position and condition of all that debris that trollers love, and every other significant sea-surface feature, such as rips, temperature breaks, and color changes, are all governed by ocean currents. Offshore anglers worth their salt know that the whereabouts of the fish and whether or not they'll be feeding are influenced more than anything else by currents and their ocean frontal zones—the leading edges of current flows—that concentrate bait, draw predators, and make hot spots hot.

Until recently, where and how those currents and their associated formations of eddies, rips, weed lines, and color changes, moved from day to day remained a mystery to everyone except the professionals who spent most of their time on the water. But now, thanks to the wizardry of sciences, including satellite and computer technology, every angler can access the same information about currents and sea temperatures that even the big-money tournament competitors use to locate fish the night before they go offshore. It's almost as easy as checking a Web site for the weather, and even easier if you subscribe to one of the services that sends the information to you.

The use of these current-flow forecasts, including sea-surface temperature Web sites and sophisticated fishing forecasts available through subscription services, has created a quiet revolution in the way many anglers approach offshore fishing.

As currents snake and meander through the oceans, they spin

off eddies, backflows, and fingers. The leading edges of these formations, called ocean fronts, create all the phenomena that we look for
offshore—the rips, color changes, and weed and debris accumula-
tions. Without knowledge of the fronts' locations, anglers—even if
they are targeting bottom structure—essentially troll blindly across
open oceans except for the limited assistance their own eyes and,
in some cases, radar, can give them. If they're working off verbal
reports from previous days, they stand a good chance of not finding
that hot bite because currents have already moved it, especially if
they're not aware enough of the ocean circulation features in those
waters to track it down.

Ocean frontal zones become hot spots for a number of reasons.
The temperature differences between the bodies of water create
a curtain past which bluewater species will not go, so they prowl
along its edge. Those temperature boundaries often form rips,
sometimes with debris, that anglers notice as stretches of calmer
water bounded by faster, rippled surface water. To know whether
the rips might produce fish, it helps to know whether they repre-
sent the clashing of ocean fronts with significant temperature differences. If the rip shows the convergence of 78-degree blue water
from a finger of the Gulf Stream and 74-degree outflow from the
Gulf (a scenario that occurs south of the reef along the Keys in the
winter), there's a good chance of finding sailfish and cobia action
there.

Mitchell A. Roffer, president of Roffer's Ocean Fishing Forecast-
ing Service based in Miami, says, "Certain fish such as mahi, marlin, swordfish, and yellowfin and other tunas travel along the edge
of the Gulf Stream and feed along the Gulf Stream frontal zones.
Not only are the eastern boundary and western boundary productive, the eddies along both sides are productive. We have also seen
eddies in the middle of the Gulf Stream that have increased productivity."

At their leading edges, fronts also carry and accumulate weeds
and debris that provide structure. One prime example of current-

Sargassum weeds
and the species
of baits that live
in them attract all
pelagic predators.

borne structure is the sargassum weed, and with it the dolphin, that
the fronts of the Gulf Stream carry to us through the summer.

In addition to debris, the fronts carry and concentrate phytoplankton, zooplankton, and baitfish at their leading edges. According to Chris Mooers, of the University of Miami's Rosenstiel School
of Marine Sciences, "All those organisms get pushed by the force of
that water to the leading edge, and that is where they stay, caught
and bounded by the movements of the water that carries them. In
turn, that's where the pelagics go to find their prey."

Fronts also mark the bounds of different kinds of ocean water. Coastal water is usually cooler, less salty, and richer in those nutrients (that give it a cloudier color) than blue water, and those variations create density differences that prevent the two waters from mixing. The boundary where they meet, seen as a color change, can last for days and start a feeding chain along its edge, which begins with the phytoplankton, zooplankton and baitfish, and moves to predators, and then, savvy anglers. Pelagics tend to hang in the blue and to eat in the green water.

"If," Roffer adds, "the organisms remain concentrated along the front for twenty-four to forty-eight hours or more, there will be a substantial concentration for larger fish to locate and feed on."

That's the kind of hot spot that a knowing angler might find at home via a computer by checking temperature breaks on sea-surface temperature charts. According to Roffer, those spots last anywhere from one day to seven days. After that time, the ocean's circulation changes will mix the surrounding waters and degenerate the optimum conditions and disperse the bait and predators.

Eddies might contain many or all of these features along the edges and are fishing destinations in the open ocean. Eddies might be created by a current's movement, from friction between a current and a land mass, from friction between two currents, or by disruption of a current's flow over massive sea mounts, such as the Steps off Florida's western coast. In any case, according to Mooers, eddies are strongly manifested in satellite imagery—both thermal and color imagery.

"Eddies themselves produce currents which are quite strong," says Mooers, "often flowing at a meter a second. These will be going in opposite directions depending on which side of the eddy you're positioned on, and the strongest currents, where the marine life concentrates, will be at the eddy's edges."

At sea, eddies are apparent by the change in current direction and speed in their water, and likely a change in the ripple pattern and even in the water color, says Mooers. However, unless anglers know that they have found an eddy and how large it might be, their discovery will be much less valuable because they won't know how to approach and fish it.

"Shallow eddies stretch about five to ten kilometers in diameter," Mooers says. "And deep eddies may stretch one hundred kilometers in diameter."

Most anglers prefer trolling in the same direction as the eddy's current since natural baits travel with the current flow. Edges might produce fish, but depending on the eddy's size and your time constraints, it may also prove effective to explore toward the eddy's center, where you can discover and fish its most productive features and areas.

Counter-clockwise rotating eddies, called cyclonic eddies in the Northern Hemisphere and also known as cold-core upwelling eddies, can become hot spots by creating the ultimate offshore oasis. In them, as Roffer explains, "The rotation of the water results in an outward flow, and this forces subsurface water up to replace the water moving outward."

These upwelling eddies bring nutrients and phytoplankton up from the sea floor toward the sunlight, which stimulates their growth. In turn, says Roffer, this brings zooplankton to feed, and then bait and predators. However, Roffer points out, "In Florida, the core does not always get colder at the surface due to the upwelling. Sometimes the increase in productivity remains deeper in the water column and does not appear to affect the surface action with tuna, wahoo, marlin, and mahi [dolphin], but swordfish action is likely to improve in either case because they feed at the lower depths."

Some anglers check reports of temperature breaks and current flows on Web sites as often in an effort to learn the patterns of circulation in their home waters. After all, oceans operate in a system similar to the earth's atmosphere, constantly moving and shifting in unstable but predictable patterns. Some Web sites have GPS coordinate overlay grids that give approximate locations of eddies, temperature breaks, and other formations, but subscription services such as Roffer's eliminate the guesswork by pinpointing their coordinate locations.

Good gaff technique requires the angler to rake the gaff point down straight across the fish's back, behind the line, as close as possible to the fish's head.

In the Keys, the Gulf Stream swings anywhere from ten to fifty miles offshore, and its strength varies plus or minus thirty percent of its total strength, according to Mooers. As it moves, the fingers, backflows, and eddies off it carry pelagics even closer to the islands. However, knowing how to take advantage of the current's positioning requires knowledge of each species' habits and preferences for water temperatures.

The free-access ocean charts, posted on Web sites often sponsored by government and university agencies, and the subscription services, all use data produced by NOAA satellites, and complex computer programs to transform it into sea surface temperatures.

The most sophisticated services also use visual information from the NASA Terra and Aqua satellites, and they combine all that data with radar, sea buoy, ship, weather, and angler reports to create their current-flow and sea temperature forecasts. Free Web sites, while providing good information, often do not use as many data sources, update their posts as frequently, or provide analysis of the data for an angler's purposes.

What anglers want, or need, will depend on their purposes, from catching dinner to winning a million-dollar tournament. But as Roffer says, "Anglers who understand the ocean circulation features and time their fishing in the areas that are most likely to provide fishing action are significantly more productive than anglers who randomly fish the ocean or target bottom structure."

Of course, ocean currents and eddies do more than bring fish our way. Our currents in Florida, such as the Loop, the Gulf Stream, and others that occasionally flow near, are all interconnected to a worldwide circulatory system that continually transports nutrients through the oceans, balances the earth's temperatures, and serves to keep the planet, and all life on it, thriving. With the stores of knowledge available at anglers' fingertips through a variety of free Web sites and through subscription services, the ways of those oceans and their currents need not be quite so mysterious anymore.

Valuable information on currents, eddies and their associated features, and how to fish them, can be found at the following Web sites:

http://roffs.com
http://nowcoast.noaa.gov
http://efsis.rsmas.miami.edu
http://sstcharts.com
http://terra.nasa.gov/
http://aqua.nasa.gov/
http://noaasis.noaa.gov/NOAASIS/a3

15

~~~~~~~~~

Offshore Extraordinary

Kite-Fishing, Pelagics on Fly, and the Shrimp Boats

If the basic techniques seem routine, maybe it's time to try something new on your boat. You may want to try kite-fishing, fly-fishing for pelagics, or an ambitious trip to one of the hottest bites in Key West: the shrimp boats.

Kite-fishing can be a fairly complex technique that most anglers, rightly so, associate with professional crews and tournament fishing. But the technique itself doesn't have to be intimidating to learn, and it can be used in any of Key West's waters for an effective presentation. Tarpon guides are now using kites, as are anglers hoping to hook sharks. Who knows where or how kites might be applied next. There's always room for innovation, and the best new techniques are often a blend of ones that already exist.

Sending up kites to suspend lines and baits may be an even truer form of fly-fishing than fly-fishing itself. From a kite line on a release clip, the fishing line lets the bait drop down onto the water for a perfect, leaderless presentation, effectively imitating a bait jumping or skipping on the surface to avoid predation. It is the method of choice in sailfishing tournaments and also highly effective on anchor, drifting or on slow-troll for tuna and kingfish.

A few other advantages make kite-fishing a valuable technique to add to the offshore angler's gamebook. Kites broaden the range of your bait spread by fanning out your baits even farther than outriggers will, and two or even three lines can be run from a single kite line. Kites also help to prevent lines from crossing each other as they often do when multiple lines are trolled from a single out-rigger, and they lessen the chances of line tangling when a fast fish hooks up because the lines are farther apart and can be quickly reeled up off the surface.

To the uninitiated, kite-fishing looks complicated, involving plenty of specific equipment and particular rigging, and it is. Even after practice, many anglers and captains still struggle to put up kites without losing them, dunking them in the sea, or tangling them, all because it's such an effective tactic. Once in the air, kite lines and the fishing lines clipped to them also need constant maintenance, so it's not a casual operation. You'll stay busy, but it's very

Capt. David Barillas sends up the kites to present baits to tuna.

Goggle eyes are the bait of choice for sailfishing.

exciting and rewarding to see a game fish take a surface-splashing kite bait.

Anglers use kites on anchor at a hot tuna bite, and they slow troll with them to cover territory for a mixed bag. But by far the most popular application for kites comes for sailfish. You won't find a boat in a sailfish tournament in the Keys without a kite. Anglers slow-troll kites over productive territory in tandem with flat-lined baits off the stern. They'll also drift with their kite baits properly positioned along the slight edge of a current break, rip, or color change where they suspect sailfish will be feeding, and they keep their baits properly placed by bumping their boat ahead and back while drifting with the current. Both tactics offer natural presenta-tion of baits and ways to cover hot territory. On the drift, anglers can also let out surface baits to drift with the current, drop jigs to the bottom, or even do both to cover almost the entire territory around them, from the top of the water column to the bottom.

Big sportfishing boats run their kite lines off the stern, bow into the wind on anchor, or drifting along with the current. Center console anglers generally can run their kite lines off the stern or bow, or both, with their beam to the drift, or with one kite off the stern if seas aren't too rough or deep to anchor.

Kites can be purchased from a variety of makers, the top ones including Bob Lewis and AFTCO, and short, stout kite rods will be needed to fly them. For convenience, kits for rigging the kite lines, including the series of larger and smaller swivels and fitted release clips, are available. Motorized kite reels and motorized handle attachments are designed to take the strain out of reeling in hundreds of yards of kite line. How to rig kite lines can be found in tackle rigging books and online sources.

Rigging the fishing line starts with a six- to eight-foot length of mainline doubled by a Bimini twist, with a ceramic ring, a float, and an egg sinker added to the line before the 60-pound snap swivel for the leader. The float works as a bright visual marker when suspended and also helps to prevent a strong live bait from pulling the line and the kite line down. The weight helps to bring the fishing line straight down to the water. To the snap swivel, loop on your leader—ten to fifteen feet of high-test mono, at least 50-pound, terminating in a 4/0 to 6/0 live-bait or circle hook. The debate rages on over which hooks work better to hook sailfish, but there's little doubt that circle hooks make the release of landed fish much easier, which is probably healthier for the fish. In 2008, it became legally mandatory that circle hooks be used in all U.S. sailfishing tournaments in Atlantic waters. The ceramic clip on the main line gets clipped to the kite line as that line lifts into the air.

Both the kite line and fishing line are let out simultaneously. The kite will fly out as far as 250 to 300 feet to position the near bait at approximately 125 feet back, and the far bait at 200 feet back. Some anglers prefer to hold their baits in the live well until the release clip reaches the proper position over the water. Once it does, they hook the bait, usually sideways through the nose or through the back, and let it drift out to the spot. Other anglers let the kite line drag the hooked bait out over the surface into position, possibly drawing strikes on the way. Either way, the process takes two anglers, one on the kite rod and one on the fishing rod, or else one very well-practiced angler at both rods.

Once you're adept at rigging and deploying kites, there are options to diversify their use. You can employ different weight kites for different wind speeds, helium balloons to fly kites on calm days, and add-on release clips to send up another fishing line on a kite line already out.

While it's hard work, most anglers who've achieved competency at kite-fishing believe that it's worth it. Keep the baits to within three feet of the surface with constant line maintenance, and those baits spread out over a color change in 200 feet will be a beautiful sight.

Pelagics on Fly Offshore

You want to catch permit on fly? Go to a Gulf wreck where permit spawn in the spring, and you can hook up to a dozen in a day.

Not only permit, which get skittish to say the least when they leave deep water to forage on the flats, but pelagics including blackfin, cobia, king and cero mackerels, sailfish, sharks, and dolphin, all yield spectacular action on fly gear in Key West's Gulf and Atlantic waters. Many of the local offshore fly-fishing techniques, only now gaining popularity elsewhere, were developed and refined thirty years ago in these waters by originators including Ralph Delph, Ken Harris, Robert Trosset, and Jose Wejebe.

Today, anglers around Key West still pursue three basic strategies for pelagics on fly: chumming behind Gulf-side shrimp boats, teasing over wrecks to bring fish to a feeding frenzy on the surface, and live chumming with pilchards on wrecks and hot spots in the open Atlantic. All the techniques involve some form of chumming to draw the fish, turn them on, and keep them by the boat. By chum-ming, anglers try to create a feeding scenario along the lines of the target species' regular feeding patterns.

The symbiosis between shrimpers and anglers has thrived for decades around the Gulf of Mexico. Come spring in the Lower Gulf, blackfins, bonito, kings, and cobia take up residence beneath the shrimp boats to feed on handouts the shrimpers toss overboard when they cull their nets. From Key West, the boats holding black-fins anchor during the day anywhere from twenty to forty miles out. Enter the angler, with chum—live or dead or bags of chum sometimes available from local marinas.

At the shrimp boats, the fish, if present, quickly respond to a few handfuls of chum thrown off your stern. Be patient, and if the tuna are there, they'll rise after a few minutes. The action behind boats can be fierce and relentless and, on a good day, will tire you out by noon. One drawback of the tactic is the distance you have to run to find the shrimp boats and the attendant price of fuel that goes with it.

Teasing with hooked baits over wrecks and switching to flies for the take can be pulse-pounding and visually stimulating too, es-pecially when big cobias, amberjacks, and barracudas get heated up below your bow. The tactic requires numbers for good wrecks and coordination among anglers. One of the challenges is to choose your fish among the many and reach it with a cast that imitates a baitfish escaping through the air. Proper presentation often results in a smashing success when the fly hits the water.

The third style, chumming with live pilchards, brings a lot of record and tackle-breaking fish close enough to boats to reach with a fly rod. Anglers use a cast net to gather pilchards in the shallows before heading to the open Atlantic to find pods of feeding black-fins and kings plus passing cobia and sailfish too. Often tuna will crash bait some distance from the boat, and while the entire pod is moving, accurate casting will be required to reach them. When you're anchored at a color change or a rip and the current's running at a few knots, you'll also need strong fish-fighting abilities to land that 30-pound blackfin, which is sounding to a depth of 100 feet as your backing dwindles.

"Fly-fishing for pelagics has changed a lot down here in the last couple of decades," says Capt. Ken Harris, who holds a number of International Game Fish Association records on fly-caught fish aboard his boat, *Finesse*. "In the mid-eighties, nothing was as cool as teasing, especially around the Gulf wrecks. We wouldn't enter a cobia in the Met Tournament that was under fifty pounds on fly. Amberjacks had to be sixty, seventy pounds to be noteworthy. Those were the early years of the Gulf wrecks. Then came the live chumming with pilchards in the early nineties, and that changed the species that we could target.

Their stunning runs and heart-stopping head shakes make kings great sport on fly gear.

"You know what's really fun behind the shrimp boats?" Harris asks. "Take a really big popper and let it float and the bonito will suck it down and spit it and finally a tuna will take it and you set the hook and hold on."

Blackfins are hard fighters, especially on the Atlantic side, in a current, every fish takes thirty, forty minutes. You take a breather before you put a line in the water.

You've got all the mackerel—king, cero, Spanish—right around the reef in the late winter and early spring. Those months, record-size cero and Spanish mackerel can be caught on a fly by anchoring over marked fish on the bar, just south of the reef, and chumming.

While you might find any of the target species here at any time of the year, spring is the peak of the pelagic fishery around Key West. Blackfin season starts in November on the Atlantic side and goes right through June on the Gulf side behind the shrimp boats. Sailfish and amberjack come in the winter and run through spring. Typically, cobia appear around November on the inshore and off-shore wrecks, and in December they move into shallow water, the harbor and the Northwest Channel, along with permit, snapper, blacktips, and bull sharks. All these fish, and others, are all present and in the greatest numbers from March to June.

The best fish to target on fly in Key West, especially for starters in the sport, may be dolphin, because their runs are fairly predictable, their numbers are plentiful, and they don't know the meaning of finicky.

Even dolphin under 10 pounds present a good challenge on light fly gear, 7- or 9-weight rods, a 4X test tippet, and no shock leader. They strike immediately when your fly hits the water, and almost every one of these colorful fish will execute head-over-tail acrobatic jumps. Quickly release the fish you don't want to keep.

When you have dolphin at your boat, don't be surprised if a marlin or a wahoo wanders into the mix. If one does, and you hook up to one on fly, you'll have performed a very rare feat for Key West. Opportunities for a wahoo on a fly come and go so fast, many times you won't have time to change a tippet before you need to cast.

Dolphin are summer crowd pleasers, and big ones present quite a challenge on fly tackle.

You've got to be rigged and ready for that sailfish rising to your wake or a cruiser-weight cobia circling your boat.

Anglers can always scale their rods to the fish, but for heavy-weight pelagics such as tuna and big kings, 12-weight are the general rod of choice—and usually more than one, all rigged and ready to cast.

You might want a popper on one, a steel leader with a fly on another, and then two others, one with sinking line, one an intermediate line with a mono leader. Also, there's a choice between anti-reverse and direct-drive reels. Direct-drive reels can be trouble for the novice when there's a big fish on. For truly big fish, such as sharks, amberjacks, and tuna, direct-drive reels let you apply much more necessary pressure than anti-reverse reels. Serious anglers always go to direct-drive reels.

As the popularity of the sport continues to grow, fly-tackle companies are making rod-and-reel outfits more affordable for novice anglers. No longer does it take $1,000 to buy sufficient gear. You can get a good outfit for $300, and even some that aren't so good for $150, plus lines, which run $35 to $75. But it's worth it to spend the extra money to get the good quality because the fish and conditions are hard on that tackle. You'll want a good reel with a solid drag that won't wilt when a fish makes a long run and one that can withstand the salt environment.

Bluewater fly-fishing doesn't need to be intimidating to beginners either and might even be more forgiving than the nerve-wracking world of the flats.

The Shrimp Boats in the Gulf

Tracking down the shrimp boats for the fish that follow them has to be one of the most exotic trips, along with swordfishing at night, available in Key West. Here's how the fairly complicated trip works.

Through their contacts with the shrimpers, local captains get the shrimp trash to chum blackfins, cobia, and bonito behind their boats. Most often, and preferably, the captains already have the big bags of bycatch at the docks in the morning from a recent, previous rendezvous with a shrimp boat, but sometimes arrangements have been made to pick up the chum from boats in the Northwest Channel on the way out in the morning. As a last resort, anglers heading out of the Northwest Channel can radio for "chum-chum" to contact shrimpers on anchor nearby and try to trade a 12-pack of beer or cola or $20 for the bycatch, but this is only a long shot. Shrimpers work at night and sleep in the day so they might not respond and cold-calling sleeping shrimpers on their boat might not get you what you want. Given the time and expense of the trips, arrangements should be set beforehand.

Once in the Gulf, and loaded with bait, the hunt for shrimp boats begins fifteen miles north of Key West. The fish hold beneath the boats, waiting for the daily cleaning of the nets which usually happens late in the day, but they're prepared to eat at anytime. If pres-

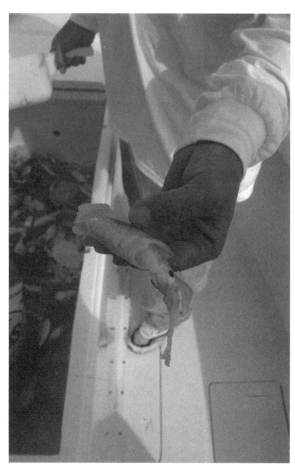

Squid is a great bait for blackfin.

ent, they will quickly respond to a couple handfuls of fresh bycatch tossed overboard as you hold by the stern of the shrimp boat.

There are a couple tricks to separating the bonito from the blackfin. Often, the bonito come up first. They're more aggressive. But be patient, and if the tuna are there, they'll surface after a few minutes. Tuna especially like pufferfish and squid, so save these baits to throw to tuna, because the bonito are less likely to take them. Also, as you drift away from the shrimp boat, the bonito will run back to it while the tuna will stick with you as long as you chum them, and that's the time to go for them on a fly.

"It used to be that the shrimpers would trade a six-pack of Coke or beer for their trash," Capt. Chris Garcia of *Cool Water* charters says, "but now they want money." If there happens to be a tournament in Key West in the next few days, as there often is in the spring, then the price of the trash gets stiff, $20 to $30, and higher for "butter," or pure mojarra, the prime bait to draw tarpon in a chumline. Anglers note: the run of tuna behind the shrimp boats coincides with prime time to chum tarpon in Key West harbor.

Garcia and a few other captains have long-standing relationships with certain local shrimpers, who often honor these alliances to the exclusion of other captains. These factors make it extremely tough, if not impossible, for a private angler to run out and garner the shrimp trash. It would be advisable, at least, for the private angler to devote a day to getting the bait. You might be able to buy from shrimpers at the docks. You can use other frozen chum behind the boats, but the trash is what the tuna and other fish expect, so it's the natural item.

Furthermore, Garcia knows what trash he wants. Either bycatch that's been culled and sacked that very morning, or frozen bycatch that's been properly dipped in preservatives and flash-frozen in the shrimper's hold, exactly as they treat the shrimp catch for market.

The bycatch is so valuable, Garcia has installed a powerful radio and antennae at his house so he can talk to the shrimp captains the night before and get their locations at sea. He'll use three to four bags per trip.

Eventually as you run northward in the Gulf, you'll spot the silhouettes of the anchored shrimp boats. Pull up to the port side and call to the deck hands, who are sometimes reluctant to confess that they have the goods until you tell them that you've already talked with their captain or offer them the right items of trade. Load the bags on board and run off to the row of shrimp boats lined up in the distance. At each one, there might be tuna waiting for you.

At the shrimp boats, toss in the chum and wait to see what shows.

Truth is, they're not supposed to sell the bycatch. Some people point out that the bycatch is in fact wasted baby fish and other species, and many of those fish are valuable game fish like red snapper. Others will say that once the fish are dead, they're no good to anybody. The conflict presents a dilemma every angler must resolve on his or her own.

part 3

Species

16

Permit, Bonefish, and Tarpon

The Flats Grand Slam

Once an angler has a good understanding of Key West's fishery, familiarity with the techniques, and an idea of the seasons for various species, the strategy really begins. Targeting a particular species among the many that are available and determining exactly how and where to catch it is the great joy of an accomplished local angler anywhere. In Key West, that accomplishment means even more since there are so many species and waters from which to choose.

There are about a hundred noteworthy game-fish species in these waters. Some very good game and food fish, such as escolar, you rarely even hear about. But without doubt, in each quadrant of the fishery, there are a few that remain the most popular. On the flats, in the backcountry, around the reef, and offshore, no book about this fishery would be complete without a close examination of each of the species in each milieu that draw anglers from around the world to Key West.

On the flats, the big three marquee species are permit, bones, and tarpon.

"Permit and bonefish are like cattle," says longtime flats guide Phil Thompson. "They move up on the flats with the tide to feed. They'll graze off a flat, and then they'll be gone the next day. Usually, neither of them will get so far up on a flat that they can't escape easily from a predator. And always," Thompson urges, "no matter where you are on a flat, have a silver-dollar sized blue crab ready,

Big "floaters" pop up in channels any time and seem to watch anglers cautiously—for good reason.

and I mean on the hook and in the water to keep it lively, for the permit that might be sneaking by."

February, March, September, and October are good months to find permit on the flats, and they're strong in the summer too. In March and April many permit will also be on the Gulf wrecks and Atlantic reef spots to spawn. And when permit come out of a channel onto a flat, they will come up moving into the current, looking for prey flowing toward them. It's good to try to approach them from deeper water toward the flats where they'll be feeding. The

Marquesas flats are the big draw for anglers looking for permit, and it's about a forty-minute run there from Key West on a good day. For the chances of encountering permit and tarpon there, it's worth it. But permit prowl many flats much nearer to Key West, from Sawyer Key to Boca Grande. You can also draw strikes from permit and bonefish too with artificial lures like D.O.A.'s two-inch weighted shrimps, whose action imitates real shrimp remarkably when scooted across the flats.

During mild tides, usually around early and late moon phases, the water won't rush up and drain off the flats so quickly, and the fish won't be moving so fast in that water. During the bigger tides, around the new moon and full moon, the fish will be quicker and more skittish, worried about being stranded in the shallows and vulnerable to sharks coming in on the flood tide. On those strong falling tides, when the flats are exposed, be sure to look for fish along the edges of the channels and just inside the channel, where they'll try to catch prey as it sweeps off the flat and where they can remain safe, far from the high shallows of the flat in receding waters.

Over time, anglers learn what kind of behavior to expect from the fish depending on the size of the tide. With this knowledge, they will be able to plan their approach with the required degree of stealth. Generally, voices on boats won't spook fish, but sounds made from the boat's hull, such as storage compartments closing or reels dropping, will signal the fish of your approach. If necessary, keep a low profile while casting, especially if the fish are close, because they will catch sight of you and run.

If permit and bonefish get spooked, your pursuit may not be lost entirely. Sometimes, they'll move off some distance but keep feeding, willingly. Generally, schools of smaller fish become more competitive for baits and less likely to leave the territory, while larger, single fish will be more particular and flighty. If you lose a school, keep your eye out for them to reappear on the flat, even while you search for new fish in the area. At all times, new fish can swim up out of the channel and onto the flats, so if you see signs of life on the flats, whether your target species, sharks, or rays, consider it a potential hot spot. Without any sign of life on a flat at the time you expect it to be hot, consider moving to a new spot.

Whatever flat you're fishing, look for floaters in the nearby channels. Floaters are permit that hang below the surface with their dorsal fins barely protruding from the water. These fish are waiting for prey to come rushing off the flats in the falling tide, and they're willing and eager to take baits. Permit are quite intelligent, with big, perceptive eyes, and you might see them raise their heads out of the water to look at you just as you attempt to look at them. In the channels, you can also attach a wine cork about three feet from your hook to help float your crab in the water longer. Simply slice the cork lengthwise and slip it over your line about three feet from your hook. Little split shots on both sides keep the cork in place.

Many anglers hold the opinion that small blue crabs are the best live bait for permit. To use one, hook the crab at the outermost flange of its shell from the bottom side first, with the hook pointing upwards. People snip off the crab's big pincher claw. One-and-a-

De-clawed crab are possibly the best bait for permit on the flats and around wrecks.

half- to 2½-inch crabs, from shell point to point, are perfect size for permit baits. To cast a crab, do not let it dive into the turtle grass, where it will naturally hide for protection. Try to lead the permit in its path, or basically try to place the crab on the permit's nose. Once the crab hits the water, start reeling to keep the crab in the water and in the permit's vision, and out of the grass. If you keep the crabs in the water while you wait to find the permit, they will last all day long.

The quest for permit on fly tackle is legendary. Guide Phil Thompson says, "Catching a permit on fly is like making a hole in one in golf. It's the pinnacle of achievement and luck together for its sport."

A 10-weight outfit is ideal for permit on a fly, with 12-pound-test minimum leader. Many anglers use fluorocarbon leader material. The Del Brown Merkin crab is the classic permit fly in the Keys. Try to hit the permit on the head with the fly, but land it quietly. Even talking about catching a permit on the fly, you run the risk of spooking all the fish in the vicinity.

Permit at the Reef and at the Wrecks

In March, April, and into May, these skittish fish make themselves much more available at reef and Gulf spawning locations, where they gather in big numbers and show their true jack qualities— aggressive and bold. Actually, permit use these same wrecks and bottom rubble locations as habitat year-round, but during these months, if you know a few of these locations, it is a sure thing to find them.

A school of permit looks like a coral head rising to the surface out of nowhere. At the Sturtevant and other wrecks, approach ready with a live crab to sight-cast to them, or anchor upcurrent from the wreck and clip an anchor buoy to your anchor line. When you hook a permit at a wreck, you can throw the buoy to get away or risk losing the fish in the bones of the sunken vessel. If there's enough current, it's better to drift away than to start your motor, which can

Slab permit, and plenty of them, school around Gulf wrecks in the spring.

spook the school when you come back to them. You need to decide beforehand whether your position requires that you throw the buoy, and if so, prepare to do it immediately on hooking a permit, because the fish will get to the haven of the wreck quickly.

Permit cruise around the wreck, but sometimes they hang down deep by it, so if you get marks on your fish finder in the middle of the column, try weights varying from split shot to egg sinkers, to get your bait down. Permit have excellent eyes, and swivels put them off, so use as clean a presentation as possible.

Sometimes the permit hang right below the surface, so try casts toward the wreck with the live crab weighted with a split shot and let it freeline toward the wreck. "Pound for pound, permit are tougher than cobia," Capt. Paul D'Antoni says. "In deep water, they run down, and they don't stop. Keep the pressure on him and his head coming up, and if he runs, help him by lowering the rod and letting him go, but stay on him."

Captain's Tip: "On the flats, permit also take a live shrimp with its tail nipped off and hooked from the back end with the hook point protruding out between its legs. Some anglers prefer to cast shrimp to permit because the shrimp can be worked more easily than a crab, which tends to immediately dive and hide. On the retrieve, a shrimp looks as though it's swimming backwards, as it does naturally. In very shallow water, the shrimp tend to hit the water more quietly, whereas a crab can splash and spook a permit if you cast too close to the permit's head."
—Capt. Dave Wiley, Outcast Charters, Summerland Key

Bonefish

Bonefishing in the Lower Keys is very good in the spring and then again in August through November. Those latter months, the waters also happen to be much less crowded with anglers. Some summer mornings can be so pristine and clear, even to be on those waters so alive with life buzzing through them can be thrilling. It's especially fine when there are no hurricanes headed to the Keys.

The fish travel in schools of similar-size fish, ranging from 3 to 5 pounds, to 10- to 13-pounders. Generally, the Lower Keys hold the edge over Key West for more and bigger bonefish, and the Middle and Upper Keys hold the biggest fish. On a lot of flats around the Mud Keys, Upper Harbor Key, the Marvin Keys, the Sawyer Keys,

Capt. Dave Wiley, of Summerland Key, likes braided lines for bones, permit, and tarpon.

and the Content Keys, anglers reliably find bonefish. The backsides of those Keys, on the ledge—essentially a mud bank with a gradual slope—that borders the Gulf, can also be productive range for bonefish. Grass flats bordering any deep channels can be good places to look for bonefish, and there are a number of small keys north of Big Pine with this terrain. Poling across those flats and scanning hard for mudding and waking fish on a rising tide usually gets good results.

Purists scoff at it, but staking out on a sand flat near a channel and chumming works well for bonefish, especially in windy or cloudy conditions when it's hard to see. Chumming can also help inexperienced anglers who may have difficulty finding or seeing the fish but who really want to hook up and feel a bonefish's speed and don't necessarily care how they do it. Anglers will crush a crab and chop up a couple shrimp and drop them down to the bottom, sometimes putting them in a cricket cage or a PVC pipe with holes drilled in it so the baitfish don't eat them. As with all chumming, a little bit of current helps to spread the chum line out to the fish.

For spinning gear, anglers use a long rod for casting distance and 6- to 12-pound line tied into a Bimini twist with a leader, usually fluorocarbon both for its reduced visibility underwater and for its added abrasion resistance compared to monofilament. Small 1/0 hooks work well because bonefish have small mouths intended for grubbing up meals off the bottom.

On fly, an 8-weight rod is typical, though in windy conditions a 9-weight might be preferred for better casting ability. Use weight-forward floating lines, and the leader length depends on the angler's casting ability and the winds. A nine-foot leader is standard, but the shorter you make it, the easier it is to cast. The longer the leader, the harder it will be to control, especially in any wind at all. For the shock tippet, usually go as heavy as possible not to break off, starting at 12-pound-test and working down if the fish seem too finicky around the fly. Move down in pound test as you will to increase the likelihood of a bite. The Crazy Charlie pattern is a classic bonefish fly, and most shrimp patterns are worth a try, considering that they are the bonefish's number-one treat to eat. Most of the world-record bonefish on fly come from the Middle Keys. Two fish, one from Big Pine, the other from Islamorada, each weighing 15 pounds, 4 ounces, both caught in the late nineties, tied for the world record in the 12-pound tippet class.

Captain's Tip: "When fly-fishing the flats, I recommend a weight-forward floating line or an intermediate sinking-tip line. The weight-forward floating line has a heavier twenty-five-foot core section shooting head that will aid in loading the rod, and the floating line will stay on the surface keeping the line out of harm's way. The intermediate sinking-tip will allow the fly to get down faster in the shallows and works well in the deeper channels where we often find tarpon early in the morning."
—Capt. Lenny Leonard, Key West

Tarpon

The Florida all-tackle record, a 243-pounder, came from Key West in 1975. The all-tackle world-record tarpon weighed 286 pounds, caught in Africa in 2003, just to give an idea of how big these fish grow.

During tarpon season, which begins in late February and peaks in April and May, everybody works the harbor. The flats boats work it early and move out when the light tackle boats start chumming. The tarpon fishing at night in the harbor makes for a great few hours of fishing close to the island. Chum with live pilchards on the outgoing tide at a spot right beside Key West, near Fleming Key Cut. That cut leads directly to Garrison Bight Marina and also to City Marina, the most popular put-in for anglers towing boats. Both are less than a mile away from good tarpon spots.

Freeline the eye-hooked pilchards behind the boat and usually you'll find young and hungry resident tarpon. If there's ever a mud line in the water by the cut, get the baits to it. Tarpon prey on bait hanging on the edge of the mud line, like sailfish at the edge of a color change offshore and redfish along the cloudy water on a flat. When you get a bite, let the fish run with the bait a second or so before hooking them, or at least trying to hook them. For these lighter tarpon, Capt. Phil Thompson likes 10-pound-test, a Bimini twist attached with an Albright-knot to a 30-pound fluorocarbon leader and a 1/0 or 2/0 circle hook. He says that the circle hooks save on abrasion to the leader when you're fighting tarpon on light tackle since they hook so often in the corner of the mouth.

When they are in the mood, tarpon take artificials too, of course, including plugs, poppers, and swimbaits. D.O.A.'s TerrorEyz, Bait Busters, and the new Big Fish Lure draw their share of tarpon on the flats and at the bridges.

Other popular places nearby to anchor for tarpon are along the banks of Calda and Bluefish channels. You can also look for tarpon on your depthfinder as you cruise up these passages. When you find them, anchor upstream and drift baits downcurrent. In the channels, look for tarpon to start feeding on the falling tide as bait washes off the flat to them. The key is to get the bait—live or cut bait—down to them. Especially as the tide moves faster, tarpon will be at the far deep end of the channel, so you can use more weight to get the bait down and bump it along the bottom, or freeline it along the current and closely monitor slack to ensure a hookup. After a hookup and a few jumps from that tarpon, it might take a few minutes for the rest of the school to settle down.

Tarpon can be found in all waters around Key West—in the harbor, in the backcountry, in the channels, in the basins, on the flats, and out by the reef, even offshore if you catch them migrating in the spring. If you really like tarpon and want to get an idea of their size and power and swagger, you can usually find a school in fifteen feet of water hanging out at Fort Zachary Taylor State Park. You can also see plenty of tarpon hanging around the cleaning tables of A&B, Sunset and King's Pointe marinas, though these aren't the wild tarpon that people want to catch; they're the domesticated ones, and anyway fishing is prohibited in marinas.

Tarpon Spots

The popular places to catch tarpon are the harbor in the spring and the channels the rest of the year. Catching them on the flats, however, turns anglers into tarpon junkies, especially during the spring migration, when schools—sometimes dozens of big tarpon—come at you in shallow water. When hooked on the flats, tarpon only have one place to go—straight up in the air—and up they go, sometimes up and up again, challenging and thrilling the anglers tight to them.

Because it's so difficult to get a hook penetrated into a tarpon's bony mouth and because they're so explosively powerful, people talk about how many tarpon they jumped as a reliable indicator of the success of their day rather than how many they landed. In various waters, jumping ten fish and landing two is a very good day. On the flats, where they're more skittish, jumping even a few fish should be considered a success. What's more, seeing tarpon is no guarantee that you'll get a hook up. Quite often they'll be rolling and lolling in the waters near your boat, antagonizing anglers targeting them, but they will not bite. Sometimes the bite turns on, and then turns off again quickly.

In the summer, the Tower flats, which stick into the harbor, are extremely productive. They're marked by four channels with water pouring in from the Gulf, and they have the Atlantic waters on the other side. A lot of tarpon, as well as permit and sharks, cross those flats. In the winter, those same flats are often exposed to high winds that make them tougher to fish unless, by chance, the tide and wind go together to produce calm enough conditions to fish. In those bad conditions, flats anglers can fish nearby channels or tuck into the lee of nearby backcountry mangrove islands to look for snook, mangrove, redfish and other species. In the spring and fall, the Tower flats get a lot of boat and jet-ski traffic which puts fish down. In late winter and spring you can also look for cobia on the flats.

When extreme weather, either hot or cold, moderates, the fish move up from the harbor's deeper channels, some of the deepest water in the Lower Keys. During these times, the nearby flats can be some of the most productive water around for tarpon. In and on both sides of the Northwest Channel, Calda Channel, and Bluefish Channel you'll find tarpon, and permit too.

The shallow flats often hold bait, and the tarpon wait in the channels, or cruise along the edges, and cross flats as the falling tide washes bait down to them. Live baits fished along those channels' edges often produce strikes. This is one scenario when some anglers will stake off within casting distance of tarpon swimming along the flat's edge. The tarpon might get hot and cold on and off during a falling tide, but if they cool off too long, you can move to another flat to look for them. On the rising tide, the tarpon get higher on certain flats, even cramming themselves up against mangrove shorelines to catch prey trying to scurry into the root systems for cover. As a rule, deeper water on a flat gives tarpon more ma-

Juvenile tarpon hang in the mangrove roots around keys and
along channels.

neuvering room to escape from approaching sharks, and they'll be
looking aggressively for food then.

Crabs, pilchards, threadfin, pinfish, smaller mullet, and shrimp
are all excellent baits for tarpon. In the channels, live baits are perfect to freeline in the current or bump along the bottom, but on
the flats, they're a bit tougher to cast to cruising tarpon. They must
be presented by leading the fish as it moves, and kept in the strike
zone and not tangled in the grass. That can also be accomplished
by suspending live baits under a small float. Cut mullet and fresh

dead shrimp can be tipped on jigs for ease of casting, and worked in a dart-and-drop motion through the water. Lures work well, both swimming and diving plugs, and so do soft baits such as D.O.A. artificial shrimp on Cal jig heads, and shad and plastic tails on jigs. D.O.A.'s new Big Fish Lure, a mullet imitation, gets strikes too. On a live bait, the angler can give a tarpon an instant to take it, and then hit them with the hook set. Tarpon will reject an artificial much more quickly, so you have to hit them quickly, without hesitation, and try to drive that hook into their bony mouths.

Anglers take spinning gear, level-wind reels, and even plug casting gear onto the flats for tarpon, and generally use 12- to 30-pound monofilament mainline and six-foot leaders of 20- to 80-pound mono or fluorocarbon, depending on the size tarpon targeted. Reels should hold at least 200 yards of line. If the fish are finicky, try lighter leaders. At the risk of breaking them off, you'll at least know if they can be enticed to strike. Around the bridges, tackle gets even heavier, and some anglers use conventional reels and stout, 30- to 50-pound boat rods to try to keep tarpon away from bridge pilings. Around the bridges, fish the bigger D.O.A. TerrorEyz for bouncing along the bottom and the lighter TerrorEyz baits for swimming through the current. The shallow running D.O.A. BaitBusters also attract strikes and hookups.

A few natural phenomena also considerably improve flats fishing for tarpon. The first, of course, is the spring migration, when thousands of tarpon come through the Keys on their way to spend the summer in cooler coastal waters around Florida, the Gulf coast, and as far north as the Carolinas. Some years the migration begins as early as March, sometimes in May. It reaches its height sometime in May or June. Those weeks, as tarpon roam the channels, harbors, and basins north and south of the main island chain, it's a matter of being on the flats when they show. The oceanside flats from Bahia Honda to the Marquesas see tarpon, and anglers for them, both night and day. The slightly deeper water in nearby Hawk's Channel, especially in spots such as Airport Buoy number 57 near Key West, hold tarpon too, but along there, as in the channels and the harbor, most of the time you lose the sight-fishing thrills.

Also in May or June, palolo worms hatch during full-moon tides and send tarpon into a feeding frenzy. Palolo worms live in the substrate of the nearshore ocean, and when they emerge, the falling tide carries the hatchlings out to sea. The worms hatch in different locations on different nights, and from Key West to Bahia Honda, it's hard to predict exactly when or where you'll see it on a given night. Many devoted tarpon anglers will come down to fish a series of days in a row hoping to see the hatch. It's the supreme opportunity to take tarpon on fly, because the fish will be roving the surface of the waters engulfing these worms aggressively. Other bioluminescent worms—locally called the green worms—hatch at night through the spring and summer and provide quite a spectacle, and good chances, to catch tarpon feeding on the surface after sunset.

One of the popular techniques to catch tarpon during the migration is to anchor at the bridges and chum, possibly with live pilchards or with block chum. You can then cast flies or baits to them. May and June are the height of the season for this approach, and it works night and day. The bite seems to move around from night to night, one night at the Seven Mile, and then the next at Moser Channel, or Bahia Honda or Niles Channel, but be assured, the tarpon are around, and you can even try to mark them with your depthfinder before you anchor. A number of basins or bays that have shallow water, five or six feet deep, are also good places to sight-fish for tarpon. Coupon Bight south of Big Pine, Cudjoe Bay, and out front of Sugarloaf are a few spots.

No doubt though, to stand on the bow of a flats skiff in only a few feet of clear, sunlit water, and wait for a school of tarpon to approach close enough to cast to them ranks among the rare angling experiences. To fight and land a 100-plus-pound tarpon amounts to an accomplishment that not many people, not even among anglers who regularly fish the Keys, can claim as their own. Put a fly rod in your hands and the level of difficulty skyrockets.

Besides calm nerves under pressure and good casting ability, standard equipment for catching tarpon on a fly includes quality gear in top condition to minimize chances of breakdown in battle. Twelve-weight rods with weight-forward floating lines are the standard. Anglers vary leader length and shock tippet weight, depending on their casting ability, winds, and the willingness of fish to strike. Longer leaders are tougher to cast but land quieter, and shorter leaders perform better in stiff winds. Also, IGFA rules dictate specific limits for the lengths of the sections and total length of the leader, from hook to fly line. Generally, 30-pound-test leader material and a shock tippet of 60- to 100-pound-test works under most conditions.

Dedicated tarpon anglers are very passionate in their pursuit. They'll debate choice of flies, stripping and hook-setting techniques, and fighting strategies for holding, turning, breaking, and bowing to jumping tarpon. And they'll hold animated discussions of the peculiarities of tarpon behavior, including their daisy chaining, air-breathing, surface popping, and rolling ways. These are all matters of concern to the relatively small crowd of tarpon-on-fly enthusiasts, each of whom could probably themselves write a book about their pursuit.

For other folks wanting to hook up to a tarpon any time of the year in Key West, a sizeable population of juvenile tarpon live year-round near the mangrove roots of backcountry islands and along the channels of the main island chain. Basically, anywhere water flows by mangrove roots, you might find young tarpon all the way down to the Marquesas. They weigh only about ten to twenty pounds, but they put up an exciting fight, either on fly or spinning tackle. When the water gets high, they hide underneath the mangrove roots for protection, but when it drops and at night, they come out to the edges of the roots and feed, and that's a terrific time to cast a fly to them, or even a live bait.

Handling Tarpon

Tarpon fishing is almost exclusively catch and release. While some tarpon die or get killed by sharks during the fight, almost everyone wants to release their fish in good condition, usually after taking a picture. For those who want trophy mounts, replicas can easily be made with measurements, and the fish released.

The battle, however, doesn't always end when you get the fish to the boat and the leader in hand; it gets critical. When landing any tarpon, no matter its weight, be very careful, both for yourself and for the fish. By the boat, big tarpon pull people into the water all the time, and if you're holding them, they yank so hard it feels like they'll pull your arm off. Add in the points of hooks and gaffs, and you get a sense of the risks that furious fish present.

If you want a picture after the release, it's easier and better to keep the fish in the water and not lift or hang it from its jaws, even briefly, for that picture. Hanging them by their jaws harms the fish, and besides, pictures look much better if you keep the fish in positions that they take while swimming in the water. Only the smaller 10- and 20-pound tarpon might be hand-lifted, supported from underneath and held horizontally for a quick photo without damage to the fish.

With the bigger fish, some guys jump into shallow water to get a picture standing next to their big tarpon boatside, and that's not a bad idea. But on that note, with the long duration of fights with those big tarpon, and permit too for that matter, bull and hammerhead sharks often home in on hooked fish as prey, so be sure that only you and the tarpon are in the water. Bulls and hammerheads will cut a 200 pound tarpon in half in a single swipe, so at the first sight of a shark, be prepared to quickly cut your line to save that fish or else sacrifice its life to that shark.

After the picture, but before the release, most fish need to be revived before they can swim away, and this might take a few minutes to an hour to bring the fish back to power. More time out of the water means more stress for the fish and only increases the time it will need to regain strength. It happens to everyone at some point, but having a fish about to be released die at your hands definitely takes some pleasure out of the catch.

Braided Lines on the Flats

Up and down the Keys, and in skinny-water fisheries all around Florida and everywhere else, more flats anglers are spooling up braided lines. For their lack of stretch, which translates into better hook sets and sensitivity to action, their narrower diameter for equivalent strength, which provides greater casting distance, and for their abrasion resistance, which means less cut-offs and more fish landed, narrow-diameter braided lines are winning more converts every season.

One advantage braided line has over monofilament is its resistance to twisting when reeling against a fighting or running fish that's testing the drag. Most of the time it may be the less experienced anglers who try to crank in as a fish pulls on the drag, but it happens to almost everyone once in a while, especially when the excitement of the fight sets in. With monofilament, reeling against the drag puts twists in the line that not only renders it harder to handle and cast, but also weakens it. Because of their suppleness and lack of memory, braided lines will not twist and weaken even if the angler reels against the drag.

Its resistance to abrasion comes in handy too, especially when bruising tarpon pull the line against barnacle-encrusted bridge pilings or streaking bonefish carry the line across the flats atop sea fans and rocks. Braided line will not sever against the little sponges and sea fans that easily cut monofilament.

The increase in casting distance braided lines provide due to narrower diameter proves extremely valuable on the flats, where you might not see too many permit or bonefish in a day. And when you do, they're often not very close. Fifty-pound-test braided line has the diameter of about 12-pound-test mono, and 30-pound-test has the diameter of about 6-pound mono. To be able to cast that extra forty or fifty feet greatly increases the angler's chances for hookups on shallow, clear flats where even the slightest movement can spook fish. Because they're thinner and lighter, braided lines also help to make softer presentations that decrease the chances of spooking wary fish.

Not only can you cast farther with narrower line, but also more of it fits on the spool—in some cases, depending on diameter, 100 yards more. That makes the difference when big bonefish can easily peel off 200 yards on their first run.

Since braided lines have no stretch, compared to roughly twenty feet of stretch per every 100 feet of monofilament, they give better hook sets and transmit way more of the action to the angler's hands. Every movement of the fish and its fight gets telegraphed to your fingertips on those lines, and you can certainly feel a bonefish pecking at a shrimp on the bottom. You may even be able to feel that shrimp twitching. The greater sensitivity in the line helps catch fish, because if they nibble too long on the bait before you hit them, they'll feel the hook and drop it.

For bonefish, many anglers use 10-pound-test-rated braided/2-pound equivalent, and for permit, 15-pound braided/4-pound, on 8- to 15-pound rated rods. For tarpon, try 30-pound braided/6-pound on a big spinner, or even 50-pound braided on a level-wind reel. For the leader, use a few feet of fluorocarbon leader for permit and bonefish, and a six-foot, 50- to 80-pound fluorocarbon leader for tarpon, switching to the lighter-weight leader when the fish act bait-shy.

The power and durability of braided lines may also provide another benefit. They may actually lessen the wear on fish by hastening the fight, and that's a big plus for survival rates in flats fisheries which are sustained by catch-and-release practices.

Along with new possibilities, the braided lines also present new challenges, and a few drawbacks. Their limp structure and slippery texture not only feel unfamiliar to monofilament users, but also the lines knot easily without careful and constant line management. If the line wraps around itself and creates a knot, then all you can do is cut that length off. To contend with its knack for knotting, anglers must practice careful and precise line management in casting, reeling, and handling by always keeping tension on the line.

Braided line's thin diameter, lack of stretch, and tensile strength combine to make it razor-like when strung tightly. The 10-pound rated line easily cuts flesh if not handled properly. Never grab the braided line during a fight, especially not the 10-pound line. Always handle the leader, which makes a good case for using slightly longer leaders with braided line.

To fill spools, most anglers will first put on twenty to thirty yards of monofilament as a base for the braided line, which can slip under, tangle, and even cut itself on the spool, if it is not carefully and tightly packed down. To get the most yardage possible for the spool, some anglers will tie the braided line directly to the spool. In either case, you must be sure that the braided line is packed down tightly on the spool by applying steady tension to the line while loading up the spool. You can tie the end of the line to a fixed pole and walk out the entire spool's length, tighten down the drag completely and reel it back onto the spool while holding tension on the line with the rod.

Angler Dave Justice created what's commonly called the Stren knot to attach braided line to fluoro leaders. Basically, it's an improved cinch knot on the braid side and a Uniknot on the fluoro side. (There's a diagram of the knot on the Stren Web site, www. stren.com.)

All captains stress the need to bow to jumping tarpon when using braided lines, or risk breaking the fish off at the leader or even breaking the rod. Bowing, basically extending the rod to a jumping fish to give it slack, becomes critical with big fish that can snap a rod with a head shake. To compensate for the line's power and lack of stretch, some anglers use longer rods with softer tips, which forgive and absorb shock better. It takes time for people to adjust to the new sense of action and control the braided lines give the equipment, and to redevelop their "touch" with palming the spool, applying rod pressure, and giving the fish free reign to run.

There may be a cost advantage to using braided lines. Though initially more expensive than monofilament, many captains who fish on a daily basis with braided lines change lines much less frequently than with monofilament, whose tendency to twist, kink, and abrade often make spools of it useless. The braided lines seem to endure the harsh conditions of sun and salt better too, though after awhile, even the braided lines fade and become less responsive.

Since braided lines are relatively new, no one has definitely determined if they save money in the long run, but as every angler knows, that really doesn't matter too much. If the lines help get more fish to the boat, then most anglers would say that they're worth it, even if they take a little practice to learn to use and a little more money to purchase them.

17

Sharks and Barracudas on the Flats

Winter Thrills

When all the rest of the action on the flats slows down in the winter, schools of barracuda warm themselves in the sunlit shallows. These fish are incredibly fast and aggressive, and can be attracted with many baits and artificials, especially green tube lures. To find the 'cudas, pole up the flats to likely holding spots, especially around white-sand patches, and cast from at least twenty feet away. Before the lure hits the water, begin reeling to get the lure moving immediately. Make the lure act as you would if a barracuda were chasing it. The plug can't move fast enough. The barracuda will give chase, take strikes nine times out of ten, and sometimes hit the lure as soon as it touches water, because they watch it fly through the air. However, once they catch sight of your boat, they'll spook. If they do, pole on and look for others in the area. Also be aware that large lemon and bull sharks hunt these same shallow waters and will attack a hooked barracuda, so be aware when handling the sharp-toothed fish near the boat to avoid a nasty surprise from an even bigger predator.

Put a light wire tippet on your fly line. The fight won't last long before they bite right through mono tippets.

The Lower Keys flats are prime grounds for chasing big sharks, both on spinning and fly tackle. The IGFA world-record for heaviest fish landed on fly is a 385-pound lemon shark, caught in the Keys (and also released after weigh-in) by Marty Arostegui and Capt. Ralph Delph in March of 2006. Not only big lemons, but also bulls, hammerheads, and spinners hunt the flats in the winter

On the flats, 'cudas take tube lures, baits, plugs, and flies, and they'll keep them unless you use a wire leader.

and spring. There's little hope of taking such a big shark on fly in the open ocean, but on the flats, sharks take an initial run toward deeper water then most often turn to fight face-to-face, which increases the angler's chances of landing them. The best time for them runs from January through March.

"On a good day," says Capt. Phil Thompson, "you'll see fifty or sixty lemons, blacktips, and bulls on the flats out to the Marquesas. The number of barracuda sunning themselves on those flats soars in the winter, and the big sharks are up there feeding on them," says Thompson. "Then in the spring, big bulls, and hammerheads too, will come up on the flats to feed on the tarpon, and they'll stay as long as the tarpon are around. If there's one thing those sharks like more than barracuda, it's tarpon."

Most days in the winter and spring, you'll have your choice of fish to battle. Want a 90-pound lemon, or a 400-pound bull? Stay away from the 300- and 500-pound nurse sharks though. They fight like heavy timber, they're not hard to hook at all, and they'll only distract you from the sportier sharks. They might even snap your 12-weight rod.

One of the keys to fighting sharks on fly tackle is to stay close to them. Recover that line, and stay within sixty to seventy feet of them, whether you motor to them or pole. Same as fighting a tarpon, keep the rod low and put the side-to-side pressure on them. When they pull right, take them left, and vice versa. That makes them mad, makes them run, and makes them burn energy.

"The hardest of all to catch are the spinner sharks," says Thompson. "Because when they jump and twist their bodies, they wrap the line around themselves and cut it. They'll even cut right through wire that way."

IGFA Rigging

To target sharks on fly, you need the strongest tackle available, rigged for maximum durability. That requires a 12-weight rod and at least a 15-pound tippet. If you're going for a record, you need to rig according to IGFA standards. To comply with those standards, Key West Capt. Rob Delph uses backing of 130-pound super braid line for its larger diameter. He nail knots the slow sinking tip fly line to three to five feet of 50-pound fluorocarbon leader with a surgeon's knot for a loop to loop connection between it and the tippet. He then puts a Bimini on the 15-pound tippet and doubles up the double line with a figure eight knot to make that loop to loop with the 50-pound leader. At the bitter end of the tippet, he ties a Bimini and Albright knots that to twelve inches of a 30-pound wire shock tippet.

Now, according to IGFA standards, the lengths of your connections matter too. There must be more than fifteen inches between the Bimini knots on either end of your tippet, and there must be less than twelve inches from your fly to the end of your shock tippet.

You can also try a shock tippet of 80-pound mono or fluorocarbon but the sharks will likely cut through it.

Rob Delph hand ties his Blood Chunk Red flies to simulate the redness of a bonito chunk, and he designs the flies for what they look like as the sharks will see them. He ties flies on circle hooks for their hooking action and their ease of release, something everyone appreciates when the shark gets boatside. You can also add a piece of Styrofoam to the fly to help suspend it in the middle of the water column against the weight of the heavy circle hook.

Find the Sharks

To meet the sharks, get out to the deep channels and flats of the keys to the west of Key West—Archer, Man, Woman Key, Boca Grande, and on the flats around the Marquesas, a vast dominion of interlocking channels, mangrove keys, and shallow turtle grass flats, where, Delph says, the lemons are feeding and spawning in January, February, and March.

Sometimes in the Marquesas you'll even find tiger sharks. Hammerheads are really difficult, if not impossible, to catch on a fly, because the long sides of the their heads, where their eyes protrude, can cut through leader material, and on a big hammerhead, that distance between the side of the head and the mouth where the hook hangs is greater than the legal limit of twelve inches of length of wire leader, so the tippet gets cut by the shark's head.

We all know fishing takes sacrifice, and in shark fishing, it's the barracuda's turn. To chum, hang a fresh-caught, butterflied barracuda off the bow to draw the sharks to the front where the angler can cast to them easily. Jacks and bonito work too. Basically, any fish with a scent will draw the sharks, and you can refresh the scent by cutting another slice into the fish occasionally.

With sufficient wind, you can drift with the breeze down a flat during the falling tide, toward a deeper channel, letting your chum line attract sharks from across the flat to your boat. Always watch

Captain Rob butter-
flies a 'cuda to get
the sharks coming.

the water level carefully to make sure you'll make it off the flat before the tide falls too low. Your other option is to anchor and let the
scent trail bring in the fish. Your choice depends on the amount and
direction of the wind.

Watch for the sharks to swim straight up the scent line toward
the boat, and select the one you want, based on its species and size.
Often, a few sharks approach at once, but depending on how hot
they are, many turn away before reaching casting range. You want
them to charge up that scent line, as if they're going to ram the boat
or try to eat the chum itself, which they will do. If they're lazy, they

may drift off as soon as they see the boat. Some anglers believe that a full-moon phase puts the sharks, like many other species, into a lazy mood during the daytime.

Sharks get less wary in the deeper water in basins and channels, but always exercise caution not to put them off. Like all flats species, noises put them down. Try to avoid slamming lids, dropping tackle, and loud footsteps on the deck. Fish will even pick up pressure from footsteps telegraphed through the water to their lateral lines. If you don't get them on their first appearance, you usually won't get them.

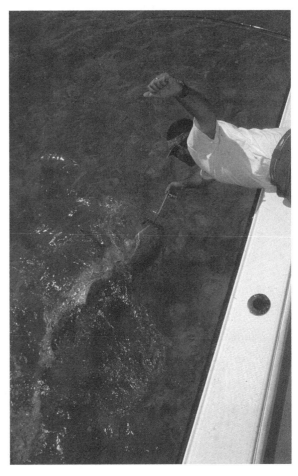

Tire out the shark well before trying to retrieve your fly.

Captain Rob says, "They're most aggressive at their first appearance, and once they see the boat, they know something's up."

To try to entice sharks out of the deeper channels, take a position at the point along the channel, but first drag your chum in the water upcurrent to increase the range of your scent line, then fall back to your point position. Sharks downcurrent of your chum will follow the scent trail back to you. The sharks come, one after another, and in pairs.

It's high-stakes fishing, targeting one species and waiting for just the right fish. It certainly takes patience and fortitude to sustain concentration while waiting for the right fish, and it takes physical strength to keep position for the right presentation of the fly. An angler might cast and strip, and withdraw the fly hundreds of times in a day.

Once you do successfully fight one of these sharks, new challenges present themselves. You'll need to wear them down. On the smaller sharks, 80 to 150 pounds, you can wear them out well enough to hold them by the leader, which you can gently pull while using a long dehooker to get the fly out. On a much bigger shark, you might have to gaff it in the tail to get a tail rope around it to hold it safely; the tail rope won't permanently damage the shark. Once that fish settles down again beside the boat, you can dehook it.

"You can also use a tailer," Rob explains, "a tool that's becoming really popular with offshore anglers to hold billfish for dehooking before release. Basically, tailers slide a cable around the fish's tail and pull it tight to hold the fish."

Whichever method you choose, plan for it in advance, and be ready with it. Sharks are opportunists, and they make a living by taking advantage of everybody else's mistakes. Exercise caution, and keep wary, and you'll stay safe in this extraordinary and exotic fishery down in the Keys.

18

Inshore Mixed Bag and Bugs

No Fuss, Fun Fishing, and Lobstering

A vivid contrast to high-stakes sharking can be seen in another inshore fishery, the mixed-bag grab-all. For a quick trip and a few fish to eat, or if you have little kids on board who need constant action to stay interested, you can't beat fishing for cero and Spanish mackerel, and other inshore fish in the harbor and patch reefs only minutes from Key West. The harbor also offers refuge from winter winds, and on the roughest days, it's the only place to fish safely.

In winter, migratory Spanish mackerel, and year-round, resident cero mackerel make good targets for a day of harbor fishing. The mackerel drill is similar to snappering—anchor, chum, and wait until the scent gets out. You'll get connected in a matter of minutes, but to what might depend on the tide. Spanish bite on any moving tide, but they might take a half an hour or so to show up. They probably bite better on slightly cloudy water. Very dirty water makes them wary of other predators. Use an oily chum such as menhaden, and figure on going through a block or two every hour. At the same time, start tossing out chunks of cut bait, a few at a time. Fresh is better, of course, but frozen threadfins, ballyhoo, or mullet work too.

Flies, spoons, live shrimp, pilchards, and cut bait—Spanish and ceros take them all. A lot of people, however, don't jig for macks on the bottom. But like their counterparts offshore, the kings, Spanish, and ceros feed on the bottom as well, and that's often where you'll find them first. By using jigs, you'll also catch everything in the

Capt. Steve Hassell holds a cero mackerel that raided his chum slick.

water column and increase your chances for plenty of action and a great day of mixed-bag fishing. Of course, such light-tackle bottom bumping attracts all the fish in the vicinity, and if you happen to hook some of the tarpon, cobia, or permit passing through the Northwest Channel area, you might be a little overmatched with 8-pound spinning tackle but it'll be fun while it lasts. Yellow jacks are a delicious fish that visit the harbor in the winter, and they make terrific sushi.

To bottom fish the harbor cuts and channels, tip your chartreuse or white ⅜- to ¼-ounce pompano jig with cut bait, or a few frozen mahua, that you're tossing into the chum line. Cast upcurrent about twenty feet to give the jig better placement on the bottom before the current picks it up again. Once it's down, twitch it to simulate the movements of a shrimp or pinfish that mackerel usually hunt along the bottom, and jig it even more if you're using a bare jig. Let it drift down current and jig it gently on the bottom. One local captain calls it "bipping it," the way you do for pompano, to make it look like a shrimp hiding on the bottom. Often, they'll hit on the retrieve in the middle of the water column.

If you're in a big school of macks, you might use a light wire, #3, attached to the leader by an Albright knot, to protect against their slashing teeth. Many anglers put a haywire twist on the wire to the jig "to give the lure a little movement."

It takes a minute to get the feel for the bottom-bumping technique. To keep your bait on the bottom, where you want it, find the right compromise between the current pulling your bait up and the weight of the rig resisting that pull. When you do, and keep your bait in the lower strike zone, you'll know it by the quick hits you get. If the current runs too strong at your spot it may disperse your chum too fast and make it hard to keep your baits down. At those times, you might try another spot where the current doesn't rip so hard, or wait it out until it slows down where you are.

Scale your tackle to the test to have the most fun with the inshore game. We use trout rods, 8-pound monofilament with a Bimini twist attached to a 25-pound leader with a blood knot, and an improved clinch knot to the terminal tackle—jig, lure, or bait hook. No matter the terminal tackle, knots are preferred to swivels for their cleaner presentation to the fish, and because in schools, resident mackerel will hit that swivel in a flash and cut you off empty-handed, with spiteful frequency.

Two main factors will make or break your hours of harbor fishing. They are first, finding a good spot with the structure to attract and hold bait and fish, and being there when the current runs swiftly to spread your chum line, but not too fast. These two conditions will also greatly influence your success bottom-fishing everywhere—at patch reefs, the reef, and deeper bottom offshore.

Usually, the inshore parade of species starts with lane snappers and includes ladyfish, mangroves, and then blue runners and a few yellowtail. It may take a few minutes for the chum's scent to get to the far-ranging Spanish mackerel, but a sudden singing drag, the strong run, and quick rise to the surface indicates the Spanish blitz has begun. When they start, it's only a matter of how close to the surface they'll come whether or not you'll get to them with a fly or a spoon.

Spanish and cero mackerel can't resist live pilchards hooked through the nose and freelined to them. While pilchards are available for cast-netting most winter and spring mornings in the shallows on Key West's southern side, it's not necessary to have them. Instead you can use cut bait or live shrimp weighted with a slip-sinker if the current runs strong—a variation of the popular "knocker rig" for deep-water bottom fishing. It's a good trick when using a slip-sinker to put it on the double line before you tie on your leader with an Albright. If you leave a tag from your heavy leader at the Albright, the slip-sinker won't get past it and foul up with the hook. Your bait will also float nicely just above the bottom, and the fish won't feel the weight as the line runs freely through the sinker. Otherwise, double wrap the line through the sinker to hold it steady a couple feet above the hook. Since some anglers say that a wire leader puts the sharp-eyed mackerel off, if you're staying with monofilament and using bait, you can also use a long-shank bait hook to put some distance between your line and the mackerel's teeth.

Nothing's guaranteed, but going after inshore species near Key West's harbor will get you into fish. It's a mixed-bag game, filled with plenty of surprises and a lot of humble virtues. You can reach the spots quickly, usually in a twenty-minute ride from local marinas. Plus the harbor can save a trip when the weather's too rough to go offshore or when nothing much turns up out there. Also, jigging in the harbor works for all the species there and guarantees action for younger, impatient anglers. The kids can usually handle the smaller fish while building their angling skills on a few strong-fighters, and if they lose a few big ones, that's a lesson too.

> *Captain's Tip*: "A few drops of menhaden oil behind the stern will bring a school of ballyhoo in your chumline up to the surface for your cast net."
> —Capt. Steve Hassell, Hassellfree Charters, Key West

Catch the Bug: Lobstering in the Keys

Gear includes a license, snorkel and fins or dive equipment, net, gloves, tickle stick, gauge, catch bag, and a dive flag either flying from your boat or rigged on a buoy trailing by a rope attached to your waist if you're snorkeling from the beach. Lobsters live almost everywhere in local waters—in the coral heads, ledges, and sand holes in the Gulf and the Atlantic, and bigger ones live along the reef walls. The nearshore patch reefs are good places for visiting boaters to begin their hunts. Lobsters even populate neighborhood boat canals, but homeowners tend to be possessive about those.

Both inshore and at the reef, there are no-take zones and preserves where lobstering is prohibited, but it's not too hard to find beaches and even state parks, such as Bahia Honda at Mile Marker 30 and Ft. Zach in Key West, where novices can begin their hunts.

At the reef or inshore, you'll want good visibility, which can be judged by scanning the ocean for differentiation among the seagrasses, sand, and rocks. You can also test it by looking straight down. If you can see bottom in five to eight feet, the visibility will be good in that area. If it's blown-out or cloudy with sand kicked up by wind and waves, not only will the lobsters be more skittish because they can't see predators, but also you won't see them either.

Summer sees the best water conditions in the Keys, with warm temperatures, good visibility, and flat calm seas most days. That

At many spots, you can swim right off the beaches and catch lobsters.

makes fine diving and spearfishing, but lobster season closes April 1 for four months for the lobsters' spawning season. The season opens the first week of August.

The two-day sport season precedes the opening of regular season by about a week, and during those days only recreational anglers can bag bugs (though by 2008 there was discussion of ending the mini-season). The sport season is like a holiday in the Keys, and in some spots, people outnumber the lobsters. Very good conditions generally prevail for the first and last two months of the season. In late fall and winter, water temperatures drop and winds often pick up to make diving conditions much tougher.

Once you're in the water and gliding over white sands, seagrasses, pumpkin-colored starfish, sea fans, and all the other life, scan holes and beneath rocks for the lobsters' antennae sensing about the currents like whiskers. When you spot one, drop down to check how well it can retreat to its hole, but be careful when you press your masked face under big coral caps, in case there's a nurse shark or moray eel ready to surprise you. Figure out your best angle on the bug and how the current will carry you once you're down. If you're right-handed, get your net in your left hand and your tickle stick in your right, and breath deep and dive.

Usually, a couple light taps on a lobster's tail with the tickle stick (a three-foot long fiberglass rod about a centimeter thick) will bring it out of its spot. Then, placing your net behind it, tap on its head until it shoots backward into your net. You can twist the net quickly to trap it. Hold the tickle stick against the net to keep it shut as you swim for the surface. Otherwise, the lobster will jump and fight to get out and likely will, only to shuttle away into the aquamarine distance or hole up again.

Once you've had a breath, measure the beast with your gauge. To be legal, its carapace must be three inches long, measured from the eyes to the back edge. The gauge slips over the carapace if it's short and should be released. You might see a dozen for every legal one. If it's a keeper, bag it and go back down for another. The limit is six per person per day, currently.

The primary defense mechanisms for lobsters are escape and camouflage. Their elaborate markings hide them against the variegated sea floor. They certainly can be quick, but after a little practice with the net you'll be fielding them like baseballs.

Good free divers can go down for more than a minute, up for a breath, and down again like a cormorant, to depths of more than thirty feet. It takes a lot of stamina and control to manage your exertions underwater, and trying to regulate your breath for an extended time makes lobstering an endurance sport. Serious divers will develop their lung capacity with practice or use scuba gear. But for beginners in reasonably good shape, if you can stay under and hold your breath for thirty seconds, you can get lobsters in a lot of spots that are less than fifteen feet deep.

Cleaning lobsters is a bit like shucking corn. With gloves on, a knife in one hand, and the lobster in the other, insert the knife under the carapace from the back edge to cut the tail free, keeping the knife parallel to the shell to get the most meat. Sever the tail and twist it off. To remove the intestine, break off part of one antenna and insert it into the anus. That loosens the intestine so that it can be easily pulled out. You can also tuck the lobsters into a paper bag and store them in a freezer for twenty minutes to make them insensate before cleaning them. You can prepare them any number of ways, all good.

19

Cobia

All about the Brown Bomber

Phil Thompson took us out to the flats, where, he says, no matter what's going on in his life, he can at least forget about it for a few hours a day. It's a great backyard to have, I said, and not a bad way to spend a late February afternoon. We had an incoming tide and good weather.

We pulled up and saw the rays mudding. Phil cut the engine and poled us over to one. He jumped down from the platform and cast, but no cobia tailed that ray. He saw another cormorant across the flat and knew by its behavior that it chased a ray, and we motored there.

"The rays actually respond to the engine sound," he said. "They'll turn to it and even follow it a bit. Who knows what they're thinking."

We came up, too quick, right on top of a big cobia piggybacking a ray. They both scooted away from us, and Phil turned in search of them. We found them a hundred yards away. This time, Phil angled the boat in such a way that the wind would push us up the flat. He cast to the ray, leading it, and keeping the jig out of the grass, brought it across the ray's back. No take. He changed from shrimp on a jig to a live crab on a circle hook.

That cobia shot out after the crab, mouthed it, and let it go. The next cast, the fish hit it with force, took it on a run, and Phil set the hook. The fight began, up and down the flat, and around the boat, for minutes, as we drifted in perfect silence, punctuated only by our happy voices.

Cobia are odd fish. They lie at the bottom like grouper and can also be chummed to the back of the boat and to the hook like snapper. They're said to be the only fish in their family, though they resemble cod to some degree and catfish to another, but they run like sharks and tug like tunas. They're very versatile and adaptable, present in great depths and in the shallows, and they thrive not only in Florida, but also around the world. Once you find them, they're as easy to catch as dolphin, and that's why it's so good to see a trend developing among devoted cobia anglers to be conservative in their catch allowances. Letting a few cobias back to swim free will help keep the stocks of their kind plentiful around Florida.

Winter is high season for tourists and for cobia in the Keys. They're both present in big numbers from January through March, and they can be found almost everywhere. Keep a lookout for the cobia anywhere you go on water, from 200-feet deep in the Atlantic, to two-foot depths in the backcountry flats and to Gulf wrecks.

In January, February, and March out beyond the reef, cobia are on the move and feeding. They will pick up jigs as deep as 200 feet, and they'll feed on the surface on live baits. In fact, cobia are often seen cruising on the surface along color changes out past the reef while anglers look for sailfish. Toss the cobia a baited jig or especially a live pinfish, and more than likely that fish will charge it. If you're trolling or drifting, try to position yourself ahead of the fish and let it approach you, because a direct approach will likely put the cobia down.

Closer to shore, in Hawk's Channel, big cobia can be found cruising and hanging around the patch reefs, and they respond to chum in these shallow waters as they do at wrecks in deeper water. Anglers anchored at these patch reefs in the winters should not be surprised to see a big cobia come to their stern sniffing around.

The Gulf is probably the most reliable place to catch cobia in the Lower Keys, because in the winter and spring the fish use the Towers and numerous wrecks as home bases. At the Towers, you'll see the cobia on the surface, often swimming in circles around the structure. When you toss a live pinfish out, it's only a matter of

Get cobia into the box fast. "Green" cobia are known to wreak havoc on the deck.

which one gets to it first. Big cobia lurk under these towers too. If they're not up top, drop live baits down for them.

At the wrecks, slack tide can be prime time for cobia. The cobia might be swimming on the surface, or down below, same as at the towers. Live pinfish go to the bottom on a Carolina rig with just enough egg weight to hit the bottom, but not so much that the fish would feel the weight. You can use swivels on cobia rigs and leave a tag end where the Bimini connects to the swivel to keep the egg weight from sliding down the leader to the hook. Standards are 15- or 30-pound-test on spinning tackle with a 50-pound fluorocarbon leader, and a 4/0 circle hook on 15-pound or a 5/0 circle with 30-pound line. Circle hooks increase the hookup ratio, ease hook removal, and lessen the damage on release fish.

"If the current is fast, hook the pinfish in the nose so he lines up with the current. If it's slow, you can hook him behind the dorsal," says Key West Capt. Paul D'Antoni, a Gulf expert. "Cobia like scent," D'Antoni says, "so you can use dead threadfin. You can also jig and toss the free-swimmers on the surface jigs with white shrimp tails or jigs tipped with squid. They're not too picky when you first get to them."

When you first get to the wrecks and towers, double and triple hookups on cobia are common, but often, after a while, the fishing slows. At all times, have a plan for boxing keepers and releasing undersize fish. "Have the box open, and clear a path straight to it," D'Antoni says. "We don't want this fish going nuts in the boat. It can crush rods in the rack and otherwise mess you up. When I stick 'em, they go straight into the box."

Quick rod work can cut the fight time in half. "Steer the fish," he advises. "If it swims left, put pressure to the right. If he dives, bring him up. Constantly control it. That way you greatly reduce the duration of the fight and therefore lessen the chances of a break-off. If it's a release fish, you'll be able let him go in better condition. Also, keep the cobia's head in the water by the boat. Don't raise it, because that's when they shake their heads and spit the hook. At your first shot, which comes early with a cobia, gaff it. If you miss, your next chance might take a long while."

D'Antoni showed a neat trick to tame the dreaded "green" cobia. If one does hit the deck, grab the fish under its gills and by its tail and bend it together, forcing its tail to its head, and it will settle down.

Around wrecks, you can experiment with baits at various depths of the water column and often come up with different species. Drop down a blue runner (after clipping its tail to slow it), and you might hook a big cobia, a black or goliath grouper, or a kingfish. Goliaths are quite common in the wrecks these days, and many local captains talk of a goliath a year permit or some restraint on the flourishing species.

Some days you can catch cobia all afternoon out in the Lower Gulf, and on other days, the bite shuts down quickly. The hotter the weather, the more critical it becomes to get out early.

Cobia on the Flats

In the clear, warm waters of the flats, cobia chase the crustaceans and baitfish that rays nose up out of the marl and sand bottom, and

Thompson lands a cobia by hand to ensure it will be healthy at release.

cormorants dive from the surface after the same prey. The scene happens only a few weeks every winter though, while packs of cobia reside in the Lower Gulf before their spring migration north. The run starts sometime in January and lasts until early April. Plenty of good-size cobia show on the flats during that time, averaging about 25 pounds, with a few 50 pounds. The much bigger cobia seem to stay in the deeper waters of the channels and wrecks of the Gulf, where you might come across 70-, 80-, even 90-pound cobia. Their schools remain in nearby Gulf waters until sometime in May, when all but a few residents migrate north to cooler water.

The two most important factors that lead cobia to move up on the flats are the water temperature and the tide phase. The water on the flats warms quickly on sunny mornings and may start the day in the high 60s but rise to the low and mid 70s by afternoon. The cobia most often appear in the later morning and during the afternoon, when water temperatures hover around 72 degrees on flats in sight of Key West—the Sea Plane Basin, the Tower Flats, and the Pearl Basin.

Play the Tides

You'll find cobia behind rays on both falling and risings tides, but the rays behave differently depending on the tide's phase. Faster-moving water leads to the best success. The rays seek strong, fast-moving water in which to feed, for a couple of reasons. First, tidal flow loosens tiny creatures from their hiding spots. And second, rays also must be moving to stir up the shrimp and creatures off the bottom, which will invariably stir up the marl, sand, and coral bottom and cloud the water around the ray while it noses—which explains why rays tend to feed upcurrent. Like permit, rays don't want to be blinded to predators by muddy water, so they'll always work into a current, which quickly carries the murky water away from them and clears their line of sight. If they're working still water, there's no current to carry the silt and sand away, a circumstance that makes them vulnerable to ambush by big bull sharks.

Rays also generally feed into the flow because the current brings the scent of their prey to them.

On the other hand, a tide that is too strong might present other problems. It might be the case that when a tide turns dramatically and water floods and rushes off the flats quickly, that the fish get skittish of being stranded in a low point. In fact, they might be hesitant to get up on the flats in the first place. That theory applies to the behavior of permit and bonefish, at least, and big astronomical high tides aren't the best for finding the cobia.

The measure of a big or low tide is how far above or below the mean tide the water level will be on that tide. GPS tide charts include that information, and you can always check how fast and hard the tide is blowing the turtle-grass blades below your boat as a measure of the strength of the tide. Prime time to find the cobia behind rays turns out to be when a high tide coincided with the afternoon sun, which warms the flats and brings the rays searching for food with the protection of plenty of water to run from sharks if necessary.

Follow the Cormorants

It's really fun how you track the cobia by looking for cormorants tagging along after rays or spotting the muds rays make as they feed. It's opportunism multiplied by four, and a great demonstration of the wiliness of living things. You feel as if you're a part of the natural feeding process of those animals even before you make a sight-cast to a cobia. Rays feed on the flats all year, and sometimes they have permit follow them. Sometimes, though, they don't mud so actively, and that's when it's especially helpful to watch for the cormorants to tip off the rays' locations. The cormorants will stick fast to feeding rays, so if the birds are skittish and flying around all over, you can bet the rays aren't feeding so intensively and will be moving fast.

Once you spot a mudding ray, go up and shut down your boat, and alert your fishing pals if it's holding a cobia or a few. About one in four rays hold cobia, and there are a lot of rays around. Stay a little bit away from the ray, but keep your eye on the cobia. If you lose sight of your ray, hunt around, because chances are it's still close by you on that flat. Pole your boat to follow that ray with the wind, or else hold the boat off the ray if the wind blows you too close. Take your shot with live bait, jig, or fly, and after the hookup, follow the fight to the finish. You can go back to that ray if there was another cobia on it, and if it's still around, or you can look for another one.

You don't have to worry too much about spooking a cobia when he's on a ray. With a ray, they're feeding aggressively, even though it sometimes takes repeated casts to get them to take the bait. In fact, sometimes it's necessary to tease them into striking, and that's why it's such a great pursuit for a fly caster, even for a beginner on fly, because the angler can see the ray, and often the cobia as well. With cobia, an angler has a lot more time and leeway than with a permit and a tarpon, and when the bite gets hot, you can hang out on a flat and catch cobia after cobia on the rays coming up to feed.

For bait, use shrimp-tipped jigs, live crabs, and flies on 9-weight rods. They'll also hit live shrimp and pilchards, and green tube lures too. The key is to have a few baits handy in case they don't go for what you first throw to them. Also, use baits that stay in different levels of the water, because the cobia might be focused more on where the bait is than on what it is. Chances are that they'll stick around to give you at least a chance to change it up. A wide array of artificials work, from Gulp! To D.O.A. BaitBusters to Bagley bucktail jigs.

The action you give the fly is more important than the pattern. Use something bright and large that gets down a few feet quickly, like a big shrimp pattern with an epoxy head that will sink quickly. And don't be afraid to cast and cast to the same fish as long as it hangs around.

"On the twenty-first cast, it might take your fly," Thompson says.

Cast in front of the ray to lead it, and draw your bait close to it as it swims, even across its back. Cobia will shoot out from that ray's side and grab your bait like it's the best piece of food they've ever seen. Hang on.

Captain's Tip: "A nice thing about cobia is that you go down west to the wrecks that are in only ten feet of water and you'll see cobia on top. A cold day in January when the sun is bright, they're up on top, sunning, and it's pretty easy fly fishing. If the cobia stay deep and you can't chum them to the surface, you can try sinking lines and streamers to get to them. Even undersize cobia give a good fight on nine-weight rods."
—Capt. Ken Harris, *Finesse* Charters, Key West

20

Black Grouper

The Big Prize

Somewhere around Key West, there's a legendary place called the Valley of the Giants, where big black grouper congregate and draw plenty of smaller grouper into their realm. Anglers drop live baits down on virtually unbreakable gear and wait for the slamming hits of big fish and the back-burning, arm-wrenching fights to begin. If you don't lift one of those big black grouper off the bottom in the first instants of the battle, you probably won't. Plenty of big grouper attack and break off bait after bait, one after another, until they make a mistake or get fed. It's not uncommon for anglers to pull up a grouper with their three last, lost hooks in its mouth.

Even beyond the Valley of the Giants, plenty of big black grouper and big muttons inhabit the reefline and wrecks near Key West. I've seen small snapper and grunts dropped down on rigs in 100 feet of water and watched their images on the depthfinder for minutes, as a big fish swims around that prey, presumably checking out its angle, and measuring its chances to get away with it. If the hit blasts away on a run and severs the line, it's likely a shark. If, for ten, fifteen minutes, the big fish swims around the bait, both their paths marked by the depthfinder, until it strikes and the heavy rod bends double and the drag screams, and the angler isn't already on that rod, then the grouper wins.

Of the many coveted species to catch around Key West, not one is more highly prized than black grouper. Local waters, especially to the west toward the Tortugas, are the best locales in all Florida to catch these great fish.

Black grouper are the best-fighting and best-tasting of the many species of grouper around Key West, among them red, snowy, scamp, yellowedge, gag, and occasionally tiger grouper. Many people would say scamp grouper tastes best and possibly snowy grouper too, and they might be right, but those fish are not powerful fighters and they don't grow as big. Black grouper are the primary target of many bottom fishermen and a catch universally respected by all anglers.

Black grouper love coral habitat. The big ones live along the reef walls, and around rocky habitat and ledges and wrecks in deeper water, and they prowl around their homes and patch reefs for food. Black grouper populate certain spots reliably, but there also seems to be a migration of fish throughout the region, including the Dry Tortugas and the Keys, that occasionally brings new fish to the same spots. Not much is known about the black grouper's migration pattern, but scientists are studying it now. But whatever the cause, a reliable grouper spot might be empty one week and hold a few good fish the next week, so it's always worth checking a known location.

Black grouper are available year-round. In the coldest months, blacks tend to migrate into shallower water, along the main reef, even showing up around patch reefs close to the islands. Backcountry and inshore waters are the nursery grounds for black grouper, and plenty of small ones are available, but few large enough to keep. Occasionally, a bridge angler will pick up a good-size fish that makes its home at the base of a bridge piling or as it moves through a deep channel. In the Gulf, wrecks and patch reefs hold black grouper and plenty of goliath grouper, known for stealing fish off the hook. Primarily, anglers look for blacks along the reef and in waters 90 to 200 feet deep and in the deeper patch reefs where they forage.

A good-size black grouper near Key West weighs 20 pounds, and 40-pound fish are fairly common among those who regularly target

Captain Delph leaders in a solidly hooked deepwater black.

them. There's no question though, because grouper are territorial and hold to specific locations around bottom structure and coral, both the size and number of black grouper increase as you move westward where there's less pressure on them, toward the End of the Bar, south of the Marquesas, and along ledges that run south of the Dry Tortugas. In those regions, 30- and 40-pound grouper are a good size, and 60-pounders are not uncommon. Occasionally, recreational anglers even land bigger fish, though not without great skill or good luck. However, those very big specimens, 60 pounds or more, carry an increased risk of holding the ciguatera toxin, and they are also important breeder individuals—two very good reasons to turn those old fish loose.

Capt. Ralph Delph, a black-grouper expert, explains that the biggest groupers are the males, and once they take up a territory, they not only draw in females, but also younger male grouper waiting for a chance to breed with the females. All black grouper begin life as females, and some change to males later in life. The largest males are so tough to land that many anglers know of specific fish in spots that they've hooked and lost repeatedly over the years. In the spring of '06, one of these, a 92-pound black, finally came aboard Capt. Rob Hammer's boat in Tortugas waters.

Black Grouper by the Numbers

One of the keys to successful grouper fishing is finding their spots and reading them correctly with your depthfinder by watching for the thick red dashes of grouper showing near the bottom. As you're drifting over these locations, drop live baits or jigs to reach the targeted fish as it rises above the bottom structure, preferably at the highest point on the fish's foray away from its hideout. That way, it will take your bait farther away from the structure, and the continuing drift of the boat will help you to pull the fish even farther away from its rocky lair. Captain Delph will sometimes give the boat a forward thrust at the point of the hookup not only to set the hook, but also to pull the fish forward a bit, before it begins its downward dive.

Big groupers will rock you up, at least once, and sometimes a few times. Inevitably, some will be lost, no matter the line test. Coral heads and other rocks shred the lines with tension and abrasion. When the fish rocks you up, all might not be lost. Open the bail, keeping only slight tension on the line, and try to trick the fish into running out. If it does, get its head coming up and try not to let it go down again. If you can control the grouper's head, you can control the fight. When possible, you can also use the boat to chase a grouper or get an extra angle on a rocked-up fish.

Black grouper love live baits—threadfin, mullet, goggle eyes, or whatever you have available—on a Carolina rig, and they'll hit jigs, baited with dead ballyhoo or with plastic tails. What tackle you use to catch them depends on how you approach them, whether on the drift or on anchor.

On the drift over targeted spots, anglers have the advantage of pulling the fish away from its protection, and they can use light tackle—8- to 15-pound-test lines and spinning gear. On anchor, at the reef, wrecks, or patch reefs, heavier tackle needs to be used to quickly lift the fish. Minimum requirements include 50- to 80-pound-test monofilament or braided lines of greater strength, with big spinning reels or even two-speed conventional reels, rods stiff as pool cues, and fast hands, good feet, and strong backs. Guaranteed, that grouper knows exactly where it's headed before it takes the bait on the run. As soon as the grouper hits your bait, hit back with force and keep it coming. You can't worry about your equipment failing or you'll lose the fish. Black grouper battles on anchor are like Ultimate Fighting Championships—fast, blunt, and brutal.

Anglers also troll along the reef and patch reefs for grouper, and this technique requires fairly heavy gear and strong connections because the hookups are abrupt and explosive. Anglers troll deeplipped lures, such as Yozuris, Mann's Stretch 25 and 30s, and Rapalas, big MirrOLures, jigs with plastic tails, and weighted ballyhoo. Some anglers use planers to get their offerings down, and others troll the deep-diving plugs on 40- or 50-pound-test or even braided line. The braided line will let those lures dive deeper. Add a swivel to your mainline and a four- to six-foot length of monofilament or fluorocarbon leader. You can control how deep those plugs dive by how much line you let out. To troll in depths of sixty to 100 feet, anglers let out 100 feet or more to get the plugs down forty feet and more.

The best depth to run baits depends on the location. Any deep ledge or coral head might hold fish, and grouper will definitely rise

Big fish, big lure, big action when grouper strike on the troll.

up off the bottom for baits. Running lures and baits too deep, how-ever, increases the likelihood of snagging. Experiment with vary-ing currents and conditions, but generally, eight- to fifteen-foot depths work around shallow patch reefs less than twenty feet deep in Hawk's Channel and in the Gulf, and generally, troll twenty to thirty feet down around deep patch reefs and deeper along the main reef. How you get your baits down depends on all the elements of your equipment, whether you use planers, mono or braided lines, and how far back you want to troll your baits. Downriggers can be used to troll around deeper reef structure, though they require careful monitoring of depths to avoid the mess and hassle of snagging the bottom.

Grouper trollers move about three to five knots. Some give a bump and go around structure to let the lures flutter to entice more bites, and some stay at constant speeds. Experiment with depths and speeds at each location to find success. Universally, grouper trollers keep moving after the hook-up to pull the fish up and away from the rocks and coral heads, often until the fish surfaces. Otherwise, every decent grouper given any slack will take all that lure and line straight to the bottom, probably for keeps.

Captain's Tip: "When bottom fishing, make sure that the rig's weight is either resting on the bottom or lifted off the bottom and suspended, but not bouncing on the bottom, puffing up the bottom sand or tearing at growth, which will definitely put off fish.

"If you want to keep the weight on the bottom, fish with it there and keep the bail open or the drag off completely and only use light thumb or finger pressure to keep line tight on the spool. This way, the rocking of the boat will allow line to pull off the spool under your thumb when necessary to keep the weight on the bottom. This technique takes lightening-fast response to a hit by setting the drag and reeling hard, hard, hard, or the grouper will assuredly rock up.

"Alternately, drop the weight to the bottom and after it hits, crank up five or six turns to make sure it rests off the bottom. The bait will still flutter at eye-level to bottom fish, but the weight won't bounce and the drag will be set in strike mode for a quicker hook-set and pressure on the fish."
—Capt. Bill Delph, Key West

21

~~~~~~~~~~

Mutton Snapper

The Pink Panther

Prevailing wisdom says optimal conditions for muttons are westerly current, full moon, and winds from any direction but the west. We had a ripping easterly current, southwesterly winds, and a quarter moon, but we also had perhaps the most important condition for a good deep bite—rich blue water. That water had moved in to 150 feet to the west, where we started, and remained farther out, at 400 feet, to the east. Without that good, purple-color water, there would be little chance at catching fish. We had muttons over a barrel every pass we made west of Key West, in about 160 feet of water.

That strong current gave us our only trouble, and it was significant. It pushed our drifting boat from 2.5 to sometimes 4 knots and literally blew us over the hot spot where we found the muttons, which ranged from 5 to 17 pounds. When we hooked one jigging, we had to run the boat back to it or else spend excessive time fighting it against that current. Each drift only took about fifteen minutes, and then we'd run back to the depths where the fish were feeding. By the end of the day, we'd drifted miles to the east and finished close to Sand Key Tower. That day, we caught them when common angling knowledge told us we wouldn't.

If blacks are the most highly sought-after grouper species in the Keys, muttons are probably the equivalent prize in the snapper clan.

Fishing for mutton snappers runs year-round consistently, but you do catch them at different depths at different times. In the spring and early summer, they can be found in shallower water, ninety to 130 feet, and can be jigged up with three- to six-ounce jigs baited with whole dead ballyhoo or using live baits on Carolina rigs. In the summer, they move out to deeper water, from 130 to 170 feet. In the fall and winter, they move back to the shallows and can often be found cruising around the islands in the deeper channels, including the Northwest Channel and Boca Grande Channel. At these times, some big muttons come very close to shore on their search for food. They'll hit live threadfins, pilchards, pinfish, mullet, and any other live baits you have. For dead baits, especially good for muttons are ballyhoo and mullet, cut kingfish, and whole flying fish.

Drifting over likely looking bottom structure, such as ledges, wrecks, and rock aggregations in 100 to 200 feet, and dropping down jigs and live baits catches a lot of muttons. A fair-size mutton runs about 10 pounds offshore, and 20-pounders are pretty common. Like black grouper, many more big fish are found to the west of Sand Key, but on very precise spots to the east, big muttons still lurk. Inshore and around patch reefs and bridges, expect fish in the 1- to 5-pound range.

The first blistering run of a big mutton tricks more than a few experienced anglers into thinking they've hooked a wahoo. The fish may run 100 yards or more, and since mutton won't hide in a hole as a grouper will, there's no sense in trying to stop that first run. (Though muttons are known to press their heads against bottom structure to provide resistance.) Simply keep tension on, and if you've maintained a connection after its first run, you can begin to work the fish up, even from deep water. Expect one or two shorter plunges downward, but the fight lessens as you bring the fish to the surface. If the fish blows its swim bladder coming up from the depths, it won't be able to dive again, but any fish that properly decompresses as it surfaces might dive again at any second. Properly releasing undersize bottom fish like muttons by ventilating their swim bladders increases the likelihood of their survival.

Full-Moon Muttons

The spring's full-moon mutton-snapper spawning bite is well-known and much heralded. The event is well-attended, especially by local anglers, who anchor up in-line at known spawning sites, and it's as much a celebration as it is angling action. However, the bite is nowhere near as easily predictable as marking off a night on a calendar. In addition to the moon phase, other variables, including water temperature, determine whether the spawn happens in May or June, and whether they bite the day before, of, or after the full moon. And until the bite happens, no one can say whether they bite in the a.m. or the p.m.

Even aside from ethical and conservation concerns over fishing a species during its spawning period, planning a trip around the full-moon spawning bite may not be the most productive strategy to catch a few muttons. As of 2007, the limit for muttons was ten per person, and who needs that many of these fish? Why the Florida Fish and Wildlife Commission doesn't lower that to five remains a mystery to most Keys anglers and captains.

According to local knowledge, full moons year-round kick the a.m. and p.m. mutton bite into action, though experienced anglers know that muttons bite on any moon phase, on any current, any time of the year. What's more important is finding the fish, from day to day, and presenting baits that they'll strike. Many local anglers will have five to ten spots in a limited area where they know muttons will visit, more than likely either wrecks, rubble, or rock aggregations near sandy, sloping sea floor. The captains usually have to check most of the hot spots before they'll find the aggressive fish.

In the hunt for muttons, the widest range of baits, presentation styles, and hot spots usually wins the day, or the night, as the case may be.

Above all, taking the time to look for muttons at a variety of depths near the reef before settling into a spot and anchoring will make a huge difference in catching fish. Will they be in ninety or 110 feet of water? It's a critical matter, and the depth might change from night to night. To save time and minimize the hard work and risks of mishap, most anglers try to keep to a minimum the number of times they will drop and retrieve anchor. They'll anchor with great care by scouting thoroughly first, both by studying the depthfinder for big dashes near the bottom—the sign of the mutton or the grouper—and by looking over at the action on boats already anchored there.

What's really surprising is how eagerly good-size—10-plus-pound muttons—take freelined cut or live baits drifted just below the surface in the current as you do for yellowtail. From my days jigging for them on the bottom in 100 to 200 feet, I'd developed an impression of muttons as bottom feeders, but when you see them hammering baits drifted 100 yards behind the boat and so close to the surface, that impression changes quickly. Imagine an 18-pounder or larger mutton nailing your bait on the drift! Truly all the snappers—yellowtail, mangrove, and muttons—feed top to bottom in the water column, depending on conditions. So it's not surprising that while you're after one species, you might catch another, because they share a lot of the same habitat, prey, and behaviors. Muttons will take live or cut baits in a chum line both at inshore patch reefs and out past the reef.

When you're out past the reef, bottom fishing in 125 to 200 feet, a slow current can be an advantage, because it lets your baits get down to the bottom on lighter tackle to entice more strikes and slows your drift over the spot to give you more time there. But when you're fishing in a chum line near the reef and the current slows down too much, all the fishing by the reef pretty much dies. When it does, it might be better to steer away from the reef and go deeper, until that current has picked back up again.

Captain's Tip: "For cut baits for mutton snappers, ballyhoo plugs work well. Take the freshest possible ballyhoo and cut it in half at a diagonal angle behind its dorsal fin and hook it under its beak on a small jig head, hook, or Carolina rig, and send it to the bottom. Also whole squid, strip baits of squid, bonito or kingfish fish belly, or big baitfish butterflied to add scent, or cut in half or split, bone-in, also work."
—Capt. Pepe Gonzalez, Key West

22

Yellowtail

The Flagship Fish of the Keys

Sometimes, you're not in the mood to troll all day, looking for weeds and birds and debris. You don't want to drift and jig, or run and gun, or fish wrecks; you want to fish and have fun and put some fish in the box. You want to get back to basics and have a blast. Go for yellowtail.

Pound for pound, yellowtail snapper are among the best fighting fish in the sea, and they're certainly one of the most reliable catches around Key West. They're available year-round, in greater or lesser quantities, often at the very same spots. Once you find them, the bite lasts as long as the tide is moving well, and most of the time, a few anglers can count on limiting out. Their sunrise–sunset colors of yellow, pink, and gold, and fighting ability make them the flagship fish of the Keys.

The preferred method of fishing for yellowtail practically differs from angler to angler, whether it's the depth, the terminal hook or jig, the rigging, or the choice of chum or baits—and they all guard their secrets. The good news is that the basic methods are the same for catching hard-fighting, good-eating, plentiful yellowtail snappers: find them, chum them, and slyly slip them the hook. Follow this basic plan, and given decent conditions, you'll find success year-round catching yellowtail snappers in the Keys. It's so dependable, yellowtailing is almost a guaranteed fall-back plan for tough days offshore, and it's always fun.

The Bar—Yellowtail Central

Yellowtail are everywhere in the Lower Keys, and you can't go in the water around the islands without seeing a few, and usually, a few schools. Even within hundreds of yards of Key West, around rocks and small patch reefs, you can anchor and successfully fish for yellowtail, and because they're so close to shore, it's a good species to target on a kayak. But like most snapper and grouper, yellowtail use the inshore waters as a nursery grounds, and when the fish mature, they move offshore to the reef and around the Bar.

The Bar, also known as the intermediate reef, is a dead, submerged reef, just south and parallel to the living reef. After the reef drops off to about 110 feet, it begins to rise to the bar, which mounts to forty-five feet below the surface, before it too drops off to the offshore deep water. That trough between the reef and the Bar makes for great habitat and foraging grounds for plenty of species. The Bar's rocky mounts that slope to sandy bottoms make perfect

Yellowtails feed on the bottom in depths greater than 150 feet.

habitat for a number of snapper and grouper species, including mature yellowtail. Numerous humps near the Bar and around the reef also hold big schools of flag yellowtail. Those schools will also hunt in deeper water, and frequent the deeper channels between the Keys, and also the rockpiles, wrecks, and towers in the Gulf.

Close to Key West, the favored place to look for yellowtail is right along the Bar, in sixty to 120 feet of water. Plenty of spots are marked on fishing maps, but a few easily accessible ones almost always hold yellowtail—south of Sand Key, Western Dry Rocks, and Toppino Buoys. Schools of flags might move in to these spots occasionally, but if you really want to find big flags, you might have to travel away from locations that get almost constant pressure. Motor west toward the End of the Bar, and search along the bar for good-looking bottom structure where fish gather.

As you go over the Bar, watch your depthfinder. First look for the big humps or sudden drop-offs where baitfish and yellowtail will gather, and then check for the fish themselves—either as big marks suspended above the humps or, most often, a solid cloud indicating a school of fish. Also check the water conditions. Most anglers prefer to fish for yellowtail in slightly cloudy, not perfectly clear blue water, because the fish can see hooks and tackle all too well in the clear water. Current should be running, but not ripping too hard. A decent current will disperse your chum and drift your baits to the fish. West-bound currents are known to be excellent for yellowtailing, but the fish will bite on east-bound current too. If no current runs, or if the water looks purple-clear, it might be better to scuttle plans to yellowtail or find a spot where other conditions prevail.

Currents right outside the reef have a mysterious relationship to tidal movements inside the reef. The current might be ripping through Key West Harbor and be calm past the reef, six miles away. For yellowtail, if it's not running at least a little where you are, you might as well find a better place.

Before you anchor, try to judge the drift of the boat over the spot to know exactly where to drop the hook, because your boat's

Porgies often turn up in chum slicks after yellowtail.

position is critical to your success. From the spot, motor into the current where you think you should anchor, and let your boat drift back. You should drift back over the spot again. It's important to put the stern of the boat twenty to fifty yards upcurrent of your marked spot to let the chum drift over the fish to attract them. If you drop the anchor on the school, they'll likely run. It's better to be too far than too close, because you can always let out a little line to get closer. So give yourself plenty of distance from the spot when you drop the hook. That way, if the anchor doesn't hold on the first drop, you'll have a chance to pull it up before it drags through the school.

Chum, Chum, Chum

Once you're well-positioned and holding anchor, begin the chumming. The standard and easy method of chumming requires approximately three frozen blocks of chum in a wide-mesh chum net for every hour of fishing, plus a bag of mahua (glass minnows) for occasional chumming and baits. But many anglers will chum *much* more heavily. To ensure a steady bite, experienced yellowtailers recommend waiting up to thirty minutes to let the fish begin feeding heavily before throwing in lines. You can also sweeten up the chum with chunks of cut bait—ballyhoo or threadfin—but whatever you use for baits, make sure it's in the chum line too. If you have access to live pilchards, yellowtail love them every time, and a few very selectively added to the chum line every once in a while keeps the bite going.

Much more complicated methods of chumming involve mixing your own chum, as most captains and serious yellowtailers do. In a five-gallon bucket, mix a few pounds of rolled oats, menhaden oil, glass minnows, a block or two of frozen block chum, and some other cut baits that you prefer. Dispense scoops of the chum every five minutes or pack a tennis ball size of chum and drop it down—what's known as a chum bomb—to the sea bottom where it will explode. Adding sand can make the chum bomb more solid, though some anglers dislike the idea because sand can smother the reef itself. If you pack your hook into one of these balls and drop it down with plenty of line in freespool, you're suddenly sandballing, a messy, but effective technique to catch yellowtail from the depths. As your chum ball disintegrates down the water column, the fish eat its pieces, including your bait. Some anglers will also drop a chum cage down to the bottom to turn on the bottom bite. Other guys will chum their yellowtail spots even when they're not fishing, to keep the fish in the area and responsive.

Usually, it will take thirty minutes to an hour to get the yellowtails going strong. Most of the time, you'll see a few flashes of yellow within minutes of dropping the chum, but the bite might not start immediately. With a little current running and proper boat position, your freelined baits will drift and drop back to where the fish are holding. Because yellowtail are wary, or smart, or keen-sighted, it becomes extremely important that you give your baits the most natural presentation possible not to put off strikes.

Yellowtail Tackle

That presentation starts with the tackle and continues with the technique. The standard Keys yellowtail setup starts with a spinning reel or plug reel and a rod rated to 8- to-15-pounds with enough backbone to stand up to the occasional pelagic that might swim into the mix. Lines might run from 6- to 15-pound-test, and to that most anglers will use an Albright knot to attach a three- to eight-foot fluorocarbon leader, which adds extra abrasion resistance and is less visible than monofilament. Some anglers Bimini twist a double line on their mainline first for added strength in the connection for fighting big pelagics, though it's generally not needed for yellowtail and may put off bites. For terminal tackle, most anglers like small 1/0 or 2/0 hooks, and a split shot or two added to get baits down. Small $\frac{1}{16}$- or $\frac{1}{8}$-ounce jigs can be used. Tackle stores in the area sell specialty yellowtail jigs, either from Fairwaters Tackle or Hook Up lures, and also Cy Flies, which are simply small hooks wrapped with a short shock of green or yellow hair. In heavier currents or greater depths, you can even try a $\frac{1}{4}$-ounce jig. Experiment with weights, even using sliding sinkers to get down, if you don't find the bite pretty quickly.

You can either try baits on a bare hook or on a jig. Whatever size jig you need to get to the depth where the fish are, tip the jig with some of the same bait going out in the chum line, whether a slim strip of squid, ballyhoo filet or chunk, or a few of the all-popular mahua. Silverside minnows, when available frozen in tackle stores, also work quite well, and small strips of kingfish or bonito belly, only 1½ inches long and cleanly streamlined, are fantastic. You can also use live eye-hooked pilchards, shrimp, or if they're around, small pinfish too.

A couple seconds before every cast, toss out a few pieces of loose chum, either mahua, silversides, or chunked ballyhoo, and cast your bait to drift down with this loose chum to help the bite. It works every time.

Only the right presentation of the bait remains. Freeline your bait, either by pulling line off with your free hand and holding line lightly on the spool by the fingertip of your rod-hand, keeping just enough pressure to feel line running, or by frequently and repeatedly lifting the rod tip straight up from the pointed-down position to let the line pull off the spool. In each technique, keep the bail wide open. Anglers say yellowtail will notice any unnatural movement in a bait's descent that comes from any resistance from a taughtly held line. Until you determine how wary the fish will be, go gently and let line fall freely, without letting out too much slack. Sense for the strike, and give the fish a second to run with it before throwing shut the bail and reeling steadily. These guys will drop the hook quickly, so act fast, but don't pull the hook out of its mouth by yanking back the rod. Most of the time, flipping the bail closed will be enough to set the hook on a fish racing away. It takes a delicate touch, or a few missed fish, to get the trick down. Don't keep the drag too tight or you'll risk pulling the hook out of their mouths.

If you're not getting solid, steady bites within forty-five minutes, you might consider moving to a new spot. There might be a predator below keeping them from feeding, or some other factor inhibiting them.

Most times, before thirty minutes passes, you'll be in a good rhythm of hooking and landing fish, usually by hand net at the boat's gunwale. You'll sense exactly when baits will reach the strike zone, and if you're in touch with your line, you'll anticipate the bite fairly accurately after a few strikes and know when to pull the trigger.

Capt. Steve Hassell displays a two-person limit of flags.

Yellowtail bigger than 4 pounds, the flags, fight like much bigger fish, and flags even try the trick of dashing to the bottom and holding ground down there—and sometimes they succeed. The big fish might take a couple runs, but as long as you keep them off the bottom where lines shred against rocks, you'll tire them out within a few minutes. Flags will also take bottom rigs meant for muttons and grouper, and they'll strike drifted, lightly weighted bottom rigs and even jigs, in waters deep as 160 feet.

While you're yellowtailing, other fish will blast into your chum line, depending on where you're fishing. Cero mackerel, bonito, blackfins, sharks, porgies, and even bottom fish such as big muttons and grouper, might make an appearance. For the bottom species, it's a good idea while yellowtailing to keep a heavy outfit weighted with a bottom rig for big fish down deep, and for the pelagics, a few handy live baits, either pilchards, threadfins, or ballyhoo, can be invaluable.

There are a number of variations on this basic yellowtail scenario to get the fish going and keep them going. In the best variation, yellowtail will rise to the surface to the chum slick in a feeding frenzy, and when they do, you can cast a fly rod to them. Other times, the fish might hold down lower, and you may need to add a split shot or two to your line to get the baits down to them.

Many anglers suspect that even in a school of average-size, 14- to 16-inch fish, bigger flags will hang at the back of the school. To get them, some anglers will put their lines on a kite and fly their baits back to get those fish. For an easier method, tie a plastic, inflatable balloon to your line a few feet from your hook and let it drift back a live bait to entice those bigger fish. When using lead-head jigs for these fish, use the lightest jigs possible to let the baits drift naturally in the current to fool the wariest, often the largest fish.

Once the school has started feeding, the action will often attract the neighborhood barracuda. The reef and the Bar are the barracudas' home waters. A 'cuda that hangs around can scare the school away, so immediately try to catch it with a chunk or live bait on a wire rig. After the fight and release, that barracuda won't be back for quite a while.

At night and even at sunset, spots along the bar close to Sand Key can be fantastic for yellowtail. But whenever you go, yellowtailing makes a classic Keys day on the water. Especially when you get the wind, tide and water conditions all in your favor, you'll have a perfect day for yellowtail, and you'll feel like you've made the best move possible for that day. When you get on them, you feel like you've struck gold.

> *Captain's Tip*: "Cubans have a saying, 'Give them the ham and cheese,' which means, when yellowtail won't come up for baits in the drift zone, put on a hunk of bonito, without skin, and a few mahua on the hook and let it drop down to them to get them going."
> —Capt. Richie Gomez, "Captain Conch," Key West

23

Dolphin

A Rite of Spring

April 10: With Joel Day
Winds 10–15 NE; Gulf Stream 15 miles out.
Three-quarter full moon and waxing.
Plenty of schoolie dolphin in 300 feet with plenty of weedlines, and also tripletail, and wahoo down below. We keep 10 dolphin and could have caught them all day long.
Question: Will dolphin be present and bite during a full moon with an easterly wind?
We'll see on Saturday, April 15.

April 15: Full moon, with Wendy and Joel. Small muttons and small red grouper jigging.
Two good gaffer dolphin—16 and 18 pounds—by weeds in 400 feet. Plenty of schoolies.

April 17:
Winds south–southwest 10–15.
Moon two days past full.
Plenty of schoolie dolphin in 700 feet. Gaffer dolphin—8, 10, 12 pounds—under turtle near weeds. Gulf Stream 10 miles out. Weeds oriented south–southwest to the north-northeast with the south-southwest winds, and somewhat scattered. Sailfish on the color change. Picked up nothing jigging for an hour.

Every April, Keys anglers watch the waters past the reef for the return of plentiful schools of big dolphin. Dolphin are aggressive and voracious feeders, strong, acrobatic fighters, and so visually stunning that you'll never forget the sight of one of these radiant blue-, green-, and gold-flecked fish in cobalt seas. When you also consider that their meat is delicious grilled, smoked, or cooked any number of ways, it's no mystery why their arrival en masse in late spring is so highly anticipated by local anglers. They are *the* fish of summer in the Keys.

Plain and simple, going for dolphin in their season is one of the great trips that every saltwater angler must make, whether in their own boat or with a charter captain. At its height, the Keys' dolphin fishery ranks among the best in the world.

Trip planning starts by knowing the timing of the arrival of the big schools of big fish. In South Florida, dolphin take to the Gulf Stream, which transports fish as it runs closer to and as it swings farther from shore. Where those warm Gulf Stream waters meet cooler near-shore water, boundaries set up where plankton, structure, weeds, and baitfish, and finally, pelagics and anglers, all gather. If dolphin and other pelagics find such a rich field of ocean, they'll hang around there for days, until conditions change. So the angler's job is to find that patch of ocean where the fish are.

Dolphin might be present off Key West at any time of the year, but in the fall through the winter, more than likely you'll come across "schoolies"—smaller fish migrating into warmer waters. The "gaffers" of 10 pounds and up, and "slammers" of 30 pounds and more, appear when the waters warm into the low and mid 80s, usually beginning in early April. Dolphin seem to prefer water temperatures in the 76- to 83-degree range.

Schools of dolphin will travel with the Gulf Stream, going northward as the waters warm, all the way to New Jersey by July and August. If you hook up to any number of big, 40- to 70-pounders— bulls or cows—that pass by the Keys, you'll have a wild fight on any tackle, any test line, from spinning gear to fly. Expect a fight with a 50-pounder to last an hour or more. The big bulls often travel with a number of female cows, and they're the most aggressive fish, often the first to hit a bait, and sometimes even a couple baits before anglers get a trolling rod in hand.

In the Keys, anglers find the biggest fish closer to the reef early in the season. Throughout May and June, it's fairly common to see good-size fish, up to 20 pounds and more, swim right up to your boat while you're drifting near the reef in 200 feet of water or even when you're anchored by the reef in eighty feet. Like most pelagics, schools of dolphin will even swarm over the reef chasing bait, though it's rare to see unless you're spending plenty of time on the water. The prime time for big fish, and plenty of them, is May 1 to June 15.

By July, waters closer to shore and the reef get so hot that the summer doldrums set in and the good fishing for many species, including dolphin, moves out deeper. By late July, you'll need to go farther offshore to find the bigger fish, as far as 2,000 to 2,500 feet deep—marlin territory—more than fifteen miles south of the reef, where the fish will be moving along with the Gulf Stream waters and staying near deeper water where they can cool themselves. Even though most anglers troll for dolphin and hook up to them on the surface, recent studies reveal that dolphin spend a good portion of their time down deep, likely to keep cool, and at night, to feed in the upwelling currents caused by cooling waters. Another run of bigger dolphin happens in late September and October, but this run doesn't match the spring migration.

The predictability of their migration heightens everyone's desire to get on them while the fish are out there early in the season, though dolphin fishing makes a good trip all summer long. Since their schools move so fast, the main variable to finding them is locating the depth where they might be feeding when you're on the water. It might be 200 feet or 1,500 feet, and it might change day to day.

Plan to troll to cover as much territory as possible to find these fast-moving fish. You'll want 8- to 20-pound spinning tackle for direct casting to schools of dolphin, and 20- to 50-pound on con-

The chum and baits that boxed the bull.

ventional trolling outfits, and 50-pound on conventional outrigger lines with the biggest baits.

A few primary indicators help anglers get on the fish. First and foremost, look for sargassum weed, the bright yellow floating weed that holds shrimp and crab and juvenile fish, and provides shade and cover for other baitfish. When the weeds string and clump up in lines that might stretch out for hundreds of yards or even a mile or more, they become foraging grounds for dolphin, nothing less than floating buffet tables. The dream scenario for dolphin anglers is to find solid weedlines, full of baits with birds working the edges—the closest thing in angling to a guarantee of catching fish. The birds, as usual, are trying to feed on the baits that the dolphin are scaring up out of the water, and when feeding, dolphin will eagerly attack a trolled bait or lure passing near them along the weedline. Anglers can also pull up to that weedline and cast jigs or baits along its edge to entice a bite.

You won't always encounter the dream scene of long weedlines, but that doesn't mean you can't find the fish. Weedlines are highly visible, provide valuable surface structure and critical habitat for juvenile baits that sustain pelagic species, serve as indicators of current boundaries to anglers, and are easy to fish. Their formation depends on current and wind direction, conditions that don't always align to create weedlines. How weeds are aligned on the water has a lot to do with wind direction. The presence of weeds is due to the currents that bring them in from the Sargasso Sea. Weedlines form due to the differential in current velocities; calmer inshore water juxtaposed to fast offshore water pushes weeds against that break, where the sargassum stays. The weed clumps will be pushed up against the edge where one current meets another, the same phenomenon that creates color changes, where plankton rich green water meets the cleaner offshore blue water. In both cases, along with weeds or different types of water, baits also get pushed up to that edge where the currents meet.

Winds do influence the surface conditions of the water, including the waves and the weeds, and the direction of the winds will govern how and in what pattern the weeds gather together. Weedlines will form in the same direction as the wind blows, and the effects of the winds' are greater the longer they are sustained in the same direction. In the Keys, sustained southerly winds will push weeds into rows perpendicular to the reef. An easterly wind will blow the sargassum into alignment with the shore and the reef, resulting in those long, wide weed lines anglers love. Sustained winds from the north will push weedlines out farther, and therefore seem to "push" the fish out farther too. A change in the direction of the wind will break up the existing weed pattern and, at least temporarily, create the condition of scattered weeds, until the clumps realign themselves along the wind's course.

You can still find fish in scattered weed, though scattered weed makes trolling a matter of constantly clearing debris off lines and baits, or even with no weed around at all, because the fish will still be out there hunting, especially along current rips and around other types of floating structure. Look for slicks, rips, and rough water in otherwise calm seas—areas that might be where currents catch and churn up bait, possibly over big bottom structure where the dolphin will be hanging around. The Ups and Downs, starting at 600 feet, out to the Wall, in 1,000 feet, are bottom structures that cause such turbulent top water, and they're both favorite dolphin grounds.

Dolphin are known to bite well in the morning, when the day heats up, and the bite can last through the late afternoon—basically, possibly at any time. What time of day they're biting can best be determined by checking up on the bite's pattern the few days previous to your trip. Your captain will know, or check with tackle store personnel, or if you have them, other local contacts.

During the slow portion of your dolphin outing, you might be better served trying other pursuits—say, super-deep jigging, jigging at a favorite deep wreck, or yellowtailing at the reef. You can style a day to your tastes and to the variety of best options that you've gleaned from recent reports.

Once you do hook up to a dolphin though, remember to watch if other fish are with it and what direction they're traveling so you can go after that school after you land your fish. If it's a school of moderate-sized fish, it's a good bet you'll find it again if you move downsea. While dolphin schools may migrate with the Gulf Stream early in the season, later in the season, they're likely to adapt to the local currents that determine the direction of travel and depth of baitfish. Bigger dolphin may be hunting into the current.

To track dolphin, it helps to know that if the fish are hunting into the current of the Gulf Stream, they are still moving to the east, because the speed of the Gulf Stream pushes them back faster than they can swim into it—as if they're on a conveyor belt that's moving to the east faster than they're swimming to the west. The west-bound direction of many big dolphin in the fall may have given rise to the notion that these fish are traveling down from the north as waters cool, the opposite of the spring migration, which is a common-sense observation based on seasonal migration patterns of many animals, especially birds. When in fact, this notion might be a fallacy. It is hoped that recent studies may yield concrete evidence one way or the other. The case may be simply that even in the fall, dolphin come up to the Keys along the Gulf Stream and travel along its path.

Along with the currents and eddies off the Gulf stream and the temperature of the water, the position of the Gulf stream itself near Key West and the Keys seems to influence where the dolphin appear on any given day. There might be eddies off the stream or offshoots that reach closer to the reef. Pelagics travel them to hunt for food, but in general, when the Gulf Stream meanders out to more than thirty-five miles away from Key West and stays out there for days, you might prepare yourself for a longer run out to find fish. Still, early in the season, when water temperatures are right for dolphin, fish might come in close. When the Gulf Stream draws nearer early in the season, you can almost count on a good day for dolphin fishing.

No matter the position of the Gulf Stream, the presence of weeds, or even the presence or absence of birds working over baits, always look for loose floating structure which provides cover and shade for bait. You'll often find pelagics like dolphin below. A floating pallet, a thick rope, a live sea turtle, a tree branch, or even a piece of lumber or a coconut might hold enough good fish to make a great morning. If nothing is near the structure, you might drop a bait down deep beneath the structure in case the fish, either dolphin or wahoo, retreated to the depths due to boat traffic around their cover.

Often, and especially when you're the first to find a piece of debris in the morning, hard-fighting and delicious tripletail will be found hanging beneath it, and if they haven't been fished over, they're usually quick to take a small, ⅛- or ¼-ounce jig baited with a strip of cut bait or a live bait tossed near their cover. Spotting a couple tripletail under debris always adds a jolt of excitement to a trolling trip, and makes one of the side perks of a day of dolphin fishing.

A few other notes on trolling for dolphin: the moon phase seems to play little or no factor at all; learn the offshore bird species—frigates, terns, boobies—and their behavior as indicators of surface

Tripletail.
Delicious.

feeding fish; sometimes after a dolphin school has tired out, you can restart the bite by simply tossing over a rigged ballyhoo and trolling away from the school; never try to gaff a free-swimming dolphin by the boat, because even small fish can wreak havoc onboard unless they've been tired out first. And release the little ones to grow up, fast as they do, to gaffers and slammers.

The Dolphin Drill

Once you've found the dolphin, the fun really begins. As soon as the first fish gets hooked, it's time to run the dolphin drill. As the angler fights the first fish, toss a few pre-cut chunks of ballyhoo into the water for chum, clear all other trolling lines, pronto, and drop a ready chum bag in the water. Bait a couple spinning rods with ballyhoo chunks for pitch baits. As the angler brings the fish boatside and holds it, watch for the rest of the school to swarm you, rod in hand. Toss the school a handful of mahua to get them going, and flick the biggest fish a chunk of ballyhoo—on spinning tackle.

As soon as you determine who has the biggest fish hooked up, let the angler with the smaller fish move to the bow and station it there by placing the rod in its holder and tightening the drag. Keeping one fish in the water by your boat, with additional chumming, will keep the entire school by your boat, and let you catch a few on jig, plugs, fly tackle, whatever you like. Many people say it's a good idea to change out this leashed fish with a fresh one every five minutes or so.

After you gaff the first fish, box it, and drop that rod on the deck, pick up another rig, all ready, and keep the school all around, hungry and feeding. Often times, other schools will come along and join the feeding frenzy, and as you drift along with your school of fish, watch for the biggest dolphin. Remember that they're so voracious that they eat each other, so be prepared for a big bull to swipe that leashed fish on the line off the bow. If you're lucky, you'll hook the bigger one too. It happens quite often.

It's also common to see a big wahoo cruise up to the edge of these feeding schools, and even marlin and sailfish crash the party, and that's when it's critical that you have the right rig ready to send to that fish. In the end, setting up on a school of dolphin to catch a few on jigs and fly tackle can get you into a whole other fight out there. Even swordfish come up to the surface for baits a lot these days. For its excitement and range of stunning possibilities, it ranks as one of the most necessary trips for any Keys angler.

Along those big weedlines with schools of feeding fish, an angler can stand on the bow of a slowly cruising boat with a rod ready to cast to the first big fish that shoots out from the weeds or up from the depths, to investigate the sound of the boat. As far as I'm con-

This is summer in the Keys.

cerned, that's one of the most exciting sight-fishing thrills, in any fishery.

The dolphin has a remarkably short, fast life, and their behavior changes as they grow. That makes a difference in how you fish for them, depending on the size fish that you're after. They can reproduce in their first year, and they live to an average age of three years.

Scientists currently believe that the oldest specimens might be five years old. They are voracious and seemingly indiscriminate feeders. They grow rapidly, by constantly consuming fish, especially flying fish. The largest grow to be 90 pounds and 6 feet long.

Early in their lives, dolphin school, and when you find a schoolie, chances are there are others nearby, which you can attract to your boat easily with the tactics described above. As they grow and age, they separate from big schools, and bulls travel with a few female cows. The largest males tend to be solitary and may be found hunting alone and in open water, often indicated by a single frigate bird diving.

Especially in the late spring and early summer around Key West, when the fish aren't so much traveling and migrating along with the Gulf Stream but have taken up temporary residence in the area, dolphin will be more likely to hang around your boat when properly enticed with chum. As the summer wears on, and the bigger fish move out to greater depths, 600 to 2,000 feet, even they may not be so likely to hang around your boat in schools, unless you find them near weedlines, where they'll have a nearby source of food.

Captain's Tip: "A whole ballyhoo on a spinning rod is the favored rig for casting to a big dolphin that swims by your boat, whether in a school or on its own.

"That's our stand-by bait in dolphin tournaments. We try to hit the bull on the head when it passes near, and we jerk the ballyhoo to make it look alive. Most of the time the bull will hit it. It's very exciting, and deadly effective."

—Capt. Rob Delph, *Second Generation*, Key West

24

King Mackerel, Blackfin Tuna, and Wahoo

Seasonal Visitors, Always Welcome

King mackerel are a seemingly ubiquitous species around Key West, scorned by some anglers for taking baits intended for other game fish and blasting tackle to pieces, and disparaged as food fish by many, perhaps because they're so plentiful. But that wasn't always the case. Only in the last decade have kingfish stocks rebounded after restrictions were placed on commercial harvesters taking their fill of kingfish. Previously, the commercial operators tracked the schools up and down the coasts with helicopters and had boats run nets around the schools, until the big schools weren't so big or prevalent.

Happily, these days the kings are back. Commercial fishermen still get them, though on a smaller scale and with tighter restrictions, and recreational anglers take their share too, sometimes when they're not even trying to catch them.

Kings are aggressive, and they fall prey to every technique in the book, from jigging to drifting dead baits, to trolling live baits, spoons, and downriggers to live-baiting. They're voracious and relentless predators. Though they can be found year-round in the Keys, they're hit and miss in the summer. But in the winter, when they migrate down from the north, it's almost hard not to catch them offshore.

From November through March in Atlantic waters, chances are you won't even have to target kingfish to find them. At the height of the run in January and February, day after day Key West charter captains can make their living by trolling threadfins or blue runners on down riggers in 150 to 250 feet off Eastern and Western Dry Rocks. The End of the Bar is another hot spot for kings.

Those same months in the Gulf, schools congregate over wrecks and in the deepwater around New Grounds, Smith Shoal, Ellis Rock, and Rebecca Shoals. For recreational anglers, close productive grounds include Edmund Lowe Shoals and Smith Shoals (49 and 2 on *Florida Sportsman's* chart for Key West), the many wrecks, and plenty of small shoals which aren't even named on charts. Blue runners are by far the favored baits when trolling, and when anchored, kings respond well to live chum and to cut bait, baited jigs, and live baits. Live pilchards take kings in quick succession, and circle hooks make releases easier. Short wire leaders keep the kingfish from cutting off lines nearly every time.

There are actually two stocks of kingfish, one from the Gulf and one from the Atlantic that migrate to the Keys. The Gulf stock has the bigger fish, and entrants in kingfish tournaments from Key West to Naples race to the Tortugas and Tail End Buoy to find winning fish of 60 and 70 pounds. Good size kings, from 20 to 40 pounds, can be found much closer to Key West though, just past the reef in 100 to 300 feet of water, feeding from the bottom of the ocean floor to the surface. Oftentimes, they'll be the predators sending up vast rafts of baitfish flying out of the water just beyond the reef.

Using Online Reports

To find the fish, remember that kings like blue-green water about seventy degrees, and most of the time they'll be on the green side of a color change, but not always. You can check temperature charts off the Web, such as Blue Water Fishfinder and Ray Tec Navigator to find that temperature break, and you can also check local Web sites where anglers post the locations of their catches, such as the

Catching baits, including blue runners, at channel markers starts many kingfishing trips.

Florida Sportsman Forum site. Also, if you're a visiting angler, don't be afraid to politely ask other anglers at the dock what's been happening. Both in person and on online, the way that you ask influences what information you'll get. Be as specific as possible about where you're fishing. Say what tackle you have, and what you want to catch and give some indication of your experience, who you'll be fishing with, and in what kind of boat. You'll more than likely get a specific and generous answer back from the online forums, at the docks, and even from tackle-store owners. Vague queries get vague responses, even if both parties have good intentions.

You can tell a kingfish strike, and a missed hookup, by the perfect slice in the bait exactly behind the hook. The speed and precision of their strikes, along with their stunning runs and hard fights are the two challenges to catching them. No matter what technique you're using, if kings are in the area, add a short bit of wire leader to minimize cut-offs. The wire won't stop them from biting, and with their laser-like eyes and razor-sharp teeth, they'll go through heavy mono leader every time, unless they're neatly hooked in the corner of the mouth. Their teeth will slice open your fingers just as easily. Many anglers won't even use swivels in their rigging with kings around because the swivel's flash attracts them. Because the water in the Keys tends to be clearer than in other locations where the kings live, anglers often use lighter tackle, 12- to 15-pound-test, to catch them.

In their fight, kings often turn and run toward the boat once they're hooked, and plenty of times anglers think they've lost the fish because of the slack line, until the king blasts off again, often pulling the hook. Never believe you've lost a king until you see the hook. To counter their first move, keep reeling hard and fast to take up the slack after the strike whether or not you feel the fish. Many times, once you come tight again, that's when the fight begins.

No one knows better how to catch big kings than Southern Kingfish Association competitors, and down to a team, their first choice of techniques in Keys waters will be trolling big live blue runners. If blue runners are not available, they'll go to Spanish mackerel or

There's plenty of smoked kingfish dip on the menu when you fish with Capt. Al White.

These teeth don't play around.

ribbon fish, which can be bought frozen and pre-rigged. To target the big Gulf kings, competitive anglers also make at least a twenty-mile run to the End of the Bar to begin trolling, and many won't put their lines in the water until they get to Tail End Buoy.

A general trolling rig for kingfish starts with 12- to 20-pound-test. To that, most anglers will add a swivel and a four- or five-foot length of fluorocarbon or monofilament leader and Albright knot on a foot to eighteen inches of 30- to 40-pound wire leader to the 3/0 or 4/0 live bait hook. Also they'll add a stinger treble hook to the lead hook with a six- to eight-inch piece of slightly heavier wire. Whether you're trolling or jigging, add that trailer hook to your terminal tackle, because kings are notorious for short-striking baits. Depending on the water clarity and the size of the bait you have, you can use heavier or lighter variations of the above wire and hook size.

Nose-hook the live bait with the lead hook and put the stinger into the lower flank of the bait, leaving slack in the wire so that the bait can swim freely. Depending on sea conditions and the quality of the baits, most anglers troll for kings at a speed of one to two knots to give the baits a natural, free-swimming presentation. On the water, keep your radio on scan and your ear tuned for what the

other captains are saying to help find the kings. If you run downriggers, drop each to a different depth from fifteen to thirty feet, and
run them back at different distances behind the boat, from fifteen to
thirty feet. Jigging in 125 to 200 feet works like a charm on kingfish
of all sizes.

Most anglers prefer to grill kings under 20 pounds and smoke
bigger ones, and if you come across one of the especially good-
eating, paler-skinned, whiter-fleshed juvenile kings that local anglers call "albinos," be sure to try it grilled.

Gaff and box kings with extreme care. Beware of their wicked
teeth. Let them die in the box before dehooking them.

Captain's Tip: "If you're out in the Gulf on a wreck for kings,
have a pinfish pitch-bait ready in the livewell for any follow-
ers that swim up, and a bucket with a few more live baits.
You need lots of rods ready for what might show—African
pompano, muttons, wahoo, amberjack. Winter and spring are
awesome out in the Gulf."
—Capt. Paul D'Antoni, Seize the Day Charters, Key West

Blackfin Tuna

In Key West, where some say that the live-baiting technique began
more than twenty years ago after commercial yellowtailers using
live pilchards discovered blackfin and yellowfin in their chum lines,
a number of Atlantic wrecks and reef locations draw and hold tuna
from November through May. The fish are nowhere near so predictable as to be present at these locations consistently throughout
the fall, winter, and spring, but rather they show for a few days at
one spot and then maddeningly move to another after a few days,
sometimes disappearing entirely from the scene for weeks, only to
reappear out of nowhere at the old haunts. While a good portion
of the yearly catch of blackfin by recreational anglers comes while
trolling lures and drifting with live baits such as threadfin in 150- to
200-foot depths and from behind shrimp boats in the Gulf, the fa-

vored method for anglers seeking blackfins is still the time-tested anchoring and live-baiting at these handful of locations—the End of the Bar, the Sub, the Rubble Pile, and the Airplane.

Live-baiting lets you stage a do-it-yourself feeding frenzy by setting up an offshore smorgasbord for the speedy pelagics. With lucky conditions, anglers might even be able to try out a variety of tackle on tuna as they hold them at bay behind their boat, including topwater plugs and flies—an otherwise fairly remote possibility when tuna schools cruise the open ocean. The technique and the locations are no secret, but as fast as these tuna move around, you have to be ready to strike or else be lucky and hit it right.

Perfect conditions might be a nice easterly breeze against a westerly current. You'll want to nose into the flow so that you can pitch your baits and they stay at the back of the boat. Locally, any westerly component in the wind is considered to have a negative effect on the fishing.

"Everybody prefers the good blue water to be in from the Gulf Stream, but we do get the tuna in green water," says Capt. David Barillas. "They're going to be where their food is, where that structure is, and you can go there and get them regardless of the exact water conditions. If I were looking for tuna, and I didn't have the Gulf Stream there, I would go to the same spots anyway, the Rubble Pile, the Airplane, the End of the Bar, the Sub."

Barillas says that these are resident fish with a wide territory. That might explain why they pop up in one quadrant and then reappear days later, miles away.

"You can target blackfins down here year-round at different places. It does seem that once the water gets too warm in the Atlantic," he says, "they move back to the Gulf and follow their food around there."

Typically, you can expect to find the bait schools and the tuna in depths of ninety to 230 feet anywhere along the reef, but the End of the Bar is a prime ground for pelagics, where deep water runs right up against the shallow reef, letting the pelagics corral baits against the reef edge. When waters at the End of the Bar shine the radiant purple of Gulf Stream origin, that always adds excitement to a day. Try to mark bait before anchoring or consider checking for them at another spot close by, such as the Sub in 230 feet, another popular live-baiting location.

"We like to see baits high in the water column," says Captain Barillas. That position indicates that they're on the run from predators and not simply resting. "It just makes it easier to get something going with our own baits if we're adding to action that's already there. When you've already spent the time it takes to catch the live baits that morning, you don't want to waste them."

If you do encounter a crowd at one of the wrecks, Barillas has some advice:

"Use proper etiquette when you anchor up. You don't want to be ahead or behind other boats," he says. "You want everybody to be in line so that everybody's chum works together. Try and give people as much space as you can, maybe seventy feet, more or less, depending on conditions. If boats are anchored really close, it's best to have your ball on the anchor line all ready to cast off so you can pull away and fight the fish away from everyone else, and then return and tie up to your anchor line. Also, don't troll through people's chum lines. You won't catch any tuna anyway with trolled dead baits when they're so focused on live baits anyway, and you'll get a lot of people angry at you."

After anchoring, take half a net full of pilchards, and out of that, scoop up a handful and bounce them off the transom into the water. That stuns them so that they don't swim away immediately. You want the baits to begin to school behind the boat, and all that commotion of a bait school draws your tuna near. You can even crush a few and toss them back to spread the scent and then bang the rest out of the net with an open palm to send them free-swimming. Repeat the process every five minutes to get the baits behind the boat.

When the seas boil and swirl behind your stern, and the pilchard that you've live-lined back takes off like a freight train, you've turned the tables on the tuna. Their trademark moves include long

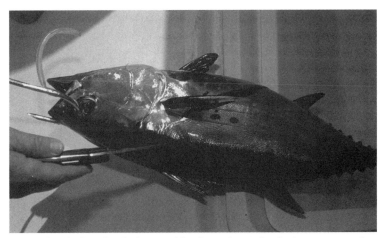

A nice blackfin hits the deck. Next, bleed it and ice it for the best taste on the plate.

runs, deep-sounding dives, and toward the end of the fight, death spirals below your boat. If one tries to walk you around your boat a few times, don't be surprised.

When a school of tuna shows up, they can surround the boat, and it pays to have gear ready to cast to them in all directions, including plugs with light wire leaders and jigs. Barillas likes No. 8 wire leader, though it may be harder for dropping back to a sailfish, but a tuna will see less of that thin wire than they will see a 50- or 80-pound mono leader that's reflecting light through it. To lighten the leader, you can also use a 25-pound fluorocarbon on 20-pound mainline to get that slightly harder, abrasive-resistant leader without adding too much up front to put the fish off. When the fish are finicky, to get strikes you can go with a double-line connection of your 20- or 30-pound mainline straight to your hook, and then fish with a very light drag. You can also put up a kite when you're anchored and in position, or if conditions are very rough and the current carries your baits away from your stern, you can try slow-trolling baits on a kite around fishy territory.

You never know where or when these tuna will turn up. When you do get them where you want them, "You only get one cast with

242 Part III. Species

each pilchard," says Capt. Brice Barr. "They're smaller baits, and whether or not they get hit, they're done after one time in the water. Use it for chum and refresh your bait for each cast.

"When you first show up," Barr says, "it might only take throwing out fifteen baits, and they're easy, *boom, boom, boom,* you've got them. Then as it gets later, and you've released a few, they get leader shy, they get smart, and they stay down. To do it effectively, you need a lot of bait.

"Sometimes," Barr says, "it's really tough to get a bait past the bonitos. One trick is to take a bonito filet and cut it into small pieces and drift those back, and most of the time tuna will eat them before a bonito does. You might also get a big wahoo with bonito chunks. Another trick is to rig a frozen flying fish and put it on a kite to get it back to the tuna. It's a bigger bait than the bonito are likely to grab, and it's a very cool bite to see, when it's suspended just out of the water on a kite."

Though they'll strike at any time, especially with live baits, prime times of the day for tunas are very early and before sunset. As the days grow longer in the spring, some local anglers don't even head out until after noon to catch the late bite at the wrecks as the sun heads down.

"It takes a fair amount of work to present live bait to tuna," says Barr, "but we've got them pretty well trained down here to eat pilchards."

Turning the tables on blackfin tuna is a thrill. *Setting* the tables for them is pretty good too. To keep their flesh the best, bleed tuna by slitting their gills or knifing the tip of their pectoral fin. The loin of blackfin can be excellent eating, especially if it's properly cared for on the boat.

Captain's Tip: "To rig the flying fish, spread its wings, put a piece of copper wire through and around one wing at the leading edge, run the copper wire through its eyes and back around the front edge of the other wing, so you've rigged the wings out. Put him up on a kite, and a lot of times he'll get bit on the way out, skipping across the water. If not, jig the flying fish up and down over the surface, and wait for that tuna to come and crash it. You can get away with a bigger hook and a heavier leader on a kite since the bait is out of the water. That's another little trick to get a blackfin instead of a bonito."

—Capt. Brice Barr, Double Down Charters, Key West

Wahoo

Higher trolling speeds, deeper bait placements, and wire leaders all make the difference when it comes to hooking up to wahoo offshore of Key West.

Wahoo are not quite an incidental catch in the Lower Keys, but it's hard to target them unless you know from the daily reports that they're around. Their runs are as hard to predict on the calendar as they are on the hook. They come and go sporadically. They seem to make almost quarterly appearances in Lower Keys offshore waters, but where they come from and where they go when they leave remains a mystery to anyone who's talking. Perhaps the lack of understanding about the species' overall migration patterns makes the timing of the runs offshore of Key West only seem surprising. Little research has been conducted on the species.

Consistently around Key West, there seem to be two big runs of wahoo, one in July and one in December, and two lesser runs, April and October. Each run lasts about two to four weeks. Their appearances may have to do with spawning or with migration patterns around the Caribbean and up and down the Gulf of Mexico. According to conventional knowledge, the days preceding the full moon provide the best wahoo bite, and a falling tide is the best tide phase. But for this species, at least in Key West, the most important tactic is to know when they're running by listening to the daily fishing reports on the docks, on the radio, or on the Web. Most years, schools of wahoo come in and out very fast.

When they're around, wahoo schools appear close to the reef, in depths from 150 to 400 feet, and farther offshore, closer to the Wall. They are usually near underwater structures. The July and

Wahoo appear sporadically around Key West, but if you get one, chances are good that a few more roam nearby.

December runs seem to have more and bigger fish, and for the Key West area, a 50-pound wahoo is a very good fish. An average fish weighs 15 to 25 pounds, though even these are formidable fighters on light tackle. When you happen to hit the bite, it's not uncommon to catch three or more wahoo on a trip, and some captains catch plenty more than that when they're as common as kingfish.

Aside from the standard strategies of looking for birds working bait, baits busting, and floating debris, you can troll in locations that are known for holding wahoo—the Western Dry Rocks, the End of the Bar, the Tail End Buoy, and of course, the Ups and Downs and the Wall. Trolling near the many lobster buoys turns up wahoo not only because the fish like to hang around the pots and the ropes, but also because the pots themselves are placed along ledges that shelter baitfish and attract predators. They'll also prowl the perimeter of a school of feeding dolphin, so always have a rod ready and rigged with a trace of wire at the terminal connection to cast to one.

Other than drifting live baits such as blue runners and threadfins in the fish's vicinity, most anglers look for wahoo by covering territory while trolling, and they troll fast, 6 to 12 knots. For the big wahoo around Key West, conventional gear will be necessary, and 50-wide reels are not too much tackle for the test. For wahoo, drag settings are kept slightly higher than for other pelagics to send the hook point through the wahoo's hard, bony mouth and to hold line

This is the kind of floating structure that almost guarantees fish, unless other anglers have already worked it over.

at those higher trolling speeds. Using mono lines, set the drag to about twenty-five percent of the line's test capacity, and on braided lines, with less stretch, to about a fifth of the line's test capacity.

A standard wahoo rig, and a good start for covering territory, employs the strongest, sharpest size 8/0 or 9/0 hooks available, crimped to six to eight feet of No. 9 single strand wire, and either a plain or skirted medium or large ballyhoo. Wahoo seem to strike with much more frequency five to thirty feet below, so the most successful presentations will be below surface. Downriggers work well for kingfish, but not so well on wahoo; their heavy lead balls come up when trolling at the higher speeds best for wahoo.

To get trolled baits below surface for wahoo, anglers use either a No. 3 or No. 5 planer or a trolling sinker known as a Z-wing on the line. Trolling sinkers drop baits down to ten feet below, depending on the boat and its speed, and they're simple to rig. There's even a trolling weight specially designed for wahoo fishing called the wahoo cigar, made by Captain Harry's in Miami. To accomplish the same purpose, deep-diving lipped plugs such as Yozuri Bonitos and Manns, weighted ballyhoo, and bullet-head lures with or without ballyhoo are also popular attractants for wahoo. Many anglers use clips on the transom that keep flatlines low to the water to help trolled ballyhoo maintain a natural appearance in the water and also to help keep a low angle in the line to increase hook up efficiency.

With their fast runs, bony mouths, and head-shaking habits, wahoo get off the hook often enough. The last thing you want to let them do is bite through your leader. When trolling for pelagics including sails and dolphin, it's common to use a monofilament or fluorocarbon leader, possibly with a trace of wire at the hook, but if you're specifically targeting wahoo and trolling at a higher speed, you can use a long four- or five-foot length of single strand wire for your leader and not worry about putting off bites. Also, when using a snap-swivel for the quick-changing of lures, most anglers will use that wire leader. Even if you're not targeting wahoo specifically, for mixed-bag pelagic fishing a few inches to eight inches of wire leader before your bait or lure will prevent a lot of cut-offs from wahoo, kings, and barracuda.

Popular skirt and lure colors for wahoo include combinations of black and purple, black and green, and black and red, though many anglers say that trolling speed and bait placement are more important than lure color. Most anglers aiming for wahoo try a mix of lures and baits in their trolling spread until they find out what works best for the day's conditions.

Chunking, or more precisely the Northeastern style of chunking for big bluefin tuna, has become another popular and successful technique for catching wahoo. Anglers anchor up at known wahoo spots such as the End of the Bar and Western Dry Rocks and begin dropping palm-sized chunks of bonito or king mackerel into their chum slicks. If the wahoo are around, they'll come to feed. Sometimes, you can even watch them take the chunks behind the boat, and it's only a matter of setting a good sharp hook into one of the chunks and freelining back with one or two other chunks to get hooked up.

Wahoo, like kingfish, lacerate bait and human flesh easily, and once you've boxed a fish, let it alone for 15 minutes before you try to take your hook or lure from its maw. One last lunge of that fish's fangs too close to your hand and you'll regret it.

Captain's Tip: "Especially during wahoo runs, if you find solid floating structure offshore, not only can you troll around it to coax out any wahoo, but also if that fails, you can drop a jig down fifty feet and deeper or troll a planer-line to see if any hold below."
—Capt. Richard Houde, Southbound Charters, Key West

25

~~~~~~~~~~~~~~~~~

Sailfish

Everybody's Billfish

Sailfish anglers talk about their days the way tarpon anglers do—as in, two-for-five or three-for-seven, mentioning how many fish they caught out of how many chances they had. They indicate their level of skill—and success—while they acknowledge the difficulty of their pursuit. And for the combined challenges of finding, hooking and successfully fighting them, sailfish probably are the sportiest fish in the Keys.

They're certainly the best chance at a billfish near Key West. Highly migratory and fast, even when they're around, sailfish move along, looking for a good food supply. They'll only hang around one location for any duration at all, say a day or two, given plenty of bait, such as sardine schools. Conditions that support large aggregations of bait rarely hold up longer than that, and when they change, the sails move.

Most often they're targeted not so much by finding the bait, but by finding conditions likely to hold bait—a good color change, temperature break, or current rip. The best sailfish anglers waste no opportunities, and they constantly scan for diving birds, especially frigates, and they run to the site of a free-jumping sail, because one sailfish often means others are in the vicinity.

Keys anglers expect sailfish to show up in schools by November, a few weeks after the first cold fronts have significantly cooled northern waters, chasing baits and their predators southward. By the middle of autumn, the local water temperatures have dropped

Follow a free-jumping sailfish and you'll often find others with it.

into the low 80s. Sailfish season runs through March and into April, peaking in February and March. In those months, it's common to see a free-jumping fish in a day's fishing around 150 and 250 feet between American Shoals and Western Dry Rocks. Anglers targeting sailfish will likely have a shot, and five or more shots at sailfish on a day's trip is a distinct possibility. At the height of each season, a few charters boats score big, with ten or more sailfish days—world-class catch numbers. During the World Sailfish Championships, held in mid-April, the winning boats average about four to five fish a day over the course of three days' fishing.

Though that tournament probably marks a height of sailfish season for Key West, lately there is a growing awareness that sailfish are really present year-round. Researchers led by NOAA's Eric Prince have identified the Wall as a summer spawning ground for sails, which might explain the prevalence of some of the year's largest fish seen cruising deeper waters, between 600 and 1,000 feet, in the months of July and August. These are the sails caught during the Drambuie Key Weat Marlin Tournament held in July. So there's at least a chance at a sailfish year-round in Key West.

Anglers target sails four primary ways:

1. Trolling live and dead baits over known productive territory and areas where likely conditions predominate—color changes, temperature breaks, current lines.

2. Looking for sails tailing in wave faces when easterly winds, prevalent in the spring, push waves up against the eastbound current.

3. Targeting bait balls schooled up by feeding sailfish, and run-and-gun method of spotting free-jumpers.

4. Kite-fishing, live-baiting, drift-fishing with live baits (sometimes with balloons) near promising conditions.

Each of these techniques has its own advantages, depending on prevailing conditions and the angler's boat, equipment, and experience.

Good sailfish baits include pilchards, ballyhoo, threadfins, and goggle eyes, but the best of all are the ones that you can get. Goggle eyes are great, because they're strong, flashy divers. They're in better supply in the spring near Key West. Ballyhoo can be chummed up to the stern of an anchored boat at patch reefs or the main reef. Birds over the chum line make ballyhoo nervous and tougher to catch with a cast net, especially when the water runs clear. In that case, the baits can be caught on a light rod rigged with 10-pound-test, a floating cork, and a bit of squid or shrimp on a long shank hook.

Anglers like live ballyhoo not only because the bait is hardy on the surface, but also because you can move fast with them, up to 6 and 7 knots, to pursue a free-jumper or a bird, and when you stop, says Capt. David Barillas, "The ballyhoo are still swimming around, doing their natural thing. Plus," he adds, "ballyhoo look so much like flying fish, which are the favorite prey of tunas and sails around here."

It's especially good to pick up some kind of live baits in the shallows or at markers around the island before you reach the reef, be-

A quick rig for a live ballyhoo is probably the most popular trolled bait for sails around Key West.

cause if you strike out at the reef for some reason, you're dead in the water.

At least bring dead ballyhoo. In a pinch, trolling dead ballyhoo works perfectly well, and many anglers devote themselves to that pursuit, saving plenty of time by not looking for baits. Live or dead, ballyhoo can be rigged multiple ways. One quick way is to put a long-shank hook point down through their bottom jaw and wrap copper wire from the eye of the hook down and around the hook shank and the bait's bottom jaw. Pin rigs are also popular. It all depends on your preference and experience.

In the prime winter season, trolling live ballyhoo can't be beat for its simplicity and its catch-all nature, because tuna, wahoo, and kingfish will also take the bait. Anglers cover the 125- to 200-foot depths in a zigzag pattern from American Shoals all the way down to the End of the Bar, trolling 3 to 7 knots, all the while watching for sailfish, the right conditions, and listening to the radio for information on what depths sails might be cruising that day.

"The sand gulley just inside the bar at the End of the Bar is also a very good place to troll," says Capt. Brice Barr, of Double Down Charters.

Probably the most popular and productive tactic sees anglers trolling along the hard edge of a good color change where many

252 Part III. Species

game fish will prowl, adding at least one dredge teaser to their trolling spread. Captain Barr will often use a live pilchard teaser, because it's simple and effective.

game fish will prowl, adding at least one dredge teaser to their trolling spread. Captain Barr will often use a live pilchard teaser, because it's simple and effective.

"Pilchards are schooling fish, and they follow the leader," Barr explains. "So you can toss out one at a time at your teaser, and they'll all join in a group, and pretty soon you've got a school following your boat, which is a pretty good setup for success. If you throw a whole big scoop, they all might swim away. It's called feeding the teaser, and pilchards are some of the only baits that will do that."

When in doubt, old standby spots prove true: south of American Shoals, south of Western Dry Rocks, and the End of the Bar—all places with good bottom structure. No matter where you troll, always watch your depthfinder for bait schools, and if you find them, concentrating some effort there usually pays off. Always have a live bait ready for a pitch rod for a cobia, tuna, or sailfish that surfaces to investigate the teaser. If you're using live bait, keep your eye on it, because when they jump around trying to escape from a predator, that tips you off to a bite about to happen and gives you the time to get set in the drop-back position.

Bigger boats commonly run two outriggers, two flatlines, and a downrigger for kings and wahoo, which muttons and grouper might take on passes near the reef.

"It's not uncommon to see two and three sails on a bait," says Captain Barr, "and when you get one, you can double and triple up. We fish our release clips really light, because you want to give a good drop back to a sailfish. A lot of the time, if we can see the fish ahead of the bite, we'll pull it down off the rigger and have the angler ready with the rod.

"Trolling speed depends on conditions that let you keep lines tight and not kill the baits, from a mile and a half to a few miles per hour. Not fast. One disadvantage to live baits," Barr acknowledges, "is that it's harder to maneuver to chase a bird or some action without bringing everything in first."

Sailfish want good feeding conditions, and if they don't have them, they'll keep on swimming to a place where they can eat without expending a great amount of energy. So what are the variables, what are the good conditions for sailfish around Key West, and how do they manifest themselves to anglers?

Water color: Sails love to feed in the powdery blue-colored water, especially when it's up against green water filled with bait. Some days the color change lines up at a perfect depth for sails, from 125 to 200 feet, but other days it runs way offshore, where it doesn't interact with the bait-holding bottom structure that sailfish hunt. Sometimes the "color change" is more of a change in the current and not so much a true change in water color, and all you'll see are "soft edges" of current differential. Scout around for that color change, or listen to the radio. Local captains will say where it is that day. The combination of auspicious currents over good bottom structure makes for the best conditions.

Current: That color change is one main variable to watch for when locating sails, as well as the strength of the current. Usually in the spring, the current comes in pretty close, and sailfish will swim and feed facing westward, heading into the usually prevailing east-bound current. A moderate east-bound current definitely helps the sailfishing, but if there's a west-bound current, the sails will be heading west with it, and it might make it easier for them to travel, so you have to hope to intercept them on their path. A lot of captains and tournament entrants will subscribe to sea-surface temperature and current services to locate temperature breaks, eddies, and current positions the night before a trip.

Time of year: In the winter, big schools of baitfish move southward into the Keys, and the sails follow them down. But in the summer, the local sailfish—possibly spawning stock—get very hungry.

"In the summer," says Captain Barr, "we get them with dead bait when we're dolphin trolling, and it seems like you can miss them again and again and they'll come back, whereas in the spring if a sail eats and you miss him, he's gone. They're a lot more aggressive in the summer."

Moon phase: Like all billfish, sails bite coming on to the full moon and after the full moon. The extra light makes them more active.

Captain Barr likes the backside of the full moon even better than the few nights before. But any time sails are around, they'll feed.

Light of day: In good clear water, there will often be an early and a late bite, when the sun doesn't shine directly on the water to make the sails wary of moving up into the surfaces where they'll easily be seen by predators. In dirtier water, says Captain Barr, there is a more consistent bite throughout the day.

"Like tuna," Barr says, "when the sun goes down, the sailfish get a little braver about making moves, and they're likely to strike especially well right before sunset."

Wind: A little wind, especially 10 to 15 knots from the east, produces waves that offer prime sailfishing conditions. Not so much because the waves turn the bite on, but because they help anglers to spot the fish. The sails use the waves' energy to surf them into the current as they hunt, making them easier to spot near the surface by keen-eyed anglers.

Captain Barr explains the phenomena: "When the fish tail, we fish differently than we do with 'riggers. We'll ride around and run and gun and cast to them, and that's really exciting. It's my favorite way to sailfish, and you can get two and three on at once.

"Usually there are big waves when the wind is against the current. Our fish are traveling east to west, into the current, to cover more ground, and they'll ride those waves to save their energy fighting the current, since the waves propel them in the direction of their hunt to find prey. They're actually trying to get out of the current a little. It's rougher for us, because we're zigzagging east, looking at them coming at us, with a couple lines baited and ready to go, and when we see them, we spin around to cast to them, sometimes right behind the boat.

"If you have strong current at your chosen depths, especially in the afternoon when the sun is high, look for those tailing fish. I've seen as many as a dozen fish tailing together, but usually it's one or two, but you never know. If you see bonitos and tunas coming by and tailing, you know you're in a good depth to see sailfish. Also big cobia. For a few weeks in mid and late March we'll get cobia in the seventy- and eighty- pound range."

To find sailfish, Barr and other local anglers put a lot of faith in frigate birds. If frigates are on a sail, a lot of time they'll sit on one spot, because sailfish work together to keep their bait in one place, sometimes quite a number of sailfish too. Whereas tuna, and dolphins, on the other hand, really push the baits and the birds have to give chase.

If you locate frigates over sailfish balling up baits and feeding, then count yourself lucky. The phenomenon happens occasionally in the winter, beginning in December around Key West, and can last for two or three days, as long as the bait and the conditions that support them in that location last. Blackfin tuna, wahoo, whale sharks, and kingfish may also join the feeding frenzy.

If you do come across a school of sailfish feeding at a bait ball, there are ways to hook up without disturbing their feeding and scattering them so that you and others can get multiple hookups. Start by hooking a live bait in the belly, stay outside the sailfish, and cast to them, says Captain Barr, and then let the bait sink. It will spin downward like one of the wounded fish they've hit to feed on.

"A lot of the time you can release that fish and turn around and try for another. If you trolled over them, you'd scatter them. Now, if you don't have what they're eating, your baits might be ignored, so it's always good to have a few different baits in your live well if you can, but either way, you'll want to watch them. Sailfish will put their sails up and swim around in circles to corral their baits. It's a memorable sight.

"Of course," Barr adds, "if that's not happening, we'll also try kite fishing, balloon fishing, drift fishing, running and gunning, and whatever else it takes.

"We have a couple ways to kite fish, either on a slow troll or a drift. We might have one rigger out, and then the kite and a couple baits on it, maybe blue runners or goggle eyes, and then big pilchards. Ballyhoo aren't really great on the kites, because they're not really heavy enough, and they'll stay on the surface, but they will make commotion. Drifting, we'll position ourselves along the color change, put the kites up, and let the current take us while I constantly bump the boat to keep the baits where the sails will be feeding."

Once you're rigged and you've found the fish, that's when the fun really begins. First, you've got to let the sail eat the bait for a while. That takes presence of mind to stay calm, but it's crucial. Give the fish five seconds to get the bait in its mouth. Wind down slow and steady until it comes tight, and if you're using a J-hook, when it does tighten, give the sail a good hookset. If you do miss him, be ready to flip your bail open right away to let the bait back again for another chance, or get it back in to rebait and shoot it out again. Most of all, wait for it to happen and don't ruin it before it does. You don't need to give such a hookset using circle hooks, but instead, keep reeling to set the hook in a running fish.

"People get so amazed watching sailfish jump and tail-walk that they stop fighting them," says Barr, "so staying tight to the fish is the second step in landing one. These fish swim up to fifty miles an hour. Your line may be going straight off the back of the boat and your fish may be jumping straight off the side of the boat, so everyone on board can help the angler locate the fish. Sometimes anglers think that they've lost them, but they haven't because after a long run, the fish started back to the angler, so keep reeling!"

Captain's Tip: "Look for pilchards on the big flats northwest of Key West by locating diving pelicans and the rippled surface water of bait schools. Sometimes a single throw of the cast net will fill your livewell, and other times, it might take a few hours to scratch up enough pilchards. Other locations for finding pilchards are the ship-channel seawall beside Fort Zachory Taylor State Park at the mouth of the harbor and in the turtle grass shallows out front of Higgs and Smathers Beach on the island's southern side. Sometimes, pilchards swarm chum lines in the channels between the islands. Great schools might be teeming in the shallows of islands farther west, by Boca Grande or even the Marquesas, but you'll only know it if somehow you're tapped into the local network of captains and anglers.

"Birds are your best ally for finding the baits, of course, pelicans and even the cormorants, when you see cormorants congregated," says Captain Barillas. "You can even tell from a distance what baits the pelicans are diving on. After the pelican dives, if his head comes up right away, he's eating pilchards. If his head stays down as he swallows, then it's the smaller glass minnows, called mahua."

Out-of-town anglers trying to live-bait on their own boats might consider catching and holding the pilchards in advance, especially if they're not familiar with local waters. There are no baitsellers offering pilchards at any price in the marinas.

"We do keep pilchards alive overnight in a big pen in our marina," says Barillas. "You lose most of your fish when you start handling them, but in that big round pen, about four feet in diameter, they survive anywhere from three to five days, and they're definitely fine for one night, so that you could get your baits the afternoon before and save a lot of fishing time the morning of your trip.

"Somebody once said that you want to have about thirty pounds of bait, and at least fifteen pounds. That's a lot of pilchards. I wouldn't say that tuna and sails are feeding on pilchards out there in the Atlantic. They're after a lot of squid, schools of sardines, but they love pilchards.

"Sand Key pilchards have a little yellow slash above their gills, and they get bigger, easily up to eight inches long. Sand Key pilchards aren't quite as hardy as the other more common species, called razor belly pilchards. Sometimes the two species mix together. But fresh, I don't think you can beat the Sand Key pilchard. They're big and flashy, and tuna and even sails love them."

—Capt. David Barillas, Key West

Blue Marlin

With Patience and Prep

If you want to find a marlin near Key West, go to Wood's Wall, the edge—or escarpment—of the continental shelf, twelve miles south of Key West. The Wall runs roughly parallel to the Keys, east–west, and drops from 800 feet down to 1,800 feet, with cracks that upwell currents, trap baitfish, and attract pelagics. It's named for Norman Wood, who, along with his friend and fishing partner Wayne Hunt, pioneered the current marlin fishery in Key West back in the seventies and eighties. These are the grounds where Hemingway used to come across marlin on his way over to Cuba.

Marlin caught near the Wall average 200 to 300 pounds in the summer, and bigger marlin appear in the fall. Many 500-pounders have been landed in recent years. October to November is a great time for big marlin. Wood and Hunt believe that in the fall, the marlin are leaving the Gulf and traveling with the Gulf Stream east along the Straits of Florida. Then in the late spring, those big fish migrate in the opposite direction against the Stream on their way west into the Gulf. Marlin follow along the Gulf Stream, so as it swings way out into the Straits of Florida, that's where they'll go. Best conditions will see the Stream over the Wall with some chop to the seas. Very calm conditions allow marlin to see trolled offerings clearly as fakes.

While Wood's Wall is a consistent producer of marlin, it's not prolific. In recent years, the Drambuie Key West Marlin Tournament, held in July around the full moon, which is known to kick

The excitement of a blue marlin boatside lasts long after the fish swims away.
Photo courtesy of Scott Greene, Drambuie Key West Marlin Tournament.

the marlin bite into full gear, has drawn about sixty boats. Those sixty boats, fishing over three days, have landed an average total of about ten blues each year. That's about eighteen days of fishing for a boat to catch a marlin, and that sounds about right judging from the results of years of local fishing reports.

The difficult aspect of catching a marlin in Key West remains being prepared for them unless you're specifically targeting them. If you are after other quarry and just happen to come across one, it will more than likely blow away your equipment. Sometimes, even those anglers targeting marlin get a surprise. One recent spring an angler was out testing his brand new $300 marlin dredge teaser in 200 feet—not usually marlin territory—when a blue came up and ripped it off and swam away with it.

If you're targeting them at the Wall, look for birds over feeding dolphin or tuna, which are prey for marlin. Such activity indicates a good area to begin trolling for blues.

Capt. Ray Rosher, who runs *The Miss Britt* in Miami and fishes tournaments around the world, routinely competes in Key West tournaments. Rosher uses stand-up tackle to make it easier for anglers to drop back baits to marlin that surface in their trolling spread. Though fighting chairs put much more pressure on fish, experienced anglers will handle most of the marlin in Keys waters on stand-up gear. Without a fighting chair in the cockpit, there's a lot more room for anglers to maneuver and work the many trolling lines in the spread. Rosher's technique can easily be adapted by anglers in center-console boats who want to try for marlin.

Captain Rosher spools six Penn 50-wide reels with 1,000 yards of combined 80-pound Spectra connected to a top-shot of 80-pound monofilament line. The Spectra line's narrow diameter affords greater yardage capacity on those smaller reels, so anglers can use them with lighter, easier-to handle stand-up rods instead of the typical marlin trolling setup of 80-wide reels on heavy bent-butt rods. With the rod held in the arms and the tip high above the head or out to the side—a difficult position to hold with the heavy bent-butt rods—anglers can more easily prepare to drop-back a bait to a marlin rising to the teasers.

In the terminal tackle rigging, a Bimini twist on the 80-pound mono mainline leads to a cat's-paw knot on a 300-pound wind-on leader (instead of a swivel) of twenty-three-foot length, followed by a six-foot 400-pound leader to lure. That setup lets the angler wind the leader all the way in and makes the mate's job of handling the leader more manageable and safer, especially when a hot blue jumps next to the boat. Rosher and his team use a floss loop to protect the line from chafing in the outrigger's release clip and to mark the line's place for proper lure placement in the trailing wake.

Rather than following preordained ideas of how fast to troll, Captain Rosher sets his trolling speed so that his baits look good in the conditions. Generally, Rosher staggers the baits, approximately twenty-, forty-, and sixty-arm lengths (each arm length equals about five feet), adjusting the lures so that they ride on the face of the waves, exactly as baitfish ride the waves. He suggests a simple technique to discover how far back to place your baits and to mark your lines at those distances. Go out on a shiny, calm day and at

Rigging a supply of marlin baits takes plenty of prep time, and the work continues throughout the day.

each rpm for your desired spread (bait or lures), you can put a mark on your line where the lure or bait rides on the wake's face.

"That way you'll know exactly how far to let them back for each rpm you want to try trolling. You want your lures to be always throwing foam and trailing smoke. Blue marlin will sometimes eat when the lure is moving incorrectly," he says, "but you're basically creating better odds that you'll get a strike with proper lure placement.

"If I do fish lures with hooks in the spread, we see a better hookup percentage with single hooks near the back of the skirt," Rosher says, addressing the one or two hook issue.

Keep in mind each lure's action. Straight-face center-hole lures, such as super-chuggers, and some straight-face offset-hole lures, such as Yaps, wobble but don't track as erratically as the slant-head, which track as much as four or five feet left to right, like an escaping baitfish. The Super Plunger head is a famous example of such a lure. It works great as a hooked lure, Rosher says, but it probably travels even more miles as a teaser because of its large size.

Captain Rosher deploys baits and hooked lures to withstand a marlin's impact, and to maximize hook-up ratios on their strikes. An optimal hookset goes into the marlin's upper jaw, and different lures make that more or less possible by the position of their hook as they travel in the trolling spread.

"An open-face lure doesn't always track in one position," Rosher says, "and so the hook point changes positions, both up and down. One advantage of a slant-head lure is that it tracks with the longer side of the slanted head up, and this allows for an upright hook placement if you control the angle of the hook with certain rigging techniques."

To fix the angle of the hook, Rosher uses a rubber stopper on the mono leader inside the head of the lure where the mono attaches to a small stainless-steel ring. Crimp the mono-to-ring attachment. The ring attaches to a short, four- to six-inch section of stainless-steel cable, and that connection gets crimped, and the cable also gets crimped onto the hook. That way nothing swivels and it stays straight. You want the point of the hook about a half inch outside the skirt of the lure.

With this setup, the hook rides in the upright position for the best placement, and if the marlin chews on the line near the hook, it's chewing on steel, not mono, with its raspy bill and powerful jaws.

Engineer your spread by choosing a variety of lures for their performance, both lateral movement and smoking action. To bring a teaser down a little on the wake, you can put a little lead ahead of the snap on your main teaser line, which is usually 200- to 300-pound mono. The teaser-leader has six feet of 400- to 600-pound mono, a length that allows the crew to quickly clear the teaser out of the water when it's being pulled from the marlin. If the teaser-leader is too long, then the fish might snatch the teaser lure and damage the rigger or take the teaser altogether.

If—when—a marlin does rise, anglers present a pitch bait in the wake behind the fish as it chases the teaser to the cockpit corner.

Once the teaser clears the water, the marlin usually falls back and eats the first bait it sees—the pitch bait. If it misses that one, it will see the other baits in the spread as it turns away.

"The advantage to those natural baits," says Rosher, "is that if the marlin strikes and misses the hook, you can give it time to eat the ballyhoo or the mackerel. The disadvantage is that the bait might get mangled, and that's when your spread becomes the back-up strategy.

"Since we get so few shots at marlin around Key West," Rosher continues, "I like to do every single thing that I can to increase our chances of a hookup if a fish does rise to our spread.

"I've done some satellite tagging that tracks the depth the fish travel in a day," he says, "and the studies show that the marlin spend their day at extremely deep depths, but they do come up at varying times during the day. The question is, what brings them up? How do you raise a marlin?"

Know all the techniques, try them all wherever you are, and see what works.

Marlin fishing demands a lot of work and expertise, but those anglers devoted to the pursuit feel that those challenges are greatly rewarded.

"To stand on the back of that boat with the rigs that I put out," says Wayne Hunt, who along with Norman Wood pioneered modern-day marlin fishing around Key West, "and to see that black shadow come up from underneath to nail them. It makes the hair on the back of your neck stand up. That was the rush."

"You're in another world when you see that fish coming," Norman Wood adds.

"Once you hook and fight a marlin," says billfish angler Kitt Toomey, "you'll never forget it in your life. It's an awesome animal, like a lion or an elephant in the animal kingdom."

If the character of the animal pursued makes for the quality of the sport, then maybe marlin fishing is one of the greatest of all outdoor sports.

Captain's Tip: "Marlin will stick around their food source—dolphin and skipjack tuna. If you're fishing live bait, you must focus on an area, possibly over structure, and troll slower than you can with lures and baits. The big benefit to naturals and lures is that you can cover much more territory."

—Capt. Ray Rosher, Miss Britt Charters, Miami

27

Swordfish

A Resurgent Fishery

Few fish are as legendary as the swordfish, titan of the world's oceans, and few people know that there's an active and productive fishery for them right off of Key West along the Wall. After over-fishing in the seventies and eighties, and restrictions on catching them in the nineties, swordfish populations are rebounding. Local anglers go after them at night, when the fish feed best, and in the summer, when the weather tends to be calmer. In 2007, swordfish-ing by day, really caught on in the Keys and South Florida. This is a practice taken from South America and developed for our waters by captains in Islamorada and Miami. By day, the swords remain very deep, so anglers must present baits such as whole squids to the bottom with heavy weights, like cinder blocks on breakaway lines, often rigged to electric reels with braided lines. Once the brick hits bottom, anglers snap it off with a quick jerk of their rod, and the baits ascend from the depths, luring strikes on the way up.

Swordfish grow to more than 2,000 pounds, though the world's record caught on rod and reel weighs a mere 1,200 pounds. We don't catch those giants here in Key West, but even a 100 or 200 pound fish—a good specimen for Key West waters—might fight an angler for an hour or two, to be lost at the last minute. Back in the seventies, at the height of the swordfishery's glory, 500- and 600-pound fish were commonly caught by recreational anglers in South Florida. The pressure on the fish, and many will primarily blame long liners, collapsed the stocks. Marine-resources management closed the fishery in the early nineties, and ten years later, stocks had recovered well enough to reopen the recreational fishery and allow commercial fishing by the buoy method, though long lining continued to be banned in the sword grounds off South Florida and in the northern Gulf. Still, some anglers express concern about how much pressure—commercial or recreational—the stocks can take at this early stage of recovery.

The traditional trip for swordfish involves going out at night, when swordfish ascend from the depths to feed. Night swordfishing has a high degree of danger and requires the utmost experience and preparation. The basic fishing principle that time spent at the dock preparing to fish equals time spent on the water fishing, definitely applies to swordfishing. To the dangers of running a boat in the dark, when collisions with unseen floating trees, abandoned rafts, even turtles, can wreak havoc on big boats, add many other risks. The deep waters beyond the Wall where anglers drift for swordfish are the shipping lanes, and huge cargo freighters passing by there won't stop for anything.

"When you see the cargo freighter's bow light lined up directly under its bridge light, that means it's headed straight at you," Capt. Brice Barr explains, "and if you don't move you'll get crushed."

In the summer, big thunderstorms blow up almost nightly out there, and if you lose power, it's way too deep to anchor, and the current runs very fast. For these reasons, many extremely accomplished and experienced captains won't swordfish at night.

The most common technique is drifting baits, very simple, though the equipment is specialized. Basically, run out to the Wall and set up before sunset to drop baits at different depths and drift along with the current. After drifting for some time, anglers pick up baits and run back to their starting spot and drift again so that they don't drift too far and make their morning run home too long.

Excellent conditions see moderate seas and no thunderstorms with the Gulf Stream right over the Wall to get bait-churning rips going and fish feeding. Some anglers believe that a bright, full moon puts the fish down, and with a darker moon the fish come to the surface to feed. However, a bright moon does provide more light for better vision. Almost all anglers concede that the most important conditions are a good, moving current and calm weather.

Experienced anglers generally use 50-wide reels spooled with hundreds of yards of high-strength line and an eight- or 10-foot length of 200- or 300-pound leader on stiff fighting rods. Since 2000, the size of fish caught has seemed to increase with each passing year, and in 2007, anglers caught a few 300-pounders along Florida's east coast and a few even bigger. Many anglers have actually started using 130-wide reels exclusively.

For rigging, start with a Bimini twist in the mainline and attach a ball-bearing swivel with an offshore knot. Crimp on the leader, and all connections to terminal tackle should also be crimped. Big 9/0 size hooks are commonly used. Popular baits are natural squid, bought frozen and rigged or bought pre-rigged and artificial squid lures. A green battery-powered light is attached to the swivel to light the bait, and some anglers loop cyalume light sticks to their leaders. To get the rig deep, tie on a breakaway weight, such as an egg sinker of twelve to twenty-four ounces, to the top of the swivel with a rubber band or to the double line above the swivel by looping the line through the sinker and securing it with a rubber band. In either position, the strike will snap the rubber band and free the weight. Anglers also bridle-rig live baits such as goggle eyes to their hooks.

Lines are suspended in position by a float bottle, holding a cyalume light inside it, attached to the mainline by a rubber band. The floating light acts as a line and strike indicator, and it still can be hard to spot those bottles beneath the waves in the darkness. Anglers drop the baits to different depths in the water, from ten feet from the surface to 300 feet down. The slack in the line as it hangs down naturally gives the swordfish a drop-back, a chance to eat the baits since they usually bat it with their bills before biting. Often, by the time you actually know that you have a bite, the fish has already pulled that line tight.

Small "pups" should be released fast. Their presence indicates bigger fish to come, maybe that very night.

"It's a very subtle bite," says Captain Barr. "You just have to keep watching and listening for the slightest movement, like a tap, on the line. There's so much slack in the line, sometimes," Captain Barr says, "you won't even know that you have a bite until the fish jumps out of the water or your bottle goes right by you."

Anglers also place big cyalume light sticks in the water by their boats to attract baits boatside and bring swords to their drift. Boats should always have at least a fighting belt available, and for big swordfish, a harness with straps will help apply needed pressure. It's also a good idea to turn off the boat's deck lights during the drifts. That extra light makes it harder to see the float lights, and also the lights of any ships nearby.

Despite its dangers, or maybe in part because of them, the challenge of night fishing for big swordfish tests anglers' limits of skill, endurance, strength, and concentration. Hook up to a good fish, and it's as if you're fighting the night itself. No matter where you do it, swordfishing makes an exotic fishing trip, and it has to be one of angling's ultimate adventures.

Captain's Tip: "Hooking a swordfish is one thing. Getting it in the boat is another. A quality flying gaff or harpoon can save you or your crew some serious injuries. And before you set to sea, check your drags with a hand scale. A properly set drag can be the difference between a sword in the boat and a pulled hook. I like to set mine at twelve to fourteen pounds. Two-speed reels also help. When a sword takes the hook it'll almost always pop to the surface. Gathering up line fast in high gear helps you stay tight, and low gear helps you pull them back."
—Capt. Rob Harris, Conchy Joe's Bait and Tackle, Key West

Capts. Rob and Missy Harris of Conchy Joe's know how to bring it home after a night on the water hunting swordfish off Key West.

On the last afternoon of a three day dolphin tournament, I watched the sickle moon coming down on our chances like a scythe. We had an hour and a half left to fish. It was time to break out the charms.

"This is my favorite lure," one of our fishing partners said, "I went back to the shop to get more and found out the guy stopped making them, but I got him to make me six more for three hundred bucks."

Within thirty minutes, we saw birds ahead at 11 o'clock and set back our trolling baits, dead ballyhoo, and the lure between them. We trolled slowly toward the diving birds. Thirty yards from the birds, a big bull rocketed into our wake, heading for that lure. The rod bent double and the drag ripped.

"Fish on!"

In Key West, you're never far from the elements of water and surprise.

Whether you strike into the Gulf, the flats, the reef, or offshore, you should find the best of what the ocean offers, not only in sport, but also in the way the ocean returns us to our senses to know that life, and its possibilities, are inexhaustible.

part 4

Appendixes

Appendix 1 Table of Baits

Table of Baits	Where to Catch Them	How to Catch Them	Prime Uses
Ballyhoo	They come to chum at patch reefs, main reef, and even in channels. Buy frozen, rigged or not.	Cast net when possible, otherwise on sabiki or small hook with a float and a tiny strip of squid bait.	Terrific surface trolling baits, live, fresh, or frozen. Will not live long down deep.
Blue Runners	At markers in near-shore waters by the island, over shallow structure, and along channels.	Sabiki rigs. Troll small spoons over shallow banks and basins.	Larger trolled for kings, sails, tuna, and bottom-rigged for big grouper. Smaller runners for bottom baits.
Bonito	Offshore and in the Gulf.	Trolling in 150 to 200, live-baiting, in the Gulf around wrecks.	Excellent live bait for marlin, live smaller fish for dolphin, in strips on jigs, and tiny strips for yellowtail snapper.
Cigar Minnows	Around patch reefs and the main reef, 30 to 60 feet deep. Also known as round scad.	Sabikis, hair hooks, gold hooks, and small hooks tipped with squid, and they respond to chum.	Very good live bait, both for pelagics and for bottom fish.
Crabs	Available in mangrove channels and canals in the Keys, but much easier to buy live at bait shops.	Almost always available at bait shops.	Claws clipped, baited by the shell point on a jig; top bait for permit, and good for tarpon too.
Flying fish	Often seen offshore, but hard to catch.	Buy frozen, rigged or not.	Terrific baits drifted, and deadly from a kite.
Goggle Eyes	Channel markers and over rocky structure in waters deeper than 20 feet, and around ship buoys offshore.	Small 1/0 hooks when they respond to chum lines.	Considered the prime live bait for sailfish, either drifted or from kites.

Appendix 1—*Continued*

Appendix 1—*Continued*

Grunts	Everywhere there is structure from the shore out to the reef, especially shallow-water patch reefs.	Small 1/0 and 2/0 hooks, respond to chum.	Live on the bottom for grouper, good bait.
Lobster, whole or heads	In shallows, by the reef, in the Gulf.	Caught in season, with license, or bought from seafood retailer (expensive).	For cubera snapper and big grouper, used whole and live, or front half on the bottom. Bait must be legal size to use.
Mahua (glass minnows)	Turtle grass and sand flats around all the keys, year-round. Buy frozen at tackle shops.	By cast net with a fine mesh, otherwise they stick in the mesh.	Great added to chum slick for snapper and grouper and a few on the hook for yellowtail.
Mojarra	Around markers and beaches in shallow water, around piers, and over turtle grass on the flats.	Cast nets when possible or small hooks and sabiki rigs.	Can be used like pinfish, but are considered the best bait to chum for tarpon, either live or dead.
Mullet	Shallows around the keys and along channels, year-round; populations increasing locally.	Cast net over schooling mullet.	Fair and hardy trolling baits, also good for cut bait and on the bottom.
Pinfish	Around structure in shallow water, by bridges, in bays and channels, almost everywhere shallow. Live at tackle shops at times.	Sabiki rigs or in cages filled with blocks of chum set in shallow water over grass.	Great snapper and grouper baits, either drifted or dropped on bottom.
Razor Belly Pilchards	Turtle grass and sand flats around keys, harbor area, along beaches, by bridges and piers, more common in cooler months.	Follow the birds, and throw big cast nets over their schools.	Live-baiting chum and bait; excellent snapper baits, good all around bait. Hardy in the livewell.
Sand Key Pilchards	Sometimes in same schools as razor bellies, but often in deeper waters too, over patch reefs and near the reef.	Cast nets, and sabiki rigs if baits stay in chum slick.	Excellent live baits to freeline and drift, can even be trolled.

continued

Appendix 1—Continued

Table of Baits	Where to Catch Them	How to Catch Them	Prime Uses
Shrimp	Shrimp run through the channels under bridges on winter nights, but much easier to buy at tackle shop.	Shrimp run much bigger in the winter season.	Great all-around inshore bait, live, fresh dead, whole, or tipped on a jig, but every fish will take this bait.
Silverside Minnows	Not local. Imported from Canada and China.	Bought frozen at tackle shops.	Like candy for yellowtail snapper.
Spanish and Cero Mackerel	Inshore over patch reefs. Spanish in winter.	1/0 or 2/0 hook, chum, bait with squid strips or shrimp, or troll with spoons.	Cut baits for bottom and for freelining, and used live trolling for kings and marlin. Need bait tube to keep alive.
Spanish Sardines	At times at the reef, usually offshore, especially in winter.	Rarely caught, but important as an indicator of activity.	When corralled by sails or tuna fish, these baits mark a great bite.
Speedos	Around the reef and around deeper patch reefs, especially late in the afternoon. Also known as redtail scad.	Anchor and chum into hoop nets and scoop up, also on small hooks baited with shrimp.	Very delicate bait. Good trolled for tuna, sailfish, and kingfish, and on the bottom, good for grouper and snapper.
Squid	Occasionally seen in schools in shallow water and around underwater boat lights offshore at night, but rarely caught live. Usually bought frozen.	Buy frozen.	Strip baits for yellowtail, whole baits for big bottom fish, occasional chum for tuna.
Threadfin Herring	At markers in the harbor, along channels, over rocky patches in 20 to 50 feet.	Unbaited #6 or #8 sabiki rigs	One of the best all-around baits for bottom fishing, trolling, and drifting.
Tinker Mackerel	Sometimes in 30 to 60 feet near the reef, also offshore, respond to chum, but more frequently seen around the mainland than in the Keys.	Sabiki rigs in chum slicks and bought frozen.	Excellent live baits trolled on surface and deep, also drifted for swordfish, and one of the favorite bottom-fish baits.

Appendix 2

Captains' Contact Information

Flats Captains

Capt. Lenny Leonard, Key West, bonefishingkeywest.com.

Capt. Dave Wiley, Outcast Charters, Summerland Key, Keywestflats.com.

Capt. Skip Nielsen, Islamorada, Florida, skipcyd@bellsouth.net.

Capt. Tim Carlile, Summerland Key, (305) 745-1503.

Capt. Phil Thompson, philkeywest@yahoo.com, (813) 325-4677.

Capt. Justin Rea, flyfishingthekeys.com, (305) 744-0903.

Center-Console Captains

Capt. David Barillas, Key West, dbarillas01@hotmail.com.

Capt. Paul D'Antoni, Seize the Day Charters, Key West, fishinkeywest.com.

Capt. Bill Delph, Key West, delphfishingcharters.com.

Capt. Rob Delph, Key West, delphfishingcharters.com.

Capt. Pepe Gonzalez, Key West, pepescharters.com.

Capt. Ken Harris, Finesse Charters, Key West, fishfinesse.com.

Capt. Steve Hassell, Hassellfree Charters, Key West, (305) 304-6853.

Sportfisher Captains

Capt. Brice Barr, Double Down Charters, Key West, doubledownsportfishing.com.

Capt. Richie Gomez, Key West, keywestcaptconch.com.

Capt. Richard Houde, Southbound Charters, Key West, southboundsportfishing.com.

Capt. Ray Rosher, Miss Britt Charters, Miami, missbritt.com.

Appendix 3

Tackle Shops along the Road

Always call way ahead of arrival to check if they have the live bait that you want. In addresses, MM means mile marker on U.S. 1. Key West is located at MM 0.

Key Largo Bait and Tackle (The Yellow Bait House), MM 102, (305)451-0921.
Islamorada Tackle, MM 81.5, (305)664-4578.
Florida Keys Outfitters, MM 81, (305)664-5423.
World Wide Sportsman, MM 81, (305)664-4615.
'Cuda Bait and Tackle, MM 90, (305)853-0191.
Faro Blanco Outfitters, 1996 Overseas Hwy., (305)743-9018.
Drag-N-Bait, 1250 Overseas Hwy, (305)743-2817.
Abel's Bait and Tackle, MM 84.2, (305)664-2521.

Marathon

World Class Angler, MM 49, (305)743-6139.
The Tackle Box, MM 48, (305)289-0540.
Big Time Tackle, MM 53, (305)289-0199.

Lower Keys

Jig's Bait and Tackle, MM 30.3, Big Pine, (305)872-1040.
Sea Boots Outfitters, MM 30, Big Pine, (305)745-1530.
Sugarloaf Marina, MM 17, Sugarloaf, (305)745-3135.
Reef Light Tackle, MM29, Big Pine, (305)872-7679.

Conchy Joe's Tackle, MM 4, Key West, (305)295-7745,
    conchyjoeskw.com.
Garrison Bight Marina, MM 4, Key West, (305)294-3093.
Key West Marine Hardware, 818 Caroline Street, (305)294-3519.
Key West Bait and Tackle, 241 Margaret Street, (305)292-1961.
Saltwater Angler, 243 Front Street, (305)296-0700.

Boater's World Stores

3022 Roosevelt Blvd., Key West, (305) 295-9232.
5001 Overseas Hwy., Marathon, (305) 743-7707.
105660 Overseas Hwy., Key Largo, (305) 451-0025.

West Marine Stores

2055 Overseas Hwy., Marathon, (305) 289-1009.
103400 Overseas Hwy., Key Largo, (305) 453-9050.
725 Caroline Street, Key West, (305) 295-0990.

Appendix 4

〜〜〜〜〜

Local Logistics

The City Marina at Garrison Bight (305-292-8167) is the local's choice for access to the harbor and beyond. The marina charges to put in and to park your trailer for the day. The boat ramp drops off suddenly; so don't back in so far that you can't see your trailer's back wheels, or you might get stuck. Boat slips are also available by the day, week, and month, and live-aboards can stay for free at the mooring field in the harbor, though that may change. There's a fuel dock and bait store right in the marina that usually has live shrimp, crab, and pinfish. Marinas at Key West Bight near Old Town have slips too.

In general, the water clarity in the Lower Keys allows boaters to navigate by sight, given sufficient daylight. In any conditions use caution—especially westward toward the Marquesas and eastward of the Harbor Keys—as there are coral heads that can subtract your lower unit in a flash. A Sea Tow policy might be a good idea.

Conchy Joe's Marine and Tackle on North Roosevelt (305-294-7745) is the tackle shop and a captain's hangout, and Cuban Joe's on Caroline Street (305-294-3519) has boat parts and tools. You can rent boats at Garrison Bight (305-294-3093) and at U.S. 1 Marina (305-296-0075). For ultimate convenience, you can pull up to your own dock after a day's fishing by staying at one of the three hotels that offer boat slips to guests—Harborside (305-294-2780, keywestharborside.com), Pelican Landing (305-296-9292), and Banana Bay (1-800-BANANA-1), bananabay.com.

Pleasures are within easy reach on the two-by-four mile island, and the best way to get to them is on bike, so consider bringing your own or renting them when you arrive. With a map and a light for night rides, you can peddle everywhere, from the beaches to the lush alleys and Old Town neighborhoods of wreckers' mansions.

Acknowledgments

Thanks to my friends, Al White, Phil Thompson, Joel and Lee Day, and Ron and Roseleen Glinski for sharing their years of knowledge and their days of adventure in Key West with me. Their generous contributions in time and teaching helped to shape this book.

I'd also like to thank Jeff Weakley, editor of *Florida Sportsman*, for his encouragement and guidance, along with the Wickstrom family and the team at Florida Sportsman Communications Network for their commitment to Florida's environments and fisheries.

My appreciation also goes to John Byram, editor-in-chief of the University Press of Florida, and his entire staff for their work on the production and creation of this book.

And of course, my life-long gratitude belongs to Wendy, my wife, Jean, my mother, and Jenn, my sister, the three women who make returning to shore worth it for me. Ed, let's fish.

Five percent of the author's proceeds from this work will be donated to the Billfish Foundation.

Index

David Conway is the managing editor of *Florida Sportsman* magazine. His articles, essays, and stories have appeared in a variety of publications, including *Cimarron Review*, *Gray's Sporting Journal*, and *Sport Fishing Magazine*.